GARDEN COUNTY PIE

Sweet and Savory Delights
from the Table of

John Michael Lerma

For Sarah —
Happy Pie Baking —
"Keep it flakey!"

John Michael

Garden County Pie

SWEET AND SAVORY DELIGHTS
FROM THE TABLE OF

JOHN MICHAEL LERMA

SYREN BOOK COMPANY
MINNEAPOLIS

Most Syren Books are available at special quantity discounts for bulk purchases for sales promotions, premiums, fund-raising, and educational needs. For details, write

Syren Book Company
Special Sales Department
5120 Cedar Lake Road
Minneapolis, MN 55416

Published by
Syren Book Company
5120 Cedar Lake Road
Minneapolis, MN 55416

Printed in the United States of America on acid-free paper

ISBN-13: 978-0-929636-84-9

LCCN 2008940590

Cover design by Kyle G. Hunter
Book design by Wendy Holdman
Cover photography and all pie photography in insert by Jennifer Frederick Terrell
Food styling by Bret Bannon
Ceramic pie dishes provided by Emile Henry

To order additional copies of this book go to www.itascabooks.com

Contents

This book is dedicated to Chad Alan Olson, my PA, my EB, life partner, and best friend. Life would taste dreadful if I couldn't share it with you. I wake up smiling each day because I can.

GARDEN COUNTY PIE

*Sweet and Savory Delights
from the Table of*

John Michael Lerma

It is utterly insufficient [to eat pie only twice a week], as anyone who knows the secret of our strength as a nation and the foundation of our industrial supremacy must admit. Pie is the American synonym of prosperity, and its varying contents the calendar of the changing seasons. Pie is the food of the heroic. No pie-eating people can ever be permanently vanquished.

—EDITORIAL, *NEW YORK TIMES,* 1902
written in response to an Englishman's suggestion that Americans
should reduce their daily pie eating to two days per week

Introduction

S INCE THE RELEASE OF MY FIRST COOKBOOK, *Garden County—Where Everyone Is Welcome to Sit at the Table,* so much good has happened.

If you are familiar with *Garden County* or have heard me on the radio or seen me on television, you know my story of being very ill and bedridden for months after surgery to remove a tumor in my throat. I couldn't continue the inactivity of lying in bed, so I began writing a cookbook. I documented years of gatherings: birthday parties, anniversary parties, Fourth of July celebrations, Thanksgiving dinners, and so on. I have stacks of stenographer's notebooks in my basement, the kind with the spiral wire at the top. My mother, Judy Lerma, used to purchase steno books for all her lists of shopping or what she needed to do. I guess I inherited that trait because today I have stacks and stacks of steno books. I cannot use any other kind; it just doesn't feel right. Actually, I have boxes of steno books documenting my every move over the years. Should I pass away, there would be left a detailed account of my life through to-do lists; menus; guest lists; grocery lists; hopes, dreams, and desires lists; places I want to travel to lists, ideas for future books I want to write; and writings and musings during plane travel of what I'm feeling. And, of course, I have dated everything. It's better than finding a daily journal or diary. But it was because of these notebooks and my documentation that I could piece together my favorite gatherings and recipes through the years and create what was a stepping-stone and unanticipated new career.

Once my cookbook was published and in bookstores, life pretty much remained the same. But then the marketing staff at Syren Book

Company started to receive feedback from bookstores like Borders in Saint Paul and the Bookcase in Wayzata, Minnesota, for book signings before the Christmas holiday. It was really touch and go for a few weeks because my partner, Chad Olson, and I had just returned from Cortona, Italy, where we host culinary vacations. We literally landed on a Friday, had no time to recover from jet lag, and had a table at the Calhoun Coffee Festival in Minneapolis, signing copies of my cookbook and chatting about cooking.

What I found so rewarding about meeting people at festivals and expos was their enthusiasm for talking about food. I would share my shortcuts and tried-and-true methods for baking cheesecake, preparing the perfect pie crust, or simply making a moist roast beef. People, or as I began to call them, "foodies," were excited and thrilled that I was taking time to speak their language about food; I was not talking over their heads and certainly not sharing recipes and ideas that couldn't be prepared in their kitchens. That was the first lesson I learned.

Three months later, I was one of many featured chefs at an expo, offering cooking demos with recipes that could be made in 15 minutes or less. I was also offering a cooking demo on making family suppers with five or fewer items. Another chef appeared before the crowd and began preparing a wonderful but complicated recipe. Five minutes into his presentation, half the audience got up and left. I felt bad for the chef but again paid attention to what the audience wanted—simplicity. So I began reviewing my menus and ideas to fit my audiences. I responded to e-mails from people who had seen me on television or at personal appearances. I began listing topics, in general, that they specifically asked me about. As I began appearing on radio, I continued to keep my topics and recipes simple but very flavorsome.

One recipe that comes to mind is my Garden-Fresh Pesto Pizza. I made it for an appearance on one of my favorite radio programs, the *Cities 97 Morning Show* with Brian Turner (BT) and Lee Valsvik. When I visit their studio, I liken it to going to a party for four or five people: BT, Lee, their producer, Chad (if he's not working that morning), and me. My Garden-Fresh Pesto Pizza is made with a pizza crust (homemade or store bought), basil pesto (homemade or store bought), and shredded mozzarella and Parmesan cheeses. That's it. It's simple but will thrill your family or guests, and it was also a recipe that commuters could re-member while driving. You see, the *Cities 97 Morning Show* plays from 6:00 until 9:00. I'm usually on around 8:00, the main commuting hour in the Twin Cities.

Not that all my recipes are so simple and easy. This cookbook is all about pies. I have some extravagant recipes in my pie repertoire, but this collection's focus is straightforward: these recipes all have at least a side-and-bottom crust. Some will include a top crust. I have pie recipes that make their own crust. I have pie recipes that have popcorn for crust. I have recipes for pies that are turned upside down. Not all of these recipes are in this cookbook, but rather all the recipes listed here can be made with homemade pie crusts or pie crust purchased at your favor-ite grocery store.

I prefer homemade pie crust, but I have the time to make it because cooking is my career. Most people who take my classes, read my articles and cookbooks, or see me on television will tell me they don't have the time for any type of baking. So I tell them that store-bought or ready-made pie crusts are not a sin or a crime. If it will help you make one of my recipes for your family and friends, then purchase the store-bought pie crust and use one of my fillings. I just want my readers and "foodies" to make pies, to enjoy an all-American desert, and see the "yummy" smiles on the faces of their friends and family as they taste each bite of pie.

During the writing of this book, I was asked to appear on *Twin Cities Live* with John Hanson and Rebekah Wood. It's a wonderful afternoon talk/variety show on KSTP, the ABC affiliate station in Minneapolis-Saint Paul. I prepared my Captain Tony's Watermelon Pie recipe. I had a pie completed for tasting after we ran through the steps to prepare the pie on live television. The looks on the hosts' faces were wonderful as they tasted a piece of my completed watermelon pie. Rebekah actu-ally took a second bite while John finished out the scene reading the cue cards. During the commercial break, the crew and other guests appear-ing on the show started cutting pieces of the pie. Satisfied "yummy" faces were all over the studio. That is the best compliment I could ever receive. I guess there is a great deal of self-sacrificing North Dakotan left in me— the satisfaction of feeding others.

Along with feeding others, I love teaching. I've been offering classes ranging from Tuscan Grilling to Holiday Baking, Italian Easter (ask me to tell you about this class sometime), and, one of my most popular, Pie Baking. My pie classes at the Chef's Gallery in Stillwater, Minnesota, are always sold out the minute they are announced, so we offer several each year. In 2008, Stephanie Jameson, director of the cooking school, and I created a Pie series. We offered a class each week focusing on one element of pie baking. The first week's topic was the pie crust. The second week we concentrated on sweet and savory pies, and so on for four more weeks. It was popular and clients could choose what they needed. After class, as I am driving home, I feel terrific. I could gauge the excitement and see the change in baking styles of my students. I could tell they couldn't wait to go to their homes and continue the pie-baking experience. I absolutely love teaching.

My first class at Kitchen Window in Calhoun Square in uptown Minneapolis was a pie class for 25 students. Each student received a ceramic pie plate and chose the type of pie they wanted to prepare in class when they registered. We had a list of six different pies from Apple Pie to Belmont Road Chicken Pie. I was running around like a chicken with its head cut off all through class, but I enjoyed it as much as the students. Sometimes I get clients who drive three to four hours to come to one of my classes. I hope they know how much I appreciate their effort because I try to give back to them, and everyone in the class, 300 percent. Who knows? Maybe I'll have my own cooking school someday.

I hope that if you are in the Twin Cities you'll join me in one of my classes at the Chef's Gallery or Kitchen Window. My company, Garden County Cooking, also offers private events such as birthday parties, anniversary parties, grooms' dinners, wedding rehearsal dinners, and much more. It's like your own private cooking class. You can contact Garden County Cooking through our Web site to book your own private event or sign up for classes at www.GardenCountyCooking.com.

I guess you can tell from this introduction that life has changed a great deal and has become extremely amusing. We started our culinary vacations to Tuscany and to the Caribbean; I write a monthly column called "Off the Eaten Path" in which I review restaurants in the Twin Cities and surrounding areas (it's a really nice gig, one Chad tells me I am never to quit). I write another monthly column, "Word of Mouth," which is about anything food I choose to write. Both columns appear in *Lavender* magazine, which is published in Minneapolis twice a month. These articles give me the chance to investigate and have fun with food. So, yes, life is busy. Along with cookbooks, classes, writing for magazines, and culinary vacations, we do have a life once in a while. We have good friends, nights around the fire pit in the backyard, and long bicycle rides.

One of my favorite pastimes is entering cooking contests, especially pie-baking competitions. I would like to invite all my readers and anyone who loves pie to enter a contest, whether at a county fair, state fair, or on the national level. Check out the American Pie Council at www.piecouncil.org. I never enjoy myself more than when I am competing or assisting in judging for the American Pie Council. When we get together for the National Pie Championship each April, it feels to me like getting together with friends and family at the holidays. It's something I can't wait for. Even if you don't win the pie contest you entered, you did it. You actually took the time to do it. That is an accomplishment on its own. Good for you.

My wish is that all my readers will find one or two pies within these pages that delight them in the making and delight their guests. I always tell my students to take my recipes and make them your own. Linda Hoskins, executive director of the American Pie Council, called me one day and told me she had baked my Vidalia Onion Pie recipe in a rectangle tart pan, cut it into squares after baking, and served it as an appetizer on her boat while entertaining celebrity chef Gail Gand. So if Linda can do that for Gail, so can you. You have permission to go wild and take one of my recipes and create something fantastic.

This all goes back to my early years on the farm with my grandma and has now taken on a life of its own. I am thrilled about this turn of events and know my grandma Thelma Anderson would be tickled pink.

Enjoy my recipes and don't forget to sing while baking. My favorite "pie song" is from Irving Berlin's 1932 musical *Face the Music*. The song was set in a self-service restaurant and sung by a group of once-wealthy people who were waiting for better times. The wisdom the lyrics impart is as timely today as it was seven-plus decades ago: life is good and there's always reason to hope, so celebrate by having another cup of coffee and another piece of pie to go with it.

Happy baking!

The History of Pie

The origins of pie actually did not come from America, but has evolved over the years into what we now call the all-American pie. It is not something that was created to be American, but somehow, we have adopted this dessert as our own and commonly use the expression, "as American as apple pie."

Pie has been around since about 2000 B.C. during the time of the ancient Egyptians. Between 1400 B.C. and 600 B.C., it's believed pie was passed on to the Greeks and then spread to Rome around 100 B.C. The early Romans' pies were sometimes made in "reeds" which were used for the sole purpose of holding the filling and not for eating with the filling.

The Romans must have spread the word about pies around Europe as the Oxford English Dictionary notes that the word pie was a popular word in the 14th century. The first pie recipe was published by the Romans and was for a rye-crusted goat cheese and honey pie.

The early pies were predominately meat pies. Pyes (pies) originally appeared in England as early as the twelfth century. The crust of the pie was referred to as "coffin." There was actually more crust than filling. Often these pies were made using fowl and the legs were left to hang over the side of the dish and used as handles. Fruit pies or tarts (pasties) were probably first made in the 1500s. English tradition credits making the first cherry pie to Queen Elizabeth I.

Pie came to America with the first English settlers. The early colonists cooked their pies in long narrow pans, calling them "coffins" like the crust in England. As in the Roman times, the early American pie crusts often were not eaten but simply designed to hold the filling during baking. It was during the American Revolution that the term crust was used instead of coffyn.

Over the years, pie has evolved to become what it is today, "the most traditional American dessert." Pie has become so much a part of American culture throughout the years that we now commonly use the term "as American as apple pie."

Used by permission of the American Pie Council

The Crust

ALL BAKERS AND COOKBOOK WRITERS SAY they have the perfect pie crust recipe or a "never fail" pie crust recipe. I call mine the Perfect Crust because it is and has been for me, whether baking pies at home, for national pie championships, or in front of the cameras for the Food Network. My hope is that when you decide to prepare a pie crust, I have given you enough information to choose a recipe that years from now you'll swear by.

Let's begin simply. I have one recipe for basic pie pastry. I used to have recipes for 8-inch, 9-inch, and 10-inch pie crusts. But I like things simple. So here's my one recipe that I have divided into one-crust and two-crust recipes for easy understanding. If you have any leftover pastry dough, wrap it tightly in plastic wrap and freeze for later use. I enjoy making fruit or leaf cutouts to decorate my edge or top crust. I've also prepared braids and decorative knots to adorn the edges or top crust.

My husband likes only two kinds of pie—warm pie and cold pie.

—AUTHOR UNKNOWN, LONGMONT, COLORADO

- The Perfect Crust
  - One-Crust Pie
  - Two-Crust Pie
- Fat
  - Butter and Margarine
  - Vegetable Shortening
  - Lard
- Kosher or Sea Salt
- Mixing by Hand
- Mixing in a Food Processor
- Blind Baking
  - Blind Baking Pie Crust
- Pie Shield
- Freezing
- Troubleshooting
- Butter and Lard Crust
- All-Butter Crust
- Buttermilk Crust
- Oil Pastry Crust
- Never-Fail Vinegar Crust
- Graham Cracker Crust
- Chocolate Graham Cracker Crust
- Cookie Crust
- Shortbread Crust
- Coconut Crust

The Perfect Crust

⸕ One-Crust Pie: Makes enough pastry for one 10-inch pie

1½ cups unbleached all-purpose flour
½ tablespoon white sugar
½ teaspoon kosher or sea salt, finely ground
¼ cup Crisco butter-flavored all-vegetable shortening, chilled
    and cut into small pieces
¼ cup unsalted butter, chilled and cut into small pieces
¼–½ cup cold water; use only as much as needed for a smooth,
    satiny dough ball
1 egg yolk and 1 teaspoon water for egg wash

1. Before beginning, all ingredients need to be cold. Combine all dry ingredients in a large mixing bowl. Add shortening and butter. Using a pastry blender or food processor (see Mixing in a Food Processor in this chapter), cut in the shortening and butter until the mixture resembles coarse meal or peas.

2. Drop by drop, add the cold water. Mix in with the fingertips, not with the hands as the palms will warm the dough. Continue mixing in water until the dough begins to hold together without being crumbly yet not sticky. Depending on where you live, dry air and humidity will be a major factor in the amount of water you use. You want a ball of pastry dough that feels like satin and holds together well, and in which you can see the small bits of fat evenly dispersed.

3. Place finished dough in plastic wrap. Fold over plastic wrap and press down to form a disk. This will make rolling out easier after chilling. Finish wrapping in plastic and place in the refrigerator for at least 30 minutes.

4. Lightly spray 8-, 9-, or 10-inch pie plate with butter or vegetable cooking spray. Roll out chilled pie dough on a nonstick fiberglass and silicone liner or other lightly floured surface. Place in pie plate, allowing excess pastry to hang over the edge. Cut away extra dough,

tuck under, and crimp decoratively. Brush sides and bottom with egg wash. This will create a cement seal between the filling and dough. Return to the refrigerator and chill until filling is ready. Add filling and brush edge with remaining egg wash for a golden sheen. Bake per recipe instructions.

Two-Crust Pie: Makes enough pastry for the bottom and top crust for one 10-inch pie

3 cups unbleached all-purpose flour
1 tablespoon white sugar
1 teaspoon kosher or sea salt, finely ground
½ cup Crisco butter-flavored all-vegetable shortening, chilled
    and cut into small pieces
½ cup unsalted butter, chilled and cut into small pieces
½–¾ cup cold water; use only as much as needed for a smooth,
    satiny dough ball
1 egg yolk and 1 teaspoon water for egg wash

1. Before beginning, all ingredients need to be cold. Combine all dry ingredients in a large mixing bowl. Add shortening and butter. Using a pastry blender or food processor (see Mixing in a Food Processor in this chapter), cut in the shortening and butter until the mixture resembles coarse meal or peas.
2. Drop by drop, add the cold water. Mix in with the fingertips, not with the hands as the palms will warm the dough. Continue mixing in water until the dough begins to hold together without being crumbly yet not sticky. Depending on where you live, dry air and humidity will be a major factor in the amount of water you use. You want a ball of pastry dough that feels like satin and holds together well, and in which you can see the small bits of fat evenly dispersed.
3. Divide dough into two pieces and place each in plastic wrap. Fold over plastic wrap and press down to form a disk. This will make roll-

ing out easier after chilling. Finish wrapping in plastic and place in the refrigerator for at least 30 minutes.

4. Lightly spray 8-, 9-, or 10-inch pie plate with butter or vegetable cooking spray. Roll out one piece of chilled dough on a nonstick fiberglass and silicone liner or other lightly floured surface. Place in pie plate and remove excess pastry to ½ inch. Brush sides and bottom with egg wash. This will create a cement seal between the filling and dough and between the edges of the bottom and top crust. Return to the refrigerator and chill until filling is ready. Roll out top crust, apply egg wash, and place on top of filled pie. Trim excess pastry, tuck under, and crimp decoratively. Brush with remaining egg wash for a golden sheen. Bake per recipe instructions.

There it is. That is my basic pie crust recipe, which has been in my family for generations. It gives you the best of both worlds regarding the fat. Crisco shortening helps give the crust integrity, fortifying and bonding it. Butter gives the crust a wonderful flavor. The two combined create the perfect crust when baked.

Of course, nothing else matters if you don't "chill, chill, chill." This is my mantra and my advice given for years during my classes, during radio interviews, and in cooking demonstrations on television. If you chill all your ingredients before you begin, and even during preparation if they become too warm, you have always have a wonderfully tender and flaky crust. What happens is that the little pieces of fat (shortening and butter) will burst open while baking and release steam, which in turn creates a flaky crust. If they are not chilled properly, they blend into the flour and liquefy rather than release steam.

I would like to take a moment to discuss nonstick fiberglass and silicone liners. I have several sizes and brands in my kitchen. At first they took the place of parchment paper on my cookie sheets and baking pans. I used them in place of greasing the pan for my cookies, rolls, and breads. One day while rolling out a pie crust, I was having trouble with my dough sticking to the countertop. I continued adding flour, but I felt it was too much. I completed the pie, and after cooling, served to friends who came to our house for a summer gathering. They loved it, but I could taste the extra flour in the crust. It was dry and ashen tasting. It was also difficult to cut when serving.

The next time I rolled out a batch of cookies, I decided to do it on a silicone liner. I removed the excess dough and placed the liner on my baking pan. While the cookies were baking, a light bulb went off in my head: Why not roll out pie pastry on a silicone liner?

So I looked forward to baking my next pie. I was on a mission. I prepared my pie dough, lightly floured (more of a sprinkle) my silicone liner, and begin to roll out my dough. It was effortless. The best part was that I could rotate the liner to roll out a perfect circle. I have a small galley kitchen and little counter space. Rolling out has always been a challenge for me. I just found a way to reduce the flour when rolling out my pie dough and discovered a way to better utilize my counter space. I was back in control and feeling pretty cocky.

Once the rolled-out dough was the correct size, I discovered another benefit of using the silicone liner. I folded over the liner and then carefully peeled it back from the dough. I then lifted the dough from the liner, placed it in my prepared pie plate, and unfolded the dough to create a perfectly rolled-out crust. It was a success. I have been using silicone liners since that day. You can see me using silicone liners on two Food Network specials while preparing pies: Food Network Challenge—The Great American Pie Cook-Off (2007) and Food Network Challenge—National Pie Championship (2008).

Fat

Many people use butter or margarine in their crusts. Unlike lard and vegetable shortening, which are 100 percent fat, butter and margarine are around 80 percent fat, so you have to boost the amount of fat in your recipe by 20 percent to get the right ratio relative to the other ingredients. In using butter and margarine, you're also adding a certain amount of water to your crust, so you may need to cut back on another liquid specified in the recipe.

Butter and Margarine

Nothing adds flavor to any dish more than butter. Crusts made with butter are extremely flavorful, for example, a Pâte Brisée, which is a standard pie and pastry dough. However, crusts made with all butter or margarine will turn out less tender and flaky than those made with lard or vegetable shortening. Lard and vegetable shortening are used in pie crusts because they have a higher melting point than butter, so an all-butter or margarine pie dough must be kept cold at all times through processing, handling, and shaping versus a crust that blends lard or shortening with butter or margarine.

Margarines can change the taste of your crust by brand. Be careful of strongly flavored brands of margarine. I choose not to use margarine unless stuck in a snowstorm stranded in the country. Real butter offers the best taste and consistency.

Also, I prefer to use unsalted butter in my pie crust for a sweeter taste. If you use regular butter rather than unsalted, omit the salt in the recipe or you will have a very salty-tasting crust.

Vegetable Shortening

As I mentioned earlier in this chapter, vegetable shortening gives your pie crust integrity and produces a flakier crust. It also makes it easier to work with than an all-butter or all-lard crust as it begins to warm in the kitchen environment. However, butter and lard add flavor, so the result of an all-vegetable shortening crust is that the flavor will not be as rich— even with a butter-flavored shortening. Crisco now offers a no trans fat all-vegetable shortening.

Lard

Lard refers to pork fat, both its rendered and unrendered forms. Lard was used as cooking fat, shortening, and a spread similar to butter. The use of lard in baking and cooking has diminished over the years due to health concerns about its saturated fat content. However, lard is having a renaissance thanks to chefs like Rick Bayless who hail its virtues in certain types of cooking.

Lard can be rendered by either of two processes, wet rendering or dry rendering. In wet rendering, pork fat is boiled in water or steamed at a high temperature and the lard, which is insoluble in water, is skimmed off the surface of the mixture, or it is separated in an industrial centrifuge. In dry rendering, the fat is exposed to high heat in a pan or oven without the presence of water (a process similar to frying bacon). The two processes yield somewhat different products. Wet-rendered lard has a more neutral flavor, snowy white color, and a high smoke point. Dry-rendered lard is somewhat browner in color and flavor and has relatively lower smoke point.

I prefer wet-rendered lard in my pie crusts. The flavor and texture are incredible. This type of lard is difficult to find in your local grocery store. I've obtained it through my local farmers' market from local butchers. They usually don't have it on hand, so you will have to ask for it and pick it up the following week. It's worth the wait.

Dry-rendered lard is easy to find at grocery stores. It gives a "brown" or cooked-fat taste to the finished pie crust. As a celebrity judge at many pie contests, I can tell when someone has use dry-rendered lard in a recipe. The crust is difficult to cut and has a texture like that of shoe leather. This type of lard is used for deep-fat and regular frying.

That said, I believe that most pie bakers were unaware of the difference in lard. They felt that the lard available at their grocer was the lard their grandmother used in her pies or the lard everyone talks about as producing the best and flakiest crusts. Now you know.

Kosher or Sea Salt

Since my first cookbook came out, I am continually asked about my recommendation to use kosher or sea salt, especially Hawaiian sea salt. I visited the Hawaiian Islands many years ago. We lived on the island of Kauai for a week, and I visited the salt ponds on the south side of the island. I also brought home 10 pounds of Hawaiian sea salt. It's coarse, sweet, and has a wonderful aftertaste. I've used it in all my cooking and baking, especially when baking pies. However, because sea salt is coarse I use a mortar and pestle to grind it into a fine powder to incorporate into pastry dough. I believe regular table salt has a "gray" taste to it and too much sodium. I prefer sea salt. Look for it at your local cooking store or fine food store.

Mixing by Hand

I prefer this method of mixing and blending. It's the way I was taught by my grandma Thelma Anderson. I can tell from the texture whether it's coarse or like satin, from the dryness of the dough if not enough water has been added, or from the stickiness if too much water has been added. By using my fingertips, I can mix together the dry ingredients with the fat without warming the dough. I can carefully knead everything together to form a ball of satiny dough. By not using the palms of my hands, I help the dough remain cold during this final mixing stage and the small pieces of fat remain intact. If I used the palms of my hands, the heat would warm the dough, melting the fat and blending everything together. The release of steam from the small pieces of fat would not take place during the baking process, and the final crust would not be flaky.

Mixing in a Food Processor

Many of my students in my pie-baking classes ask me if I know how to prepare pie pastry in a food processor. I guess I have such a "hands on" reputation that it's a logical question. I have used a food processor to successfully prepare my pie pastry, and here are my recommendations:

1. Chill your food processor bowl and blade in the freezer or refrigerator.
2. Follow your favorite pie pastry recipe. Add all your dry ingredients to the food processor bowl. Close the top and pulse once or twice to incorporate well.
3. Add your chilled fats cut into small pieces.
4. Close the top and pulse quickly 1-2-3-4-5-6 times. Remove the top of the processor and check pastry dough. The incorporated fat and dry

ingredients should resemble coarse meal or small peas. If not, cover processor with top and pulse one more time.

Note: I have never had to pulse more then seven times to achieve the "coarse meal or peas" stage.

5. Pour the contents from the bowl of the food processor into a chilled mixing bowl. Add recommended chilled water from recipe and begin mixing with fingertips until ball of dough forms. Continue to follow recipe instructions.

Never add water to the food processor bowl and process. This will blend the fats with the dry ingredients. The release of steam from the small pieces of fat will not take place during the baking process, and the final crust will not be flaky.

Blind Baking

Blind baking is just another term for prebaking. It refers to a pie crust that is partially or completely baked before it is filled. This is usually done for cream or custard fillings that are already cooked but will not be baked or to help keep the crust from becoming soggy from a wet fruit filling.

When you blind bake a pie crust, follow the recipe for preparing the dough. After placing it in the pie pan, prick the sides and bottom of the crust with a fork. This allows excess steam to be released and keeps the dough from puffing. Line the crust with parchment paper or a coffee filter if you don't have parchment paper, and fill with baking beans or beads. Push the beans or beads up against the sides and evenly around the bottom.

Bake following the pie recipe. Carefully remove the parchment paper with beans or beads. Let cool completely on a rack before filling. Some recipes suggest chilling before filling. If the recipe requires filling and additional baking, cover edges with a pie shield to prevent excessive browning or burning.

Blind Baking Pie Crust

1½ cups unbleached all-purpose flour
½ tablespoon white sugar
½ teaspoon kosher or sea salt, finely ground
¼ cup Crisco butter-flavored all-vegetable shortening, chilled
    and cut into small pieces
¼ cup unsalted butter, chilled and cut into small pieces
¼–½ cup cold water; use only as much as needed for a smooth,
    satiny dough ball
Crisco butter-flavored cooking spray

1. All ingredients should be cold. Combine all the dry ingredients in a large mixing bowl. Add shortening and butter. Using a pastry blender, cut in the shortening and butter until the mixture resembles coarse meal or peas.
2. Drop by drop, add the cold water. Mix in with the fingertips, not with the hands as the palms will warm the dough. Continue mixing in water until the dough begins to hold together without being crumbly yet not sticky.
3. Place dough in plastic wrap. Fold over plastic wrap and press down to form a disk. This will make rolling out easier after chilling. Finish wrapping in plastic and place in the refrigerator for at least 30 minutes.
4. Lightly spray a deep 8-, 9-, or 10-inch pie pan. Roll out dough and place in pie plate, allowing the excess pastry to hang over the edge. Trim excess dough, tuck under, and crimp decoratively. Prick side and bottom of crust with a fork. Chill in the refrigerator for at least 30 minutes or freezer for 15 minutes.
5. Preheat the oven to 400 degrees. Line the pastry shell with parchment and baking beans or beads. Bake the shell for 12 minutes. Remove the paper and beans/beads and return to the oven for 12 more minutes or until golden. Cool.

Makes enough pastry for one 10-inch single-crust pie.

Pie Shield

A pie shield is an indispensable tool for preventing the edges of your prize pie from burning before the center of the pie has fully baked. There are many types of pie shields available on the Internet or at your favorite cooking store. When I began baking pies, my grandma and I would use tinfoil to create a shield over the pie edges. Foil sometimes falls off, however, and creates an unevenly baked edge. Today there are reusable aluminum pie shields you simply place over the edges. I have had the aluminum shield stick to my edge if I have any leakage from the filling, so I suggest spraying the inside of your pie shield with cooking spray before placing on the pie and baking. I just started using the new reusable solid silicone pie shields. They are fantastic and require no cooking spray beforehand. Both aluminum and silicone shields are dishwasher safe.

Freezing

Most pie crusts, tightly wrapped in plastic wrap, may be refrigerated for up to one week or frozen for up to one month. I have sealed several batches of completed pie pastry with my home food vacuum and placed them in the freezer up to six months with no freezer burn. Be sure to remove from the freezer and bring almost to room temperature before rolling out. You want chilled, but not frozen, pastry dough to roll out. This is an excellent time-saving technique.

Troubleshooting

* Always make deep slits in the top crust of any fruit pie. This will allow steam to be released from the pie to prevent the filling from becoming soft and soggy.

- If your crust is becoming too dark before the filling is ready or bubbly, place a piece of tinfoil over the entire top crust. You can also reduce the temperature of the oven.
- Shiny metal pie plates do not brown pie crusts properly. Use glass, ceramic, or dark metal pie plates.
- Spray pie plate with cooking spray before adding pie crust. This will ensure that your pie will not stick to the pie plate after baking even if the filling has leaked. Trust me; I've used this technique and it has served me well, especially in front of judges on national television.
- Brushing an egg wash (one egg yolk and one teaspoon cold water) on the bottom and sides of an unbaked pie crust before filling will create a barrier between the filling and crust that will prevent it from becoming soggy.
- Do not use an egg wash on your pie crust before blind baking. It will create a glue bond between the parchment paper and the crust. The top layer of the pie crust will be removed when you take out the parchment paper.
- When baking at a high altitude, slightly increase the liquid in your pie pastry dough. Otherwise the crust may become too dry in baking. Use as little flour as possible when rolling out.

ϯ Butter and Lard Crust

1½ cups unbleached all-purpose flour
½ tablespoon white sugar
½ teaspoon kosher or sea salt, finely ground
¼ cup wet-rendered lard, chilled and cut into small pieces
¼ cup unsalted butter, chilled and cut into small pieces
¼–½ cup cold water; use only as much as needed for a smooth,
    satiny dough ball
1 egg yolk and 1 teaspoon water for egg wash

1. Before beginning, all ingredients need to be cold. Combine all dry ingredients in a large mixing bowl. Add lard and butter. Using a pastry blender or food processor (see Mixing in a Food Processor in this chapter), cut in the lard and butter until the mixture resembles coarse meal or peas.

2. Drop by drop, add the cold water. Mix in with the fingertips, not with the hands as the palms will warm the dough. Continue mixing in water until the dough begins to hold together without being crumbly yet not sticky. Depending on where you live, dry air and humidity will be a major factor in the amount of water you use. You want a ball of pastry dough that feels like satin and holds together well, and in which you can see the small bits of fat evenly dispersed.

3. Place finished dough in plastic wrap. Fold over plastic wrap and press down to form a disk. This will make rolling out easier after chilling. Finish wrapping in plastic and place in the refrigerator for at least 30 minutes.

4. Lightly spray 8-, 9-, or 10-inch pie plate with butter or vegetable cooking spray. Roll out chilled pie dough on a nonstick fiberglass and silicone liner or other lightly floured surface. Place in pie plate, allowing the excess pastry to hang over the edge. Trim excess dough, tuck under, and crimp decoratively. Brush sides and bottom with egg wash. This will create a cement seal between the filling and dough.

Return to the refrigerator and chill until filling is ready. Add filling and brush edge with remaining egg wash for a golden sheen. Bake per recipe instructions.

Makes enough pastry for one 10-inch single-crust pie.

∱ All-Butter Crust

When handling an all-butter crust, make sure you keep the dough cold. If you feel the dough becoming soft or sticky, immediately place in the refrigerator until well chilled and then continue. Also, if using a food processor, place the bowl and blade in the freezer before processing. You'll be rewarded with the best-tasting pastry dough for your award-winning pie filling recipe.

> 1½ cups unbleached all-purpose flour
> ½ tablespoon white sugar
> ½ teaspoon kosher or sea salt, finely ground
> ½ cup unsalted butter, chilled and cut into small pieces
> ¼–½ cup cold water; use only as much as needed for a smooth, satiny dough ball
> 1 egg yolk and 1 teaspoon water for egg wash

1. Before beginning, all ingredients need to be cold. Combine all dry ingredients in a large mixing bowl. Add butter. Using a pastry blender or food processor (see Mixing in a Food Processor in this chapter), cut in the butter until the mixture resembles coarse meal or peas.
2. Drop by drop, add the cold water. Mix in with the fingertips, not with the hands as the palms will warm the dough. Continue mixing in water until the dough begins to hold together without being crumbly yet not sticky. Depending on where you live, dry air and humidity will be a major factor in the amount of water you use. You want a

ball of pastry dough that feels like satin and holds together well, and in which you can see the small bits of fat evenly dispersed.

3. Place finished dough in plastic wrap. Fold over plastic wrap and press down to form a disk. This will make rolling out easier after chilling. Finish wrapping in plastic and place in the refrigerator to chill for at least 30 minutes.

4. Lightly spray 8-, 9-, or 10-inch pie plate with butter or vegetable cooking spray. Roll out chilled pie dough on a nonstick fiberglass and silicone liner or other lightly floured surface. Place in pie plate, allowing excess pastry to hang over the edge. Cut away extra dough, tuck under, and crimp decoratively. Brush sides and bottom with egg wash. This will create a cement seal between the filling and dough. Return to the refrigerator and chill until filling is ready. Add filling and brush edge with remaining egg wash for a golden sheen. Bake per recipe instructions.

Makes pastry for one 10-inch single-crust pie.

Buttermilk Crust

1½ cups unbleached all-purpose flour
½ tablespoon white sugar
½ teaspoon kosher or sea salt, finely ground
¼ cup Crisco butter-flavored all-vegetable shortening, chilled and cut into small pieces
¼ cup unsalted butter, chilled and cut into small pieces
¼ cup cold buttermilk or more, if needed

1. Before beginning, all ingredients need to be cold. Combine all dry ingredients in a large mixing bowl. Add shortening and butter. Using a pastry blender or food processor (see Mixing in a Food Processor in this chapter), cut in the shortening and butter until the mixture resembles coarse meal or peas.

2. Drop by drop, add buttermilk. Mix in with the fingertips, not with the hands as the palms will warm the dough. Continue mixing in buttermilk until the dough begins to hold together without being crumbly yet not sticky. You may use anywhere from ⅛ cup to ¼ cup of cold buttermilk. Depending on where you live, dry air and humidity will be a major factor in the amount of water you use. You want a ball of pastry dough that feels like satin and holds together well, and in which you can see the small bits of fat evenly dispersed.

3. Place finished dough in plastic wrap. Fold over plastic wrap and press down to form a disk. This will make rolling out easier after chilling. Finish wrapping in plastic and place in the refrigerator to chill for at least 30 minutes.

4. Lightly spray 8-, 9-, or 10-inch pie plate with butter or vegetable cooking spray. Roll out chilled pie dough on a no-stick fiberglass and silicone liner or other lightly floured surface. Place in pie plate, allowing excess pastry to hang over the edge. Trim excess dough, tuck under, and crimp decoratively. Brush sides and bottom with egg wash. This will create a cement seal between the filling and dough. Return to the refrigerator and chill until filling is ready. Bake per recipe instructions.

Makes pastry for one 10-inch single-crust pie.

⨍ Oil Pastry Crust

This is the most requested recipe from pie fans and enthusiasts. I've only prepared this crust a couple of times and use it exclusively for my savory pies. I've been told this is very good for sweet pies, too, so you can be the judge. My grandma used to say this was the easiest of pie pastries to make because of the liquid fat. She didn't need to use as much fat, and she could roll and reroll her oil crust without the dough becoming coarse.

> 2 cups unbleached all-purpose flour
> 1 tablespoon white sugar
> 1 teaspoon kosher or sea salt, finely ground
> ½ cup vegetable oil or extra virgin olive oil*
> ¼ cup cold whole milk

1. In a medium mixing bowl, combine flour and salt. Add vegetable oil and milk. Mix briskly to combine dry and liquid ingredients until a dough forms into a ball.
2. Divide the dough in half. Roll dough between two sheets of wax paper to about ⅛-inch thickness.

*Using extra virgin olive oil will change the taste of your pastry dough— you will taste a difference. I've used extra virgin olive oil while in Italy for both savory and sweet pies.

John Michael's Time-Saving Tip: Because this pastry dough is prepared with oil, it must be used immediately. Storing in the refrigerator will separate the oil from the dough, resulting in seepage.

𝆑 Never-Fail Vinegar Crust

This was always my favorite recipe in Grandma's collection. I enjoyed the term "never fail." To be truthful I've only tried this recipe once in my pie career and that's when I was 17. It worked beautifully. Since then I've mostly used my "Perfect Crust" recipe at the beginning of this chapter. It's always worked well for me and, well, I'm a creature of habit.

2 cups unbleached all-purpose flour
2 teaspoons white sugar
1 teaspoon kosher or sea salt, finely ground
¾ cup lard or shortening, chilled, or ½ cup lard or shortening
    and 4 tablespoons unsalted butter, chilled
2 teaspoons white vinegar
1 egg
Up to ¼ cup cold water, if needed

1. Measure flour, sugar, and salt into a medium mixing bowl. Drop the fat by pieces into the flour mixture. With a pastry blender or food processor, cut the fat into the flour mixture until it resembles coarse meal or peas. Add vinegar and egg. Using your fingertips, mix in liquids, adding water only as needed to create a ball of pastry dough that feels like satin and holds together well, and in which you can see the small bits of fat well dispersed.
2. Wrap the ball of dough in plastic wrap and place in the refrigerator to mature and chill 4 hours or longer. Remove the dough from the refrigerator about 30 minutes before rolling or it will be difficult to work. Prepare and roll as you would for any pie crust.

Makes two 8- or 9-inch pie crusts.

⸗ Graham Cracker Crust

1¾ cups graham cracker crumbs
2 tablespoons light brown sugar, firmly packed
½ teaspoon ground cinnamon
Pinch of salt
6 tablespoons unsalted butter, melted
Crisco butter-flavored cooking spray

1. Preheat oven to 350 degrees. Spray pie plate with cooking spray and set aside.
2. Combine the graham cracker crumbs, brown sugar, cinnamon, and salt in a large mixing bowl. Using your fingertips, mix together. Add the butter and incorporate well, mixing first with a fork, then with your hands, rubbing thoroughly to form evenly dampened crumbs.
3. Spread the crumbs evenly and loosely in the pie plate, pressing them into the bottom and up the side. Refrigerate for 10 minutes.
4. Bake for 8 to 10 minutes. Cool on a rack. Refrigerate 15 minutes before filling.

Makes one 9-inch graham cracker crust.

⸗ Chocolate Graham Cracker Crust

1¼ cups graham cracker crumbs, fine
¼ cup white sugar
¼ cup Dutch processed cocoa powder, unsweetened
⅓ cup unsalted butter, melted
Crisco butter-flavored cooking spray

1. Preheat oven to 350 degrees. Spray pie plate with cooking spray. Set aside.
2. Stir together the crumbs, sugar, cocoa powder, and butter until the mixture is combined. Press mixture into the bottom and up the side

of prepared pie plate. Chill for 30 minutes. Bake for 7–10 minutes. Cool completely before adding filling.

Makes one 9-inch crust.

✦ Cookie Crust

I love this crust because it tastes like my grandma's sugar cookies. I have used this recipe for many of my pies, but the most popular were my Key Lime Delight Pie and my John Michael's Citrus Delight Pie.

> 2 cups all-purpose flour
> 1 stick chilled unsalted butter, diced
> 2 tablespoons white sugar
> 2 large egg yolks
> Pinch of kosher or sea salt, finely ground
> 2 tablespoons cold water

1. Sift the flour into a mixing bowl and use pastry blender to cut in the chilled butter until it resembles coarse meal. Add the sugar, egg yolks, salt, and water. Mix to a soft dough.
2. Roll out the pastry on a lightly floured surface and use to line a deep 9-inch pie pan or 8½-inch fluted flan pan, allowing the excess pastry to hang over the edge. Prick the pastry bottom and chill for 30 minutes.
3. Preheat the oven to 400 degrees. Trim the excess pastry from around the edge of the pastry shell. Line the pastry shell with parchment and baking beans or beads.
4. Bake the shell for 10 minutes. Remove the paper and beans or beads and return to the oven for 10 more minutes. Cool.

Makes pastry for one 9-inch single-crust pie.

Shortbread Crust

3 cups unsalted butter, softened
⅝ cup light brown sugar
⅝ cup confectioner's sugar
4½ cups unbleached all-purpose flour
Crisco butter-flavored cooking spray

Preheat oven to 325 degrees. Spray a 9-inch pie plate with cooking spray. Set aside. Using your fingertips, mix butter, sugars, and flour together in a medium mixing bowl. Blend together into a dough ball. Press with fingertips into a 9-inch pie pan and place in the refrigerator for 2 hours. Bake for 15 minutes or until lightly golden around the edges.

Coconut Crust

2 cups flaked coconut
4 tablespoons unsalted butter, melted

Combine the coconut and melted butter in a small bowl. Press into the bottom and up the side of an 8- to 9-inch pie plate. Bake at 325 degrees until the coconut is lightly browned, about 15 minutes. Cool completely while preparing filling.

Now, go out to your kitchen and bake a pie. As my good friend and fellow champion pie baker Phyllis Bartholomew says, "Keep it flaky."

Fruit and Berry Pies

I'M GOING TO BEGIN THIS CHAPTER by getting right into the nitty-gritty about which apples to use for the perfect pie. I am asked this question continually, and those who ask it appreciate an answer. Growing up with an expert baker, my grandma Thelma Anderson, helped me understand which apples work—and which do not. Here's the list:

The Best Apple for Pies

MY FAVORITES

* Golden Delicious
* Granny Smith

SWEETNESS AND TARTNESS FOR PIES

* Jonathan
* Jonagold
* Winesap
* Pippin

SWEET CHOICES FOR PIES

- Braeburn
- Fuji
- Mutsu
- Pink Lady
- Suncrisp
- Rome Beauty
- Empire

GOOD TART BAKING APPLES

- Idared
- Macoun
- Newton Pippin
- Northern Spy

APPLES THAT BECOME MUSHY WHEN COOKED

- McIntosh
- Cortland
- Red Delicious

This isn't the perfect list, but it does offer my favorites that I have found work well in my pies. McIntosh, Cortland, and Red Delicious are wonderful eating apples. I've also used them in my applesauce recipes, but do avoid them for pies. They become runny and mealy.

There, now that that is out of the way, let's hope choosing apples for your pie will not be such a chore. I like to use several varieties of apples for my apple pie recipes. Try a couple of varieties in your recipes and you will be surprised at how wonderful your filling tastes.

I've been baking fruit and berry pies for decades. As a teenager, I would make extra money during the holidays by baking pies for the neighbors and family friends. Everyone enjoyed my "mile-high" apple pies and my pumpkin pies made with real pumpkin. I would go home right after school and bake until late. Thanksgiving was the busiest time, and everyone wanted their pies delivered Wednesday evening, the night before Thanksgiving. Fortunately, I had my driver's license the minute I turned 16 or Mom or Dad would have had to drive me. I treasured those customers who offered to pick up their pies.

There were so many recipes I could have listed in this chapter with wonderful berries you would find in eastern North Dakota or northern Minnesota, but I wanted to be as inclusive as possible. I wanted my readers to be able to find the ingredients at their corner market or favorite grocery store. I left out my gooseberry recipe and ground-cherry recipe. They may appear in future cookbooks.

If there is one word of advice I can give for making a perfect fruit or berry pie, it would be to start with the freshest ingredients. Don't purchase your blueberries, strawberries, or raspberries because they are on sale and you think you'll have time to make a pie. I've done this so many times and find I don't have the time to bake with them. I end up with moldy berries. Because of my hectic calendar I sometimes schedule my baking time. That way I'm sure I will use the ingredients I've purchased and I have something fun to look forward to.

The recipes in this chapter are my favorites. Although it's not a definitive list, it does include my favorites and some that I have entered in pie competitions and won. Because fruit and berry pies are perfect with a top crust, I've added instructions for decorating the top crust with stenciling, a technique I call "piemaling." I hope you'll try it sometime and delight your guests. I've also added instructions for easy lattice crusts that make a pie look wonderful. Nothing says "home and garden" more than a lattice. I make my lattice crust strips wide or thin and very precise. A top crust can also be decorated with a variety of cutouts made with miniature cookie cutters. There is no limit to what you can do to decorate your pies.

Enjoy these recipes and let me know what you think of them. Of course I had to throw in one pie that will surprise you: my Avocado Pie. It has a wonderful taste—if you enjoy avocados. I always like to find fruits, berries, citrus, and, yes, even onions to make pies with. I hope you will try even my most outlandish recipes along with my standards.

Happy pie eating!

∮ Grandma's Secret Apple Pie

I prepared this pie on the Food Network Challenge—The Great American Pie Cook-Off. Because we were at a high altitude in Denver, I forgot that the filling wouldn't cook properly. I had studied the effects of high-altitude baking on pie crusts, toppings, and other factors but forgot to consider the filling. The judges thought it tasted of flour. Oh well, that's why they call it a challenge.

I also told the story of why this was called Grandma's Secret Apple Pie: she would add good-quality rum or bourbon to the filling—"about a smidgen." I have measured that out to be about one tablespoon. Of course, you're welcome to use more or less or omit altogether. I think it adds a smooth taste. Enjoy.

Try to find the best apple butter possible to spread on the bottom crust before filling. It changes the flavors beautifully. I have canned my own apple butter for decades. The recipe is in my first cookbook, *Garden County—Where Everyone Is Welcome to Sit at the Table.* I truly believe it is the best apple butter recipe I have ever tasted.

Crust

   3 cups unbleached all-purpose flour
   1 tablespoon dark brown sugar
   1 teaspoon kosher or sea salt, finely ground
   ½ cup butter-flavored all-vegetable shortening, chilled and
      cut into small pieces

I simply don't know why
I should be so fond of apple pie.
And when I'm offered it with cheese
OR cream, I always say: "Yes, please."
And no one has to ask me twice
I'll ALWAYS take another slice.

—IVY O. EASTWICK, "APPLE PIE"

½ cup unsalted butter, chilled and cut into small pieces

½–¾ cup cold water; use only as much as needed for a smooth, satiny dough ball

Butter-flavored cooking spray

1 egg yolk and 1 teaspoon water for egg wash

1. All ingredients should be cold. Combine all the dry ingredients in a large mixing bowl. Add shortening and butter. Using a pastry blender, cut in the shortening and butter until the mixture resembles coarse meal or peas.

2. Drop by drop, add the cold water. Mix in with the fingertips, not with the hands as the palms will warm the dough. Continue mixing in water until the dough begins to hold together without being crumbly yet not sticky. Divide dough into two pieces and place one piece of dough in plastic wrap. Press down to form a disk. This will make rolling out easier after chilling.

3. Lightly spray a deep 9-inch pie pan with cooking spray. Roll out second piece of dough and place in pie plate, allowing the excess pastry to hang over the edge. Lightly brush sides and bottom of crust with egg wash. Chill in refrigerator for 10 minutes before filling.

Makes pastry for one 9-inch double-crust pie.

Filling

6 to 8 apples (Cortland, Granny Smith, or other baking apples), peeled, cored, and sliced

¼ cup good-quality apple cider

1 tablespoon rum or rum extract (optional)

2 tablespoons freshly squeezed lemon juice

2 teaspoons pure vanilla extract or paste

¾ cup white sugar

¼ cup cornstarch

½ teaspoon kosher or sea salt, crushed

1 teaspoon cinnamon

¼ teaspoon nutmeg

¼ teaspoon allspice

¾ cup apple butter for spreading on bottom of pie crust

2 tablespoon unsalted butter, cut into bits for dotting

1. Preheat oven to 425 degrees. In a dutch oven or large stockpot over medium heat, stir together the apples, cider, rum, lemon juice, and vanilla. Mix in the dry ingredients until well combined. Using a heat-resistant spatula, stir gently until apples release their juices and mixture begins to thicken. Remove from heat and let cool.

2. Remove chilled pie crust from refrigerator and spread bottom and sides of pie crust with apple butter. Carefully spoon cooked apple mixture into pie crust, patting mixture with spatula to fill in air pockets. Dot with butter.

3. Before applying top crust, brush bottom crust edge with egg wash (this will create a glue bond between the top and bottom crusts). Cover pie with top crust, vent, and trim overhang. Turn edges under flush with the rim; crimp all around to make a decorative stand-up edge. Cover edges of the crust with a pie shield to prevent excessive browning.

4. Bake for 15 minutes. Lower the oven temperature to 375 degrees and bake for 30 to 40 minutes longer, or until the top is golden brown and filling is bubbly. Remove pie shield during the last 20–25 minutes of cooking time. Let cool on a wire rack.

Serves 8–10.

John Michael's Helpful Hint: This is a perfect two-crust pie to decorate using my "piemaling" technique; see the "Decorating Your Pie" chapter for instructions.

In order to make an apple pie from scratch, you must first create the universe.

—ISAAC ASIMOV

⨍ Caramel Apple Pie

At Christmastime, my grandma Thelma Anderson would make pecan brittle. I love making it, and especially eating it, to this day. She would use her pecan brittle in this recipe for her topping, and it was wonderfully chewy and crunchy. It was a lovely combination. If you cannot find pecan brittle or don't have time to make your own, simply purchase toffee bars to use instead. It's a wonderful pie either way.

Crust

   3 cups unbleached all-purpose flour
   1 tablespoon dark brown sugar
   1 teaspoon kosher or sea salt, finely ground
   ½ cup Crisco butter-flavored all-vegetable shortening, chilled
      and cut into small pieces
   ½ cup unsalted butter, chilled and cut into small pieces
   ½–¾ cup cold water; use only as much as needed for a smooth,
      satiny dough ball
   Crisco butter-flavored cooking spray
   1 egg yolk and 1 teaspoon water for egg wash

1. All ingredients should be cold. Combine all the dry ingredients in a large mixing bowl. Add shortening and butter. Using a pastry blender, cut in the shortening and butter until the mixture resembles coarse meal or peas.
2. Drop by drop, add the cold water. Mix in with the fingertips, not with the hands as the palms will warm the dough. Continue mixing in water until the dough begins to hold together without being crumbly yet not sticky. Divide dough into two pieces and place one piece of dough in plastic wrap. Press down to form a disk. This will make rolling out easier after chilling. Refrigerate for at least 30 minutes.
3. Lightly spray a deep 9-inch pie pan with cooking spray. Roll out second piece of dough and place in pie plate, allowing the excess pastry to hang over the edge. Lightly brush sides and bottom of crust with egg wash. Chill in refrigerator for 10 minutes before filling.

Makes pastry for one 9-inch double-crust pie.

Filling

  6 cups apples (Jonathan, Jonagold, Winesap, Pippin, Granny Smith),
     peeled and sliced
  1–2 tablespoons freshly squeezed lemon juice, about half a lemon
  ½ cup light brown sugar, packed well
  ½ cup white sugar
  ¼ cup unbleached all-purpose flour
  1 teaspoon cinnamon, preferably China cassia
  ¼ teaspoon freshly grated nutmeg
  ¼ teaspoon fine sea salt
  1 teaspoon pure vanilla extract or paste
  4 tablespoons heavy cream
  4 tablespoons unsalted butter

1. Preheat oven to 450 degrees. In a large mixing bowl, sprinkle apple slices with lemon juice. Set aside. In a medium mixing bowl, combine light brown sugar, white sugar, flour, cinnamon, nutmeg, and salt. Mix well and add to apples. Using a spatula, toss gently to blend. Add vanilla and cream.
2. In a large heavy-bottom skillet, melt butter. Add apple mixture and cook about 8–10 minutes or until the apples have begun to soften. Remove from heat and gently spoon into prepared pie crust. Set aside and prepare topping.

Topping

  ½ cup unbleached all-purpose flour
  3 tablespoons white sugar
  1 tablespoon unsalted butter

I went to sit in the bus station and think this over. I ate another apple pie and ice cream; that's practically all I ate all the way across the country, I knew it was nutritious and it was delicious, of course.

—JACK KEROUAC, *ON THE ROAD*

4 ounces pecan brittle (see recipe in the "Decorating Your Pie"
   chapter) or 2 toffee bars, crushed

1. In a medium mixing bowl, combine flour and sugar. Using a pastry
   blender or a fork, mix in the butter until crumbly. Stir in the crushed
   pecan brittle. Sprinkle over pie.
2. Roll out remaining pastry. Lightly brush egg wash around edge of pie;
   this will act like a cement bond between the top and bottom crust.
   Cover pie with top crust, vent, and trim overhang. Turn edges under
   flush with the rim; crimp all around to make a decorative stand-up
   edge. Cover edges of the crust with a pie shield to prevent excessive
   browning. Brush top of crust with egg wash.
3. Bake pie at 450 degrees for 15 minutes. Reduce heat to 350 degrees
   and bake for an additional 45 minutes or until the top is golden
   brown. Remove from oven and sprinkle with vanilla sugar. Cool on
   wire rack.

Serves 8–10.

John Michael's Helpful Hint: This is a perfect two-crust pie to decorate
using my "piemaling" technique; see the "Decorating Your Pie" chapter
for instructions.

🍴 Apple Honey Pie

Instead of sweetening this filling with sugar, I use honey, which gives the
pie a pleasant flavor. Walnuts add a fantastic flavor and crunch, but you
can substitute pecans if you wish.

Crust

   3 cups unbleached all-purpose flour
   1 tablespoon dark brown sugar
   1 teaspoon kosher or fine sea salt, finely ground

½ cup Crisco butter-flavored all-vegetable shortening, chilled
and cut into small pieces
½ cup unsalted butter, chilled and cut into small pieces
½–¾ cup cold water; use only as much as needed for a smooth,
satiny dough ball
Crisco butter-flavored cooking spray
1 egg yolk and 1 teaspoon water for egg wash

1. All ingredients should be cold. Combine all the dry ingredients in a large mixing bowl. Add shortening and butter. Using a pastry blender, cut in the shortening and butter until the mixture resembles coarse meal or peas.
2. Drop by drop, add the cold water. Mix in with the fingertips, not with the hands as the palms will warm the dough. Continue mixing in water until the dough begins to hold together without being crumbly yet not sticky. Divide dough and place in plastic wrap. Press down to form a disk; this will make rolling out easier after chilling. Refrigerate for at least 30 minutes.
3. Lightly spray a deep 9-inch pie pan with cooking spray. Roll out dough and place in pie plate, allowing the excess pastry to hang over the edge. Cut away excess dough. Lightly brush sides and bottom of crust with egg wash. Chill in refrigerator before filling and baking.

Makes pastry for one 9-inch double-crust pie.

But I, when I undress me
Each night upon my knees
Will ask the Lord to bless me,
With apple pie and cheese.

—EUGENE FIELD, 1980

Filling

5½ pounds of baking apples (Granny Smith, Jonathan, Jonagold,
    Winesap, Pippin)
¼ cup walnuts, coarsely chopped
⅓ cup seedless raisins
2½ cups water
1¼ cups honey
1 teaspoon ground cinnamon, preferably China cassia
1 teaspoon freshly squeezed lemon juice
¼ teaspoon freshly grated nutmeg
⅓ cup cornstarch

1. Preheat oven to 350 degrees. Peel, core, and slice apples; combine in mixing bowl with nuts and raisins. Set aside.
2. In a medium heavy-bottom saucepan, combine 2 cups water, honey, cinnamon, lemon juice, and nutmeg. Over medium heat, bring to a boil. Mix cornstarch with remaining ½ cup water and add to honey mixture. Cook and stir until thickened and clear. Pour hot honey mixture over sliced apples and toss to coat evenly.
3. Carefully spoon apple filling evenly into prepared pie shell. Brush outside edge of crust with egg wash; this will act like a cement bond between the top and bottom crusts. Cover apple filling with top crust. Seal edges with crimping of choice. Cut slits in top crust so that steam can escape; brush with egg wash. Cover edges of the crust with a pie shield to prevent excessive browning. Bake for 10 minutes. Reduce heat to 300 degrees and continue baking for 35 minutes.

Serves 8–10.

⨍ Carpe Diem Blueberry Pie

I called this "Carpe Diem Blueberry Pie" because I used a clock face stencil with roman numerals to decorate the top crust. It was very pretty and accentuated the pie perfectly. I state in the recipe that frozen blueberries can be used in this recipe, but fresh are better. It's a wonderful and simple recipe. Load up this puppy with tons of blueberries, and your guests will be delighted.

Crust

> 3 cups unbleached all-purpose flour
> 1 tablespoon dark brown sugar
> 1 teaspoon kosher or sea salt, finely ground
> ½ cup Crisco butter-flavored all-vegetable shortening, chilled
>   and cut into small pieces
> ½ cup unsalted butter, chilled and cut into small pieces
> ½–¾ cup cold water; use only as much as needed for a smooth,
>   satiny dough ball
> Crisco butter-flavored cooking spray
> 1 egg yolk and 1 teaspoon water for egg wash

1. All ingredients should be cold. Combine all the dry ingredients in a large mixing bowl. Add shortening and butter. Using a pastry blender, cut in the shortening and butter until the mixture resembles coarse meal or peas.
2. Drop by drop, add the cold water. Mix in with the fingertips, not with the hands as the palms will warm the dough. Continue mixing in water until the dough begins to hold together without being crumbly yet not sticky. Divide dough into two pieces and place one piece of dough in plastic wrap. Press down to form a disk. This will make rolling out easier after chilling. Refrigerate for at least 30 minutes.
3. Lightly spray a deep 9-inch pie pan with cooking spray. Roll out second piece of dough and place in pie plate, allowing the excess pastry to hang over the edge. Lightly brush sides and bottom of crust with egg wash. Chill in refrigerator before filling.

Makes pastry for one 9-inch double-crust pie.

Filling

> 7 cups blueberries fresh or frozen; if frozen, thaw and drain
> 1 cup white sugar
> ¼ cup cornstarch
> 1 teaspoon lemon zest
> 2 tablespoons freshly squeezed lemon juice
> ½ teaspoon allspice
> 2 tablespoons unsalted butter for dotting

1. Preheat oven to 425 degrees. In a large heavy-bottom saucepan over medium heat, gently blend blueberries, sugar, cornstarch, lemon zest, lemon juice, and allspice with a heat-resistant spatula or back of wooden spoon. Simmer, gently stirring, until filling is thickened. Cool to lukewarm.
2. Gently spoon cooled filling into chilled pie crust. Dot filling with butter.
3. Before applying top crust, brush bottom crust edge with egg wash; this will create a cement bond between the top and bottom crust. Cover pie with top crust, vent, and trim overhang. Turn edges under flush with the rim; crimp all around to make a decorative stand-up edge. Cover edges of the crust with a pie shield to prevent excessive browning.
4. Place finished pie on the lower rack of the oven and bake for 15 minutes. Lower the oven temperature to 350 degrees, move the pie to the upper rack, and bake for 35–50 minutes longer, or until the filling is bubbly and the crust is golden. Remove pie shield during the last 20–25 minutes of cooking time. Let cool on a wire rack.

Serves 8–10.

John Michael's Helpful Hint: This is a perfect two-crust pie to decorate using my "piemaling" technique; see the "Decorating Your Pie" chapter for instructions.

⸙ Grandma Anderson's Cherry Pie

This pie's name gives credit to Grandma Anderson, but it's not my grandma Thelma Anderson but my great-grandmother Gunhild Anderson, my grandpa's mother. I found this in Grandma Thelma's recipe book. She wrote, "This is Gunhild Anderson's recipe. It's very good." Enough said. I don't have many of my great-grandmother's recipes and hope I find more in the future. Great-grandmother Gunhild Anderson was a beautiful woman with a full head of white hair. That's how I remember her. My grandpa Julien Anderson adored her, so this recipe is in honor of her memory.

Crust

3 cups unbleached all-purpose flour
1 tablespoons white sugar
1 teaspoon kosher or sea salt, finely ground
½ cup Crisco shortening, chilled and cut into small pieces
½ cup unsalted butter, chilled and cut into small pieces
½–¾ cup cold water; use only as much as needed for a smooth, satiny dough ball
Crisco butter-flavored cooking spray
1 egg yolk and 1 teaspoon water for egg wash

1. All ingredients should be cold. Combine flour, sugar, and salt in a large mixing bowl. Add shortening and butter. Using a pastry blender, cut in the shortening and butter until the mixture resembles coarse meal or peas.
2. Drop by drop, add the cold water. Mix in with the fingertips, not with the hands as the palms will warm the dough. Continue mixing in water until the dough begins to hold together without being crumbly yet not sticky.
3. Divide dough into two pieces and place each in plastic wrap. Fold over plastic wrap and press down to form a disk. This will make rolling out easier after chilling. Finish wrapping in plastic and place in the refrigerator for at least 30 minutes.

4. Lightly spray a 9-inch pie plate with cooking spray. Roll out second piece of dough and place in pie plate, allowing excess to hang over the sides. Cut away excess dough. Brush with egg wash. Return to the refrigerator until filling is ready.

Makes pastry for one 9-inch double-crust pie.

Filling

4 cups sour cherries, pitted (2 pounds fresh or 2 16-ounce cans, water-pack, drained)
⅓ cup white sugar
¼ cup unbleached all-purpose flour
1½ tablespoons freshly squeezed lemon juice
¼ teaspoon pure almond extract
2 tablespoons unsalted butter

1. Preheat oven to 425 degrees. In a medium mixing bowl, combine cherries, sugar, flour, lemon juice, and almond extract. Gently spoon the mixture into the prepared pie crust and dot with butter.
2. Brush pie crust edge with egg wash to create a cement bond. Attach top crust and vent to release steam if using a full crust. May also top with a lattice crust. Brush with remaining egg wash. Protect edges of pie with a pie shield to prevent excessive browning or burning. Bake for 30 minutes or until the filling is bubbly and crust turns golden. Cool on a wire rack completely before serving.

Serves 8–10.

We stopped at a camp where there were some tables, and ate the whole peach pie, still warm from Irish Mary's oven . . . We poured cream from the jar onto the pieces Father cut for us, and thick sweet juices ran into delicious puddles.

—M. F. K. FISHER

ƒ Triple Crown Cherry Pie

Winner: Honorable Mention Professional Division in the Crisco Classic Cherry Category 2008 APC Crisco National Pie Championship and featured on the Food Network Challenge—National Pie Championship

Crust

3 cups unbleached all-purpose flour
1 tablespoon dark brown sugar
1 teaspoon kosher or sea salt, finely ground
½ cup Crisco butter-flavored all-vegetable shortening, chilled
    and cut into small pieces
½ cup unsalted butter, chilled and cut into small pieces
½–¾ cup cold water; use only as much as needed for a smooth,
    satiny dough ball
Crisco butter-flavored cooking spray
1 egg yolk and 1 teaspoon water for egg wash

1. All ingredients should be cold. Combine all the dry ingredients in a large mixing bowl. Add shortening and butter. Using a pastry blender, cut in the shortening and butter until the mixture resembles coarse meal or peas.
2. Drop by drop, add the cold water. Mix in with the fingertips, not with the hands as the palms will warm the dough. Continue mixing in water until the dough begins to hold together without being crumbly yet not sticky. Divide dough into two pieces and place one piece of dough in plastic wrap. Press down to form a disk. This will make rolling out easier after chilling. Refrigerate for at least 30 minutes.
3. Lightly spray a deep 9-inch pie pan with cooking spray. Roll out second piece of dough and place in pie plate, allowing the excess pastry to hang over the edge. Lightly brush sides and bottom of crust with egg wash. Chill in refrigerator while preparing filling.

Makes pastry for one 9-inch double-crust pie.

Filling

> 2 (14-ounce) cans pitted dark sweet cherries
> 2 (14-ounce) cans pitted sour cherries
> 1 (10-ounce) jar maraschino cherries
> 1 freshly squeezed lemon, about 4 tablespoons
> 1½ teaspoons gourmet cherry extract
> 1½ cups white sugar, divided
> ½ teaspoon red food coloring
> ¼ teaspoon pure vanilla bean paste
> ⅔ cup cornstarch
> ¼ cup cherry preserves
> 2 tablespoons unsalted butter for dotting

1. Preheat oven to 425 degrees. Pour all three types of cherries into a colander set over a bowl and drain. Reserve ¾ cup of the drained juice. Transfer the cherries to a medium mixing bowl. Add the lemon juice, cherry extract, and ¾ cup sugar. Stir gently with the back of a wooden spoon or rubber spatula to mix well. Set aside and let the flavors mellow for about 15 minutes.

2. In a heavy-bottom saucepan over medium heat, combine the reserved ¾ cup of cherry juice with the remaining ¾ cup sugar, food coloring, vanilla, and cornstarch. Blend together well. Cook for about 5 minutes, or until well heated through. Add cherries and cook for about 5 minutes longer, stirring gently and constantly, until the mixture thickens. Spread the cherry preserves evenly over the bottom of the chilled pie crust. Cover with the thickened cherry filling. Dot filling with butter.

3. Before applying top crust, brush bottom crust edge with egg wash; this will create a cement bond between the top and bottom crusts. **For a decorative top crust:** Before attaching top crust, place stencil on top of rolled-out dough. Slowly roll over the stencil with rolling pin to adhere stencil to dough. Brush over stencil with egg wash. Using sugars, spices, and cocoa, or dusting powder, sprinkle over open areas of the stencil. *If dough becomes too warm, place in refrigerator to chill.* Carefully remove stencil, being mindful not to spill

excess sprinkling items outside the stencil area. Attach top crust, crimp decoratively, and vent. Cover the edge with a pie shield to prevent excessive.

4. Place finished pie on the lower rack of the oven and bake for 15 minutes. Lower the oven temperature to 375 degrees, move the pie to the upper rack, and bake for 35–45 minutes longer, or until the filling is bubbly and the crust is golden. Remove pie shield during the last 20–25 minutes of cooking time. Let cool on a wire rack.

Serves 8–10.

John Michael's Helpful Hint: If you prefer a tart cherry pie, reduce the total quantity of sugar to ⅔ cup and use ⅓ cup of sugar for each of the additions.

Concord Grape Jam Pie

I grow my own concord grapes on two arbors in my backyard garden. I can tell when it's time to harvest the grapes because the backyard is filled with the smell of sweet purple grape juice. It's an impossible odor to describe, but it's one of the most delightful things on my list of enjoying life. One evening a friend came over for a backyard gathering. She walked under the arbor with large hanging clusters of concord grapes. She asked why I would hang clusters of plastic grapes in the garden. I smiled and told her they were real.

Each fall, I process tons of concord grapes to make our family's old recipe of Concord grape jam. There is no better Concord grape jam on the grocery store shelves, and we love sharing it during the holidays in gift baskets. This pie recipe is also an old family recipe that includes two of my favorite things—pie and Concord grape Jam.

Crust

> 3 cups unbleached all-purpose flour
> 1 tablespoon white sugar
> 1 teaspoon kosher or sea salt, finely ground
> ½ cup Crisco all-vegetable shortening, chilled and cut into
>   small pieces
> ½ cup unsalted butter, chilled and cut into small pieces
> ½–¾ cup cold water; use only as much as needed for a smooth,
>   satiny dough ball
> Crisco butter-flavored cooking spray
> 1 egg yolk and 1 teaspoon water for egg wash

1. All ingredients should be cold. Combine all the dry ingredients in a large mixing bowl. Add shortening and butter. Using a pastry blender, cut in the shortening and butter until the mixture resembles coarse meal or peas.
2. Drop by drop, add the cold water. Mix in with the fingertips, not with the hands as the palms will warm the dough. Continue mixing in water until the dough begins to hold together without being crumbly yet not sticky.
3. Divide dough into two pieces and place each in plastic wrap. Fold over plastic wrap and press down to form a disk. This will make rolling out easier after chilling. Finish wrapping in plastic and place in the refrigerator for at least 30 minutes.
4. Lightly spray a 9-inch pie plate with cooking spray. Roll out dough and place in pie plate. Brush with egg wash. Return to the refrigerator until filling is ready. Prepare Lattice Crust (see instructions in the "Decorating Your Pie" chapter). If using a full crust, cut vents in the top to release steam.

Makes pastry for one 9-inch double-crust pie.

Filling

¼ cup water
¼ cup freshly squeezed lemon juice
¼ cup cornstarch
2½ cups (20 ounces) Concord grape jam
2 tablespoons unsalted butter

1. Preheat oven to 425 degrees. In a medium mixing bowl, combine water, lemon juice, and cornstarch; gently stir in jam. Gently spoon into prepared pie crust. Dot with butter and cover with full or lattice crust. Brush with remaining egg wash. Protect edges of pie with a pie shield to prevent excessive browning.
2. Bake 35–45 minutes or until crust is golden and filling is set, not jiggly.

Serves 8–10.

Fresh Raspberry Pie

This is one of my simplest recipes for a pie. I love raspberries, and our garden produces tons from the 4th of July until Minnesota's first hard frost. I freeze several vacuum bags of raspberries, but fresh raspberries are better for this recipe. The true taste of raspberry will burst through with every bite. Add a scoop of raspberry gelato or sorbet to enhance this pie.

Crust

3 cups unbleached all-purpose flour
1 tablespoon dark brown sugar
1 teaspoon kosher or sea salt, finely ground
½ cup Crisco butter-flavored all-vegetable shortening, chilled
    and cut into small pieces
½ cup unsalted butter, chilled and cut into small pieces

½–¾ cup cold water; use only as much as needed for a smooth,
    satiny dough ball
Crisco butter-flavored cooking spray
1 egg yolk and 1 teaspoon water for egg wash

1. All ingredients should be cold. Combine all the dry ingredients in a large mixing bowl. Add shortening and butter. Using a pastry blender, cut in the shortening and butter until the mixture resembles coarse meal or peas.
2. Drop by drop, add the cold water. Mix in with the fingertips, not with the hands as the palms will warm the dough. Continue mixing in water until the dough begins to hold together without being crumbly yet not sticky. Divide dough into two pieces and place one piece of dough in plastic wrap. Press down to form a disk and place in refrigerator. This will make rolling out easier after chilling. Refrigerate for at least 30 minutes.
3. Lightly spray a deep 9-inch pie pan with cooking spray. Roll out second piece of dough and place in pie plate, allowing the excess pastry to hang over the edge. Lightly brush sides and bottom of crust with egg wash. Chill in refrigerator while preparing the filling.

Makes pastry for one 9-inch double-crust pie.

Filling

6 cups fresh raspberries (frozen can be used, but thaw
    and drain first)
7 tablespoons unbleached all-purpose flour
¾ cup white sugar
2 tablespoons unsalted butter

1. Preheat oven to 425 degrees. Pick over berries to remove stems and leaves. In a medium mixing bowl, gently combine berries, flour, and sugar. Let sit for 10 minutes. Gently spoon filling mixture into prepared pie curst. Dot with butter.

2. Before applying top crust, brush bottom crust edge with egg wash; this will create a cement bond between the top and bottom crusts. Cover pie with top crust, vent, and trim overhang. Turn edges under flush with the rim; crimp all around to make a decorative stand-up edge. Cover edges of the crust with a pie shield to prevent excessive browning.

3. Place finished pie on the lower rack of the oven and bake for 15 minutes. Lower the oven temperature to 350 degrees, move the pie to the upper rack, and bake for 35–50 minutes longer, or until the filling is bubbly and the crust is golden. Remove pie shield during the last 10 minutes of cooking time. Let cool on a wire rack until at room temperature.

Serves 8–10.

John Michael's Helpful Hint: This is a perfect two-crust pie to decorate using my "piemaling" technique; see the "Decorating Your Pie" chapter for instructions.

Blackberries and Cream Pie

Crust

1½ cups unbleached all-purpose flour
½ tablespoon white sugar
½ teaspoon kosher or fine sea salt, finely ground
¼ cup Crisco butter-flavored all-vegetable shortening, chilled and cut into small pieces
¼ cup unsalted butter, chilled and cut into small pieces
¼–½ cup cold water; use only as much as needed for a smooth, satiny dough ball
Crisco butter-flavored cooking spray
1 egg yolk and 1 teaspoon water for egg wash

1. All ingredients should be cold. Combine all the dry ingredients in a large mixing bowl. Add shortening and butter. Using a pastry blender, cut in the shortening and butter until the mixture resembles coarse meal or peas.
2. Drop by drop, add the cold water. Mix in with the fingertips, not with the hands as the palms will warm the dough. Continue mixing in water until the dough begins to hold together without being crumbly yet not sticky.
3. Place dough in plastic wrap. Fold over plastic wrap and press down to form a disk. This will make rolling out easier after chilling. Finish wrapping in plastic and place in the refrigerator for at least 30 minutes.
4. Lightly spray a deep 9-inch pie pan or 8½-inch fluted flan pan. Roll out dough and place in pie plate, allowing the excess pastry to hang over the edge. Trim excess, fold under, and crimp decoratively. Brush with egg wash. Return to the refrigerator until filling is ready.

Makes pastry for one 9-inch single-crust pie.

Filling

5 cups fresh blackberries (frozen can be used, but thaw
     and drain first)
3 large eggs, slightly beaten
½ cup white sugar
⅓ cup unbleached all-purpose flour
¼ teaspoon fine sea salt
1½ teaspoon pure vanilla extract or paste
1 cup heavy cream

1. Preheat oven to 400 degrees. Place blackberries in prepared pie crust. In a large mixing bowl, combine eggs, sugar, flour, salt, vanilla, and cream. Blend well. Gently pour filling mixture over blackberries. Cover edge of the crust with a pie shield to prevent excessive browning. Remove last 10 minutes of cooking time.

2. Bake for 30–40 minutes or until the crust is golden and the filling in the center has become set. Cool on a rack. Garnish with Sweetened Whipped Cream (see recipe in the "Decorating Your Pie" chapter).

Serves 8–10.

⸏ Tutti Frutti Pie

This pie has the astonishing flavors of apple, plum, red grape, and sweet cherry. It's a perfect pie to serve for an afternoon tea or birthday gathering.

Crust

> 3 cups unbleached all-purpose flour
> 1 tablespoon dark brown sugar
> 1 teaspoon kosher or sea salt, finely ground
> ½ cup Crisco butter-flavored all-vegetable shortening, chilled
>   and cut into small pieces
> ½ cup unsalted butter, chilled and cut into small pieces
> ½–¾ cup cold water; use only as much as needed for a smooth,
>   satiny dough ball
> Crisco butter-flavored cooking spray
> 1 egg yolk and 1 teaspoon water for egg wash

1. All ingredients should be cold. Combine all the dry ingredients in a large mixing bowl. Add shortening and butter. Using a pastry blender, cut in the shortening and butter until the mixture resembles coarse meal or peas.
2. Drop by drop, add the cold water. Mix in with the fingertips, not with the hands as the palms will warm the dough. Continue mixing in water until the dough begins to hold together without being crumbly yet not sticky. Divide dough into two pieces and place one piece of

dough in plastic wrap. Press down to form a disk and place in refrigerator. This will make rolling out easier after chilling.

3. Lightly spray a deep 9-inch pie pan with cooking spray. Roll out second piece of dough and place in pie plate, allowing the excess pastry to hang over the edge. Lightly brush sides and bottom of crust with egg wash. Chill in refrigerator while preparing the filling.

Makes pastry for one 9-inch double-crust pie.

Filling

4 cups apples (Jonathan, Granny Smith, etc.), cored, peeled, and sliced
1 cup ripe plums, peeled and sliced
½ cup red seedless grapes, halved
½ cup sweet cherries, pitted (frozen can be used but thaw and drain first)
⅓ cup unbleached all-purpose flour
½ cup white sugar
½ teaspoon cinnamon, preferably China cassia
½ teaspoon freshly grated nutmeg
2 tablespoons unsalted butter

1. Preheat oven to 425 degrees. In large mixing bowl, gently combine fruit. Mix in flour, sugar, cinnamon, and nutmeg. Gently spoon into prepared pie crust. Dot with butter cut into small pieces.
2. Top with full crust with decorative vents for release of steam, or lattice crust (see Lattice Crust in the "Decorating Your Pie" chapter). Brush with remaining egg wash. Protect edges of pie with a pie shield to prevent excessive browning. Bake for 40–50 minutes or until the filling is bubbly and crust turns golden. Cool on a wire rack completely before serving.

Serves 8–10.

⨍ Peach Almond Pie

Crust

1½ cups unbleached all-purpose flour
½ tablespoon white sugar
½ teaspoon kosher or sea salt, finely ground
¼ cup all-vegetable shortening, chilled and cut into small pieces
¼ cup unsalted butter, chilled and cut into small pieces
¼–½ cup cold water; use only as much as needed for a smooth, satiny dough ball
Butter-flavored cooking spray

1. All ingredients should be cold. Combine all the dry ingredients in a large mixing bowl. Add shortening and butter. Using a pastry blender, cut in the shortening and butter until the mixture resembles coarse meal or peas.
2. Drop by drop, add the cold water. Mix in with the fingertips, not with the hands as the palms will warm the dough. Continue mixing in water until the dough begins to hold together without being crumbly yet not sticky.
3. Lightly spray a 9-inch pie pan with cooking spray. Roll out dough and place in pie plate, allowing the excess pastry to hang over the edge. Trim excess, tuck under, and crimp decoratively. Prick bottom and sides with a fork. Chill for 30 minutes before baking.
4. Preheat the oven to 400 degrees. Line the pastry shell with parchment and baking beans or beads. Bake the shell for 10 minutes. Remove the paper and beans or beads and return to the oven for 10 more minutes. Cool.

Makes pastry for one 9-inch single-crust pie.

Filling

> 1 (8-ounce) package cream cheese, room temperature
> 1 (14-ounce) can sweetened condensed milk
> 2 large eggs
> 3 tablespoons amaretto liqueur, divided
> 1½ teaspoon pure almond extract, divided
> 3 medium peaches, peeled and sliced
> 2 tablespoons peach preserves

1. Reduce oven temperature to 375 degrees. In a large mixing bowl, beat cream cheese until fluffy. Slowly add sweetened condensed milk. Continue beating until smooth. Add eggs one at a time until well incorporated. Add 2 tablespoons amaretto and 1 teaspoon almond extract. Pour mixture into prepared pie crust. Bake for 25 minutes or until set. Remove from oven and cool completely.

2. Once pie has come to room temperature, arrange peach slices on top of filling. In a small heavy-bottom saucepan, combine preserves and remaining amaretto and almond extract. Stir continuously over low heat until hot but not boiling. Let cool slightly and then spoon over top of pie and arranged peach slices. Chill 2 to 4 hours before serving.

Serves 8–10.

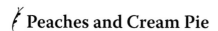 Peaches and Cream Pie

Crust

> 1½ cups unbleached all-purpose flour
> ½ tablespoon dark brown sugar
> ½ teaspoon kosher or sea salt, finely ground
> ¼ cup Crisco butter-flavored all-vegetable shortening, chilled
>   and cut into small pieces
> ¼ cup unsalted butter, chilled and cut into small pieces

¼–½ cup cold water; use only as much as needed for a smooth,
   satiny dough ball
Crisco butter-flavored cooking spray
1 egg yolk and 1 teaspoon water for egg wash

1. All ingredients should be cold. Combine all the dry ingredients in a
   large mixing bowl. Add shortening and butter. Using a pastry blender,
   cut in the shortening and butter until the mixture resembles coarse
   meal.
2. Drop by drop, add the cold water. Mix in with the fingertips, not with
   the hands as the palms will warm the dough. Continue mixing in
   water until the dough begins to hold together without being crumbly
   yet not sticky. Place dough in plastic wrap. Press down to form a disk
   and place in refrigerator. This will make rolling out easier after chilling. Refrigerate for at least 30 minutes.
3. Lightly spray a deep 9-inch pie pan with cooking spray. Roll out
   dough and place in pie plate, allowing the excess pastry to hang over
   the edge. Cut away excess dough, tuck under, and crimp decoratively.
   Lightly brush sides and bottom of crust with egg wash. Chill in refrigerator for 30 minutes while preparing the filling.

Makes pastry for one 9-inch single-crust pie.

Filling

7 fresh peaches, peeled, pitted, and halved
1 cup white sugar
2 large eggs, slightly beaten
1 cup heavy cream

1. Preheat oven to 425 degrees. Place peach halves, cut side down, in
   one tight layer on bottom of prepared pie crust. In a large mixing
   bowl whisk together sugar, eggs, and cream. Blend well. Gently pour
   filling mixture over peaches.
2. Bake for 15 minutes. Reduce oven temperature to 375 degrees. Continue to bake for 35 minutes or until filling center is set. Cool on

a rack until almost at room temperature. Garnish with Sweetened Whipped Cream (see recipe in the "Decorating Your Pie" chapter).

Serves 8–10.

ƒ Avocado Pie

The avocado is a tropical American tree of the laurel family. Its fruit has a large egg-shaped pit but technically is a berry. It's also known as the alligator pear because of the bumpy texture of its skin. I found this recipe in Grandma's collection with a note years ago. She had received this recipe from a woman in California during the Great Depression. I believe they had been friends in North Dakota. Avocados were plentiful in California, and this woman wrote Grandma that she made the most delicious pie with them. I don't actually remember Grandma making this pie, but I have several times. The recipe was difficult to transcribe because it read: "Half a juice glass lime juice, half a juice glass lemon juice. A can of condensed milk small cream and small sour cream." It took awhile, but I finally cracked the code. Most of the family recipes are written like this.

Crust

  1¾ cups graham cracker crumbs
  2 tablespoons light brown sugar, firmly packed
  ½ teaspoon ground cinnamon, preferably China cassia
  Pinch of salt
  6 tablespoons unsalted butter, melted
  Crisco butter-flavored cooking spray

1. Preheat oven to 350 degrees. Spray pie plate with cooking spray and set aside.
2. Combine the graham cracker crumbs, brown sugar, cinnamon, and salt in a large mixing bowl. Using your fingers, mix together. Add the

butter and incorporate well, mixing first with a fork, then with your hands, rubbing thoroughly to form evenly dampened crumbs.

3. Spread the crumbs evenly and loosely in the pie plate, pressing them into the bottom and up the side. Refrigerate for 10 minutes.
4. Bake for 8–10 minutes. Cool on a rack. Refrigerate 15 minutes before filling.

Makes one 9-inch graham cracker crust.

Filling

¼ cup freshly squeezed lime juice
¼ cup freshly squeezed lemon juice
1 envelope unflavored gelatin
3 medium-size very ripe avocados, more for garnish
1 (14-ounce) can sweetened condensed milk
½ cup heavy cream
½ cup sour cream

1. In a medium mixing bowl combine lime juice, lemon juice, and unflavored gelatin. Let gelatin soften ("bloom") for 5 minutes. Set aside.
2. In a food processor or blender, blend gelatin mixture, avocados, and sweetened condensed milk. Gently pour into prepared pie crust. Place in refrigerator and chill for at least 2 hours or until filling center is set and firm.
3. Meanwhile, in the bowl of a standing mixer with the whisk attachment, whip the heavy cream and sour cream together until stiff peaks form. Serve slices of pie with whipped topping and garnish with a thin slice of avocado.

Serves 8–10.

Cream and Custard Pies

CREAM AND CUSTARD PIES are usually associated with clowns at the circus or in comedy shows on television. It was much more exciting to throw a cream or custard pie in someone's face than it was to throw a fruit or berry pie. Clowns just got more bang for their buck with all the filling flying everywhere and targets wiping creamy goop out of their eyes. It's classic and fun. But cream and custard pies are no joke to make. They can be difficult to master, and the risk of ending up with a runny filling is high.

As I learned more about baking on the farm in my grandma's kitchen, I was most fascinated by preparing pies. Around the age of 10, I remember learning to make a basic Custard Pie. Grandma had several variations on this recipe, one being Carrot Custard Pie, but the best and simplest was Custard Pie lightly sprinkled with freshly ground nutmeg. This was my favorite.

My repertoire grew in the pie-baking arena, and soon I could prepare my favorite Banana Butterscotch Pie. Grandma taught me by example how to cook the filling until it was just right and would hold its shape after being poured into a pie crust and chilled in the refrigerator. She showed me how to remove small lumps of cornstarch or flour or other items that hadn't blended well by straining the cooked filling through a fine-mesh sieve. She also showed me how to whisk quickly to blend all the ingredients so that straining with a sieve would not be necessary. Grandma had many techniques, and they all worked. She would quote the *Farmer's Home Journal,* her mother, Grandma Gertrude "Dean" Knutson—Grandma Dean later remarried John Johnson who was in the North Dakota legislature (she thought Grandma Dean was the best cook and baker), and her sisters Berget Anderson and Alice Fladland. Baking was in our family.

One of the simplest techniques for preparing the perfect cream or custard pie that Grandma shared with me was to start with clean bowls and utensils. She instructed me to wipe bowls with a clean kitchen towel before beginning in case of dust or unseen debris. Grandma said that small particles of dust, salt, and other things could crystallize while the filling was cooking, which could ruin or prevent the filling from setting properly. This was especially true when caramelizing sugar. So to this day, I wipe down my utensils, bowls, food processors, and pans.

All of this advice came to a head in March 2007, when the Food Network invited me to participate in a Food Network Challenge—The Great American Pie Cook-Off. I was asked to submit three recipes, one for a fruit pie, one for a cream or chocolate pie, and one that I felt was my signature pie. There would be three rounds, 90 minutes each, to prepare our pies and present to a panel of judges. There would be a live audience, and we would compete for a prize of $10,000. I was thrilled to be invited but couldn't think of anything else for a week.

For my submissions I chose my Grandma's Secret Apple Pie (the secret being the rum she added to the filling without Grandpa knowing), my Coconut Cream Dream Pie (a recipe I found when I had returned home to Grand Forks, North Dakota, for the holidays), and my Key Lime Delight Pie. My Key Lime Delight Pie was not my signature pie, but I was playing it safe and being conservative for the first time in my life. Hey, it was for a Food Network gold medal and $10,000. My signature pie was and will always be my Vidalia Onion Pie. I could kick myself for not preparing it for that Food Network Challenge.

During the actual filming, we began at 5:30 a.m. with a breakfast call and organization time. The first round was actually fun for me. I was overconfident and baked my Grandma's Secret Apple Pie with no issues. However, the filming took place in Centennial, Colorado. I was prepared for high-elevation baking but forgot that water doesn't boil at high altitudes, so why would my filling bubble and thicken? It would not, and the judges tasted a great deal of flour. The pie was beautiful in its presentation but was not very tasty. When the scores were announced I had tied for fourth place. Now the pressure was on.

My next pie was my Coconut Cream Dream Pie. I worked through the preparation in my mind before we began. When the clock started, I was off. Everything went well and my filling cooked up beautifully. The pie gods were smiling upon me.

Once the pie was poured into the prepared crust, I placed the pie in the freezer to cool the filling. We were escorted to the Green Room before serving our pie to the judges. The time off the floor was supposed to be around 20 minutes, but it dragged out to 40 minutes. I was concerned my pie would be frozen by the time I sliced it.

I was escorted back into the studio, sliced my Coconut Cream Dream Pie and plated the portions, and it was served to the judges. The slice was perfect. Food Network Challenge host, Keegan Gerhard, commented that what he liked about my pies was that I made them a mile high. And I do. My recipe for Coconut Cream Dream Pie could make two pies in regular pie tins, but I enjoy using deep dish pie plates and piling on the topping. The judges also enjoyed it. When the scores were announced, my Coconut Cream Dream Pie was number one in the second round. It received the highest score of any pie during the entire challenge. I was in shock. This high score actually placed me on top. I couldn't concentrate and that wasn't a good thing. The final round was about to begin.

I prepared my Key Lime Delight Pie and presented to the judges. The blind-baked crust wasn't completely done, and I lost points for that. The judges also commented that this was not my signature pie. They said they knew my reputation and asked why I had played it safe. I was embarrassed and explained that I would never play it safe again.

Fortunately, my Coconut Cream Dream Pie was given such a high score that in the final analysis, I was awarded third place with a Food Network bronze medal. I was so happy. It was like winning the Oscar for baking pies. I wore the medal home on the airplane, kept it next to my bedside, and wore it to pie events. I couldn't have been prouder. However, I finally had to have it professionally matted and framed. I had worn it so much the inscription on the back of the medal was beginning to wear off.

One month later, I prepared my Coconut Cream Dream Pie at the National Pie Championship in Celebration, Florida. I won First Place Professional Division in the Cream Category. My pie had a very good year, and so did I.

𝑓 Aloha Joe® Pineapple Paradise Pie

I named this pie after a good friend of mine—even though we have never met in person. Aloha Joe has the best Hawaiian music radio show. I listen through the Internet at AlohaJoe.com. I sent Joe a copy of my first cookbook, and he asked me to call in for a live interview. A year later, Joe asked if I would call in monthly and talk about food and share recipes with his listeners. I was honored. I had also promised Joe that I would name a recipe after him and his radio show in my next cookbook, so here it is. I prepared this recipe for the APC Crisco National Pie Championship in 2008. The judges loved it, but although it got great scores, it didn't win. Too bad—it's a lovely creamy pie that reminds me of the islands.

Crust

 1 cup graham cracker crumbs
 ⅓ cup unsalted butter, melted
 ¼ cup white sugar
 ⅓ cup chopped macadamia nuts
 ½ cup shredded coconut
 Butter-flavored cooking spray

1. Preheat oven to 375 degrees. Spray a 9-inch pie plate with cooking spray. Set aside.
2. Using your hands or a food processor, combine graham cracker crumbs, melted butter, and sugar. Mix in macadamia nuts and coconut. Press crumb mixture into prepared 9-inch pie plate. Bake for 8–10 minutes until lightly toasted. Remove from oven. Chill in refrigerator until ready to use.

A boy doesn't have to go to war to be a hero; he can say he doesn't like pie when he sees there isn't enough to go around.

—E. W. HOWE

Filling

1 can (16-ounce) crushed pineapple, in heavy syrup or natural juice
2 tablespoons cornstarch
½ cup white sugar
3 large eggs, room temperature
2 envelopes (¼ ounce each) unflavored gelatin
¼ cup freshly squeezed lime juice
2 tablespoons dark rum or rum extract
2 cups heavy cream, whipped

1. Drain pineapple; reserve the liquid. Add water to pineapple liquid to make 1 cup. In a heavy-bottom saucepan, combine ½ cup of the pineapple liquid, cornstarch, and sugar. Separate eggs. Beat egg yolks into the cornstarch mixture. Soften gelatin in the remaining ½ cup pineapple liquid.

2. Heat cornstarch and egg yolk mixture over very low heat until it just starts to thicken. Stir in the gelatin and blend until it dissolves. Add lime juice, rum, and drained pineapple. Remove from heat and cool mixture. When pineapple mixture is completely cool, beat the egg whites until they hold firm peaks. Fold whipped cream into the pineapple mixture; then fold in the egg whites. Pour mixture into the chilled crust. Return to the refrigerator and chill for at least 4 hours or overnight. Garnish with Sweetened Whipped Cream (see recipe in the "Decorating Your Pie" chapter), fresh sprigs of mint, and slices of lime.

Serves 8–10.

Apricot Coconut Cream Pie

Crust

1½ cups unbleached all-purpose flour
½ tablespoon white sugar
½ teaspoon kosher or sea salt, finely ground

¼ cup Crisco butter-flavored all-vegetable shortening, chilled
  and cut into small pieces
¼ cup unsalted butter, chilled and cut into small pieces
¼–½ cup cold water; use only as much as needed for a smooth,
  shiny dough ball
Crisco butter-flavored cooking spray

1. All ingredients should be cold. Combine all the dry ingredients in a large mixing bowl. Add shortening and butter. Using a pastry blender, cut in the shortening and butter until the mixture resembles coarse meal or peas.
2. Drop by drop, add the cold water. Mix in with the fingertips, not with the hands as the palms will warm the dough. Continue mixing in water until the dough begins to hold together without being crumbly yet not sticky.
3. Place dough in plastic wrap. Fold over plastic wrap and press down to form a disk. This will make rolling out easier after chilling. Finish wrapping in plastic and place in the refrigerator for at least 1 hour.
4. Lightly spray a deep 9-inch pie pan or 8½-inch fluted flan pan. Roll out dough and place in pie plate, allowing the excess pastry to hang over the edge. Cut away excess, tuck under, and crimp decoratively. Prick bottom and sides with a fork. Chill in the refrigerator for at least 30 minutes.
5. Preheat oven to 400 degrees. Line the pastry shell with parchment and baking beans or beads. Bake the shell for 12 minutes. Remove the paper and beans or beads and return to the oven for 12 more minutes or until golden. Cool.

Makes pastry for one 9-inch single-crust pie.

Filling

2 cups shredded coconut, divided

½ cup apricot nectar

1 (15-ounce) can apricots, cut into small pieces, drained, and
separated

1 tablespoon pure almond extract

8 egg yolks

1¼ cups white sugar

⅔ cup cornstarch

2 tablespoons unsalted butter, melted

2½ cups milk

1 cup cream of coconut

1 teaspoon pure vanilla bean extract or paste

1 cup heavy whipping cream

1. Lightly toast 1 cup shredded coconut in oven. Remove and cool. Set aside.
2. In a small bowl, mix apricot nectar, apricot pieces, and almond extract. Set aside.
3. Combine egg yolks and sugar. Beat with electric mixer until pale yellow and fluffy. Add cornstarch and melted butter. Blend well and set aside.
4. Heat milk but do not boil. Stir in cream of coconut. Gradually add egg and cornstarch mixture, stirring constantly over medium-low heat until filling begins to thicken. Add vanilla.
5. Remove filling from heat and let cool.
6. In a mixing bowl, whisk or beat heavy whipping cream on high until it begins to thicken and forms stiff peaks. Set aside.
7. Strain cooled filling through fine-mesh sieve to remove any lumps. Fold in whipped cream, 1 cup of shredded coconut, and apricot pieces in nectar with pie filling and pour into prepared pie crust. Chill.

Topping

1¼ cups heavy whipping cream
3 tablespoons confectioner's sugar
2 teaspoons pure vanilla extract or paste
3 tablespoons apricot preserves, melted and cooled

Whisk or beat heavy cream until it begins to thicken. Gradually add confectioner's sugar and vanilla. Continue beating until stiff peaks form. Gently fold in ½ cup toasted coconut and apricot preserves. Pipe or spoon over top of pie. Sprinkle remaining toasted coconut. Refrigerate until mixture has cooled and set.

Serves 8–10.

Banana Butterscotch Pie

This recipe is a nice alternative to Banana Cream Pie. I'm a big fan of butterscotch, so, of course, this was one recipe that I learned to prepare at the very early age of 10. Wow, that was back in 1971. I enjoy telling our daughter, Heather, that I watched *The Brady Bunch* when it was a brand-new show. So make this pie, slice yourself a piece, and watch a rerun of your favorite 1970s sitcom.

Crust

1½ cups unbleached all-purpose flour
½ tablespoon white sugar
½ teaspoon kosher or sea salt, finely ground
¼ cup Crisco butter-flavored all-vegetable shortening, chilled and cut into small pieces
¼ cup unsalted butter, chilled and cut into small pieces
¼–½ cup cold water; use only as much as needed for a smooth, satiny dough ball
Crisco butter-flavored cooking spray

1. All ingredients should be cold. Combine all the dry ingredients in a large mixing bowl. Add shortening and butter. Using a pastry blender, cut in the shortening and butter until the mixture resembles coarse meal or peas.
2. Drop by drop, add the cold water. Mix in with the fingertips, not with the hands as the palms will warm the dough. Continue mixing in water until the dough begins to hold together without being crumbly yet not sticky.
3. Lightly spray a deep 9-inch pie pan or 8½-inch fluted flan pan. Roll out dough and place in pie plate, allowing the excess pastry to hang over the edge. Cut away excess, tuck under, and crimp decoratively. Prick bottom and sides with a fork. Chill in the refrigerator for 30 minutes.
4. Preheat oven to 400 degrees. Line the pastry shell with parchment and baking beans or beads. Bake the shell for 10 minutes. Remove the paper and beans or beads and return to the oven for 10 more minutes. Cool.

Makes pastry for one 9-inch single-crust pie.

Filling

¾ cup brown sugar, packed tightly
5 tablespoons unbleached all-purpose flour
½ teaspoon kosher or sea salt
2 cups whole milk
2 egg yolks, slightly beaten
2 tablespoons unsalted butter
1 teaspoon pure vanilla extract or paste
3 ripe bananas, sliced

1. In a heatproof bowl or double boiler, combine sugar, flour, and salt. Slowly pour in milk and stir or whisk to blend well. Cook until thickened, stirring constantly. Cover and cook an additional 10 minutes, stirring occasionally.

2. In a small bowl, add 2 tablespoons of hot mixture to egg yolks to raise their temperature and prevent cooking the eggs. Add egg yolks to hot mixture and stir or whisk continually; cook 1 minute longer. Add butter and vanilla and cool to room temperature.
3. Place alternate layers of cooled filling and bananas in prepared pie crust. Refrigerate for 2 hours before serving. Top with meringue or Sweetened Whipped Cream (see recipe in the "Decorating Your Pie" chapter).

Serves 8–10.

Blackberry Cream Pie

If blackberries are unavailable, try raspberries, blueberries, strawberries, or ground-cherries.

Crust

1½ cups unbleached all-purpose flour
½ tablespoon white sugar
½ teaspoon kosher or sea salt, finely ground
¼ cup Crisco butter-flavored all-vegetable shortening, chilled and cut into small pieces
¼ cup unsalted butter, chilled and cut into small pieces
¼–½ cup cold water; use only as much as needed for a smooth, satiny dough ball
Crisco butter-flavored cooking spray
1 egg yolk and 1 teaspoon water for egg wash

1. All ingredients should be cold. Combine all the dry ingredients in a large mixing bowl. Add shortening and butter. Using a pastry blender, cut in the shortening and butter until the mixture resembles coarse meal or peas.
2. Drop by drop, add the cold water. Mix in with the fingertips, not with the hands as the palms will warm the dough. Continue mixing in

water until the dough begins to hold together without being crumbly yet not sticky.

3. Place dough in plastic wrap. Fold over plastic wrap and press down to form a disk. This will make rolling out easier after chilling. Finish wrapping in plastic and place in the refrigerator for at least 30 minutes.

4. Lightly spray a deep 9-inch pie pan or 8½-inch fluted flan pan with cooking spray. Roll out dough and place in pie plate, allowing the excess pastry to hang over the edge. Cut away excess, tuck under, and crimp decoratively. Brush with egg wash and return to the refrigerator until filling is ready.

Makes pastry for one 9-inch single-crust pie.

Filling

1 cup white sugar
⅔ cup unbleached all-purpose flour, divided
2 large eggs, lightly beaten
1⅓ cups sour cream
1 teaspoon pure vanilla extract or paste
3 cups fresh or frozen blackberries, thawed if frozen
⅓ cup firmly packed brown sugar
¼ cup toasted pecans, chopped
3 tablespoons unsalted butter, room temperature

1. Preheat oven to 400 degrees. In a medium mixing bowl, mix together sugar, ⅓ cup flour, eggs, sour cream, and vanilla. Whisk or stir until smooth. Gently fold in blackberries with a silicone spatula. Pour mixture into prepared pie crust.

2. Bake for 30–35 minutes or until center is set.

3. In a medium mixing bowl combine remaining ⅓ cup flour, brown sugar, pecans, and butter. Mix well. Sprinkle over hot pie. Return pie to oven for 10 minutes or until golden brown. Cool on a wire rack. Garnish with Sweetened Whipping Cream (see recipe in the "Decorating Your Pie" chapter) and whole blackberries.

Serves 8–10.

∮ Cantaloupe Cream Pie

This is a wonderfully delicious pie in the summer. You may also use chucks of cantaloupe instead of balls. I have mixed honeydew melon balls with cantaloupe balls. I have also used a mixture of frozen fruits and berries. Visit your local farmers' market for a variety of melons to use in this recipe.

Crust

> 1½ cups unbleached all-purpose flour
> ½ tablespoon white sugar
> ½ teaspoon kosher or sea salt, finely ground
> ¼ cup butter-flavored all-vegetable shortening, chilled and cut into small pieces
> ¼ cup unsalted butter, chilled and cut into small pieces
> ¼–½ cup cold water; use only as much as needed for a smooth, satiny dough ball
> Butter-flavored cooking spray

1. All ingredients should be cold. Combine all the dry ingredients in a large mixing bowl. Add shortening and butter. Using a pastry blender, cut in the shortening and butter until the mixture resembles coarse meal or peas.
2. Drop by drop, add the cold water. Mix in with the fingertips, not with the hands as the palms will warm the dough. Continue mixing in water until the dough begins to hold together without being crumbly yet not sticky.
3. Place dough in plastic wrap. Fold over plastic wrap and press down to form a disk. This will make rolling out easier after chilling. Finish wrapping in plastic and place in the refrigerator for at least 1 hour.
4. Lightly spray a deep 9-inch pie pan or 8½-inch fluted flan pan. Roll out dough and place in pie plate, allowing the excess pastry to hang over the edge. Cut away excess, tuck under, and crimp decoratively. Prick bottom and sides with a fork. Chill in the refrigerator for at least 30 minutes.

5. Preheat oven to 400 degrees. Line the pastry shell with parchment and baking beans or beads. Bake the shell for 12 minutes. Remove the paper and beans or beads and return to the oven for 12 more minutes or until golden. Cool.

Makes pastry for one 9-inch single-crust pie.

Filling

    1 envelope unflavored gelatin
    ½ cup freshly squeezed orange juice
    1 large cantaloupe, halved and seeded
    ¼ cup white sugar
    2 teaspoons orange zest
    1 cup heavy whipping cream
    ⅓ cup apricot jam
    2 tablespoons Grand Marnier

1. In a small heavy-bottom saucepan, combine gelatin and orange juice. Let stand for 5 minutes to "bloom." Cook over low heat, stirring continually until gelatin has dissolved. Do not boil. Remove from heat and set aside.
2. Scoop melon into balls, about 2 cups. Set aside. Scoop out remaining melon from rind and cut into pieces. Using a blender or food processor, puree melon pieces, sugar, and orange zest until smooth. Strain mixture through a fine-mesh sieve to remove any melon flesh or pieces.
3. Add strained mixture to gelatin mixture and whipping cream. Blend well and refrigerate until slightly thickened.
4. Pour into cooled, prepared pie crust. Spread evenly. Top with melon balls and return to refrigerator for at least 2 hours or until well set.
5. Before serving, heat jam in a small heavy-bottom saucepan until melted; stir in Grand Marnier. Spoon evenly over pie.

Serves 8–10.

⸕ Coconut Cream Dream Pie

Winner: Bronze medal—Food Network Challenge—The Great American Pie Cook-Off 2007 and First Place Professional in the Cream Category at the APC Crisco National Pie Championship 2007

This is the famous recipe that was extremely successful in 2007. I am so happy it did well at both the Food Network Challenge and the APC Crisco National Pie Championship. In April 2008, I was filming another Food Network Challenge that will air in fall 2008. Keegan Gerhard, the host of the Food Network Challenge, came over to greet me when I walked into the room where the challenge was to be filmed. After a handshake and greeting, Keegan's first comment was, "Your Coconut Cream Pie is still the best pie I have ever tasted." I was truly honored, since Keegan was named one of the nation's top 10 pastry chefs of 2002 and 2004 by both *Chocolatier* and *Pastry Art & Design* magazines.

Crust

> 1½ cups unbleached all-purpose flour
> ½ tablespoon white sugar
> ½ teaspoon kosher or sea salt, finely ground
> ¼ cup Crisco butter-flavored all-vegetable shortening, chilled and cut into small pieces
> ¼ cup unsalted butter, chilled and cut into small pieces
> ¼–½ cup cold water; use only as much as needed for a smooth, satiny dough ball
> Crisco butter-flavored cooking spray

1. All ingredients should be cold. Combine all the dry ingredients in a large mixing bowl. Add shortening and butter. Using a pastry blender, cut in the shortening and butter until the mixture resembles coarse meal or peas.
2. Drop by drop, add the cold water. Mix in with the fingertips, not with the hands as the palms will warm the dough. Continue mixing in water until the dough begins to hold together without being crumbly yet not sticky.

3. Lightly spray a deep 9-inch pie pan or 8½-inch fluted flan pan, Roll out dough and place in pie plate, allowing the excess pastry to hang over the edge. Cut away excess, tuck under, and crimp decoratively. Prick bottom and sides with a fork. Chill in the refrigerator for 30 minutes.

4. Preheat oven to 400 degrees. Line the pastry shell with parchment and baking beans or beads. Bake the shell for 10 minutes. Remove the paper and beans or beads and return to the oven for 10 more minutes. Cool.

Makes pastry for one 9-inch single-crust pie.

Filling

2 cups shredded coconut, divided
8 egg yolks
1¼ cups white sugar
⅔ cup cornstarch
2 tablespoons unsalted butter, melted
2½ cups whole milk
1 cup coconut cream
2 teaspoons pure vanilla extract or paste, divided
2 cups heavy whipping cream, divided
3 tablespoons confectioner's sugar

1. Lightly toast 1 cup of shredded coconut in oven, about 7 minutes. Remove and cool. Set aside.

2. Combine egg yolks and sugar. Beat with electric mixer until pale yellow and fluffy. Add cornstarch and melted butter. Blend well and set aside.

A homemade pie with a flaky crust is one of life's great joys. Such a crust is airy, yet has texture. It makes its presence known without being assertive. It displays one of the great struggles of the universe, the tension between being and nothingness, right there in a 9-inch pie pan.

—ROB KASPER, *BALTIMORE SUN*

---

3. Heat milk but do not boil. Stir in coconut cream. Gradually add egg and cornstarch mixture, whisking or stirring constantly over medium-low heat until filling begins to thicken. Add 1 teaspoon vanilla.

4. Remove filling from heat and let cool.

5. In a mixing bowl, whisk or beat 1 cup of heavy cream on high until it begins to thicken and forms stiff peaks. Set aside.

6. Strain cooled filling through fine-mesh sieve to remove lumps if needed. Fold in whipped cream and 1 cup of shredded coconut with pie filling and pour into prepared pie crust.

7. Whisk or beat remaining heavy cream on high until it begins to thicken. Gradually add confectioner's sugar and remaining teaspoon of vanilla. Continue until stiff peaks form. Fold in toasted coconut and spread over top of pie. Refrigerate until mixture has cooled and set.

Serves 8–10.

Custard Pie

This simple yet delicious recipe was a family staple for years. Grandma would serve it without whipped topping but instead added sliced, freshly picked strawberries to adorn the top of the pie or any fruit or berries of the season. I added a couple of her variations to this recipe that I enjoyed and still do. Her Carrot Custard Pie was fun to make. I would grate the carrots with her box grater. The carrots add an interesting sweet taste that the lemon juice enhances. Try it for a little something different.

Crust

    1½ cups unbleached all-purpose flour
    ½ tablespoon white sugar
    ½ teaspoon kosher or sea salt, finely ground
    ¼ cup Crisco butter-flavored all-vegetable shortening, chilled
        and cut into small pieces
    ¼ cup unsalted butter, chilled and cut into small pieces

¼–½ cup cold water; use only as much as needed for a smooth,
    satiny dough ball
Crisco butter-flavored cooking spray
1 egg yolk and 1 teaspoon water for egg wash

1. All ingredients should be cold. Combine all the dry ingredients in a large mixing bowl. Add shortening and butter. Using a pastry blender, cut in the shortening and butter until the mixture resembles coarse meal or peas.
2. Drop by drop, add the cold water. Mix in with the fingertips, not with the hands as the palms will warm the dough. Continue mixing in water until the dough begins to hold together without being crumbly yet not sticky.
3. Place dough in plastic wrap. Fold over plastic wrap and press down to form a disk. This will make rolling out easier after chilling. Finish wrapping in plastic and place in the refrigerator for at least 30 minutes.
4. Lightly spray a deep 9-inch pie pan or 8½-inch fluted flan pan with cooking spray. Roll out dough and place in pie plate, allowing the excess pastry to hang over the edge. Cut away excess, tuck under, and crimp decoratively. Brush with egg wash and return to the refrigerator until filling is ready.

Makes pastry for one 9-inch single-crust pie.

Filling

4 large eggs, slightly beaten
¼ teaspoon kosher or sea salt
½ cup white sugar
3 cups milk, scalded

½ teaspoon pure vanilla extract
    or paste
Freshly ground nutmeg

1. Preheat oven to 450 degrees. Combine eggs, salt, and sugar. Slowly add milk and vanilla.
2. Pour mixture into prepared pie crust and sprinkle with nutmeg. Cover pie crust edge with pie shield to prevent excessive browning. Bake for

10 minutes. Reduce temperature to 325 degrees and bake for an additional 30–40 minutes, or until a knife inserted in center comes out clean. Cool on rack. Top with Sweetened Whipped Cream (see recipe in the "Decorating Your Pie" chapter) and your favorite sliced fruit.

Serves 8–10.

Grandma's Variations

Carrot Custard Pie: Add 1 cup peeled and grated carrot, ½ teaspoon freshly squeezed lemon juice and 3 additional tablespoons of sugar to the custard before baking.

Caramel Pie: Caramelize sugar and add to scalded milk before combining milk with egg mixture.

John Michael's Helpful Hint: Several older recipes called for scalded milk; that is, milk brought to nearly a boil (185 degrees) in a heavy-bottom saucepan or double boiler. Scalding served three purposes: to kill harmful bacteria that may have spoiled the food being prepared, to destroy enzymes that may have affected the way the milk performs in the recipe, and to raise the temperature of the milk to speed up results. With modern pasteurization, bacteria and enzymes are already destroyed, so scalding is no longer necessary. However, heating the milk helps to encourage growth of yeast in breads, to better dissolve other ingredients (help melt butter, dissolve sugar more easily), to promote bacteria growth for recipes such as making yogurt, or to increase the amount of flavor that is released from some ingredients such as vanilla beans.

If you decide to scald milk:

◆ Keep heat to medium, use a heavy-bottom saucepan, and stir continually.

◆ Heat milk in a double boiler and stir occasionally.

◆ Heat milk in a heatproof glass container in the microwave oven.

◆ Use an instant-read thermometer to read temperature. Do not exceed 82°C/180°F, and do not boil milk.

✒ Lava Flow Pie

This pie is a lot of fun, and children enjoy assisting with decorating the top of the pie to resemble a volcano and lava flow. A fruity and creamy filling makes this a perfect recipe for a summer picnic or summer holiday gathering.

Crust

> 1½ cups unbleached all-purpose flour
> ½ tablespoon white sugar
> ½ teaspoon kosher or sea salt, finely ground
> ¼ cup butter-flavored all-vegetable shortening, chilled and
>   cut into small pieces
> ¼ cup unsalted butter, chilled and cut into small pieces
> ¼–½ cup cold water; use only as much as needed for a smooth,
>   satiny dough ball
> Butter-flavored cooking spray

1. All ingredients should be cold. Combine all the dry ingredients in a large mixing bowl. Add shortening and butter. Using a pastry blender, cut in the shortening and butter until the mixture resembles coarse meal or peas.
2. Drop by drop, add the cold water. Mix in with the fingertips, not with the hands as the palms will warm the dough. Continue mixing in water until the dough begins to hold together without being crumbly yet not sticky.
3. Place dough in plastic wrap. Fold over plastic wrap and press down to form a disk. This will make rolling out easier after chilling. Finish wrapping in plastic and place in the refrigerator for at least 30 minutes.
4. Lightly spray a deep 9-inch deep pie dish. Roll out dough and place in pie plate, allowing the excess pastry to hang over the edge. Cut away excess, tuck under, and crimp decoratively. Prick bottom and sides with a fork. Chill in the refrigerator for 30 minutes.

5. Preheat oven to 400 degrees. Line the pastry shell with parchment and baking beans or beads. Bake the shell for 10 minutes. Remove the paper and beans or beads and return to the oven for 10 more minutes. Cool.

Makes pastry for one 9-inch single-crust pie.

Filling

1 cup coconut cream
1 cup fresh pineapple puree
½ cup dark or white rum or extract
½ cup white sugar
¼ cup cornstarch
¼ cup pineapple juice
½ cup heavy whipping cream
1½ cups strawberry puree, more for decorating top of pie

1. Combine coconut cream, pineapple puree, rum, and sugar in a medium heavy-bottom saucepan over medium heat. Stir occasionally, heating just until sugar has dissolved.
2. Mix cornstarch and pineapple juice and add to saucepan. Heat until filling thickens, stirring constantly, and cook one minute longer. Remove from heat and cool.
3. In a mixing bowl, whisk or beat heavy cream on high until it begins to form stiff peaks form. Fold into cooled pie filling.
4. Pour strawberry puree into prepared pie crust. With a spoon, spread puree over bottom and sides of crust. Pour filling over strawberry puree. Chill for at least 4–5 hours or overnight.

Topping

1 envelope unflavored gelatin
¼ cup cold water
2 cups heavy whipping cream
½ cup confectioner's sugar
1½ teaspoons pure vanilla extract or paste

1. Refrigerate a mixing bowl at least 15 minutes to chill.
2. In a small saucepan, combine gelatin and water. Let stand 1 minute. Over low heat dissolve gelatin, stirring constantly. Do not boil. Remove from heat and cool to room temperature.
3. In chilled bowl, place whipping cream and gradually add dissolved gelatin, beating with electric mixer on low speed until well blended. Beat on medium-high speed 5 minutes or until thickened. Add sugar and vanilla; beat on high speed 5 minutes or until soft peaks form.
4. Spoon whipped topping on pie, building a cone in the center resembling a volcano. Spoon remaining strawberry puree from top of cone to resemble lava flowing down.

Serves 8–10.

Nessy's Nesselrode Pie

Winner: Third Place Amateur Division for Pies Made with Splenda, APC Crisco National Pie Championship 2006. (The contest challenged bakers to use only Splenda as the sweetener. You may use equal amounts of white sugar as a substitute for Splenda.)

Crust

> 1¼ cups chocolate wafer or cookie crumbs
> 1 tablespoon Splenda® No Calorie Granular
> 5 tablespoons unsalted butter, melted
> Butter-flavored cooking spray

1. Preheat oven to 350 degrees. Spray 9-inch pie plate with cooking spray and set aside.
2. Add chocolate wafers or cookies to food processor or crush with mortar and pestle. Pulse until wafers or cookies are broken down. Add Splenda. Mix well. Pour butter over crumb mixture and process until mixture begins to hold together.

3. Spread crumb mixture in pie plate and press into the bottom and up the side.
4. Bake for 10–12 minutes. Cool and place in refrigerator for 10 minutes before filling.

Filling

1 tablespoon good-quality rum or extract
¼ cup candied fruit, chopped
2 teaspoons unflavored gelatin
2 cups whole milk, divided
½ cup Splenda No Calorie Granular
½ teaspoon fine sea salt
3 large eggs, separated
1 cup heavy whipping cream
Chocolate curls or shavings, for decorating

1. In a small bowl, combine rum and candied fruit. Set aside.
2. Sprinkle gelatin in a small bowl and pour ½ cup of the milk over it. Let stand 5 minutes to soften.
3. In a heavy-bottom saucepan over low heat, combine ¼ of the Splenda, the remaining milk, and salt. Stir in the gelatin mixture. Cook, stirring constantly, until the gelatin dissolves.
4. Whisk in the egg yolks and cook, stirring, until thick enough to coat the spoon. Do not boil. Pour the mixture over the candied fruit and rum. Set in a bowl of ice water to cool.
5. Whisk or beat the cream until soft peaks form. Set aside.
6. With an electric mixer, beat the egg whites until they hold soft peaks. Add the remaining Splenda and beat just enough to blend. Fold a large dollop of the egg whites into the cooled gelatin mixture. Pour into the remaining egg whites and carefully fold together. Fold in the whipped cream.
7. Pour into the chilled pie shell and chill for at least 2 hours or until firm. Decorate with chocolate curls or shavings.

Serves 8–10.

⸔ Norwegian Mocha Pie

I embellished the name of this pie by adding "Norwegian." Nothing means Norwegian, to me, more than coffee. My grandma and grandpa would drink coffee night and day. I remember them having a cup of coffee before bed. If I drank a cup of coffee before bed I would be up all night. Caffeine affects me strangely. So, this recipe is in honor of all my Norwegian relatives and their many cups of coffee that got them through the worst of times and the best of times.

Crust

>   1½ cups unbleached all-purpose flour
>   ½ tablespoon white sugar
>   ½ teaspoon kosher or sea salt, finely ground
>   ¼ cup Crisco butter-flavored all-vegetable shortening, chilled
>   and cut into small pieces
>   ¼ cup unsalted butter, chilled and cut into small pieces
>   ¼–½ cup cold water; use only as much as needed for a smooth,
>   satiny dough ball
>   Crisco butter-flavored cooking spray

1. All ingredients should be cold. Combine all the dry ingredients in a large mixing bowl. Add shortening and butter. Using a pastry blender, cut in the shortening and butter until the mixture resembles coarse meal or peas.
2. Drop by drop, add the cold water. Mix in with the fingertips, not with the hands as the palms will warm the dough. Continue mixing in water until the dough begins to hold together without being crumbly yet not sticky.
3. Lightly spray a deep 9-inch pie pan or 8½-inch fluted flan pan. Roll out dough and place in pie plate, allowing the excess pastry to hang over the edge. Cut away excess, tuck under, and crimp decoratively. Prick sides and bottom with a fork. Refrigerate for 30 minutes.

4. Preheat the oven to 400 degrees. Line the pastry shell with parchment and baking beans or beads. Bake the shell for 10 minutes. Remove the paper and beans or beads and return to the oven for 10 more minutes. Cool.

Makes pastry for one 9-inch single-crust pie.

Filling

¼ cup ground coffee
2 cups whole milk, scalded (see Custard Pie recipe
    in this chapter for instructions on scalding)
¾ cup white sugar
⅓ cup unbleached all-purpose flour
¼ teaspoon kosher or sea salt
1 ounce (1 square) semisweet baking chocolate
2 large eggs, slightly beaten
1 large egg yolk, slightly beaten
1 tablespoon unsalted butter
1 teaspoon pure vanilla extract or paste

1. In a heavy-bottom saucepan, add coffee to milk while you scald it. Strain through a fine-mesh sieve to remove grounds from milk.
2. In a double boiler or heatproof bowl over simmering water, combine sugar, flour, and salt. Stir in milk and cook until thickened, stirring constantly. Add chocolate and continue cooking an additional 10 minutes, stirring occasionally.
3. Combine eggs and egg yolk in a small mixing bowl. Add 2 tablespoons of the hot mixture to eggs to incorporate before adding eggs to the hot mixture. Cook for 2 additional minutes. Remove from heat and add butter and vanilla; cool. Pour into prepared and cooled pie crust. Refrigerate for at least 2 hours or until filling is set before serving. Serve with Sweetened Whipped Cream (see the "Decorating Your Pie" chapter for recipe).

Serves 8–10.

✟ Sugar Cream Pie

This recipe is also very good in a graham cracker crust. It just depends on your mood, taste, or what you and your family enjoy.

Crust

> 1½ cups unbleached all-purpose flour
> ½ tablespoon white sugar
> ½ teaspoon kosher or sea salt, finely ground
> ¼ cup Crisco butter-flavored all-vegetable shortening, chilled and cut into small pieces
> ¼ cup unsalted butter, chilled and cut into small pieces
> ¼–½ cup cold water; use only as much as needed for a smooth, satiny dough ball
> Crisco butter-flavored cooking spray

1. All ingredients should be cold. Combine all the dry ingredients in a large mixing bowl. Add shortening and butter. Using a pastry blender, cut in the shortening and butter until the mixture resembles coarse meal or peas.
2. Drop by drop, add the cold water. Mix in with the fingertips, not with the hands as the palms will warm the dough. Continue mixing in water until the dough begins to hold together without being crumbly yet not sticky.
3. Lightly spray a deep 9-inch pie pan or 8½-inch fluted flan pan with cooking spray. Roll out dough and place in pie plate, allowing excess pastry to hang over the edge. Cut away extra, tuck under, and crimp decoratively. Prick sides and bottom with a fork. Chill in the refrigerator for 30 minutes.
4. Preheat the oven to 400 degrees. Line the pastry shell with parchment and baking beans or beads. Bake the shell for 10 minutes. Remove the paper and beans or beads and return to the oven for 8 more minutes. Cool.

Makes pastry for one 9-inch single-crust pie.

Filling

> ¾ cup white sugar
> 2½ cups half-and-half
> ¼ teaspoon kosher or sea salt
> ¼ cup dark brown sugar, packed
> ¼ cup cornstarch
> ½ cup unsalted butter, cut into pieces
> 1 teaspoon pure vanilla extract or paste
> ⅛ teaspoon cinnamon

1. Preheat oven to 325 degrees. In a medium heavy-bottom saucepan, combine sugar, half-and-half, and salt. Bring to a boil, stirring occasionally.
2. In another heavy-bottom saucepan, combine brown sugar and cornstarch. Gradually stir or whisk in hot half-and-half mixture. Add butter. Cook over medium heat, stirring or whisking constantly for about 5 minutes until boiling and thickened. Turn heat down and simmer for 1 additional minute. Remove from heat and stir in vanilla.
3. Pour filling into prepared, lightly baked pie crust. Sprinkle with cinnamon. Bake for 20 minutes or until the top of the pie is golden. Cool on rack. Filling will thicken as it cools. Refrigerate at least 4 hours or overnight before serving.

Serves 8–10.

Il Rifugio Tiramisu Pie

Il Rifugio is a 300-year-old stone villa in the Etruscan hills outside Cortona, Italy. It is encircled by more than 500 olive trees and has its own chestnut grove. Chad and I have been visiting and living at Il Rifugio for several years. We offer our Tuscan Gathering culinary vacations each year to groups of enthusiastic cooks of all levels. We have baked some wonderful pies and offer a "Pie in the Italian Sky" week each November that focuses on both sweet and savory pies along with our regular Italian itinerary.

Il Rifugio (www.sojourninItaly.com) is so special to me that I named this Tiramisu Pie after it. It represents the beauty and awe I find each time I step out onto the terrace at Il Rifugio and look down the hill to the small village of Montanare and to Cortona across the valley and up the mountain on the other side. It's an amazing sight. I hope you enjoy this pie and I hope you will join us in Tuscany, where we can prepare this special pie together in gracious surroundings. Oh, did I forget to mention? We'll uncork incredible Tuscan wines to help us along the way to baking a perfect pie.

Crust

    1⅓ cups chocolate wafer crumbs (about 30 cookies)
    2 tablespoons white sugar
    1 teaspoon instant coffee granules
    ⅓ cup unsalted butter, melted
    Cooking spray

1. Preheat oven to 375 degrees. Spray pie pan with cooking spray. Set aside. In a medium mixing bowl, combine cookie crumbs, sugar, and coffee granules. Drizzle with butter and stir until well blended. Press evenly into the bottom and side of a 9-inch pie plate. Bake for 8 to 10 minutes. Cool on a rack to room temperature before filling.

Makes one 9-inch pie crust.

Filling

    2 ounces semisweet baking chocolate, coarsely chopped
    4 large egg yolks
    ¼ cup white sugar
    ¾ teaspoon unflavored gelatin
    3 tablespoons brandy, warmed
    1½ cups Mascarpone cheese, room temperature
    ¾ cup heavy whipping cream
    1 tablespoon coffee-flavored liqueur
    2 teaspoons unsweetened cocoa powder, preferably Dutch processed
    1 teaspoon instant coffee granules

1. In a double boiler or heatproof bowl over a saucepan of simmering water, melt chocolate, stirring occasionally. With a spatula or pastry brush, gently spread over the inside of the cooled pie crust. Refrigerate for 10 minutes or until the chocolate is set.

2. In a heatproof bowl, using a whisk or electric hand mixer, beat egg yolks until pale and starting to thicken. Place over a saucepan of simmering water. Add sugar in a thin, steady stream, beating constantly until tripled in volume and having the consistency of softly whipped cream, about 5–6 minutes. Scrape down bowl occasionally with spatula. Remove from heat.

3. In a small mixing bowl, sprinkle gelatin over brandy; let stand for 5 minutes to "bloom." Beat into egg mixture for 1 minute.

4. Place Mascarpone in a separate large mixing bowl. Using an electric hand mixer, beat in egg mixture on low speed until smooth. In another mixing bowl, whip cream; fold into Mascarpone mixture. Transfer half into a separate mixing bowl. Stir together liqueur, cocoa, and coffee granules until granules have dissolved. Fold into one of the bowls. Scrape coffee mixture into prepared and cooled crust, smoothing with rubber spatula. Refrigerate for 30 minutes or until softly set. Gently spread remaining Mascarpone mixture over top. Return to refrigerator for at least 4 hours or until fully set before serving.

Topping

2 teaspoons unsweetened cocoa powder, preferably Dutch processed
Shaved dark chocolate

With a fine sieve, sprinkle cocoa powder over pie. Decorate edge of pie with chocolate shavings. To make shaving a chocolate bar easier, microwave for 5 seconds. Also use a vegetable peeler rather than a knife.

Serves 8–10.

Pie Fun Facts

According to a 2006 survey by Crisco® and American Pie Council:

- One out of four Americans prefer apple pie, followed by pumpkin or sweet potato (17%), anything chocolate (14%), lemon meringue (11%) and cherry (10%)

- Nearly twice as many people prefer their pie unadorned as those who like it "a la mode" with either ice cream or whipped cream topping

- Three out of four Americans overwhelmingly prefer homemade pie, while 13 percent enjoy pie from a bakery or pastry shop—only one percent said they head to the diner for their favorite slice

According to a 2006 survey conducted by Four Points by Sheraton:

PIE BY THE NUMBERS

- 36 million Number of Americans who identify apple pie as their favorite

- 47% Americans for whom the word "comforting" comes to mind when they think of pie

- 6 million Number of American men ages 35-54 who have eaten the last slice of pie and denied it

- 27% Americans who believe chocolate pie is the most romantic to share with someone special

- 1 in 5 Proportion of Americans who have eaten an entire pie by themselves
- 113 million Number of Americans who have eaten pie for breakfast
- 42% Americans who prefer to eat their pie with ice cream
- 75 million Number of Americans who prefer to drink milk with their pie
- 32% Americans who prefer no crust on top of their pie
- 90% Americans who agree that a slice of pie represents one of the simple pleasures in life
- 9% Americans who prefer to eat their pie crust-first
- 7% Americans who have passed off a store-bought pie as homemade
- 18% Men who say their wife makes the best homemade pie
- 2% Women who say their husband makes the best homemade pie

PIE PERSONALITIES

If you love ...	You are likely to describe yourself as ...
Apple Pie	Independent, realistic and compassionate
Pecan Pie	Thoughtful and analytical
Chocolate Pie	Loving
Pumpkin Pie	Funny and independent

PIE PREFERENCES

- More than one-third of Americans have eaten pie in bed
- Nearly one in four women believe that they make the best pie—better than Mom or Grandma
- More than a third of Americans have craved pie in the middle of the night
- If you lined up the number of pies sold at U.S. grocery stores in one year, they would circle the globe and then some.

- If you lined up the number of pies sold at U.S. grocery stores during Thanksgiving, they would span more than half the globe.

- The majority of pies purchased are bought at a grocery store or supermarket.

- The first mention of a fruit pie in print is from Robert Green's *Arcadia* (1590): "thy breath is like the steame of apple-pyes."

- The wet bottom molasses pie, Shoo-fly pie, was used to attract flies from the kitchen.

- Oliver Cromwell banned the eating of pie in 1644, declaring it a pagan form of pleasure. For 16 years, pie eating and making went underground until the Restoration leaders lifted the ban on pie in 1660.

- The wealthy English were known for their "Surprise Pies" in which live creatures would pop out when the pie was cut open.

- Pumpkin pie was first introduced to the holiday table at the pilgrim's second Thanksgiving in 1623.

- Pie was not always America's favorite dessert—in the 19th Century, fruit pies were a common breakfast food eaten before the start of a long day.

- At one time it was against the law to serve ice cream on cherry pie in Kansas.

- "As easy as pie" is an American expression. In the 1890's, "pie" was a common slang expression meaning anything easy, a cinch; the expression "easy as pie" stemmed quite readily from that.

- The airplane Buddy Holly died in was named the "American Pie."

- Boston Cream Pie is a cake, not a pie.

- Pies are favorite props for humor, particularly when aimed at the pompous. Throwing a pie in a person's face has been a staple of film comedy since the early days of the medium, and real-life pranksters have taken to targeting politicians and celebrities with their pies, an act called "pieing."

STATE PIES:

* Key Lime pie was just adopted in the state of Florida as the official pie of Florida in 2006.
* The state of Vermont adopted apple pie as the official state pie in 1999.

Used by permission from the American Pie Council

Chocolate Pies

*T*HERE IS MUCH TO BE SAID ABOUT the magical properties of chocolate. Women are not the only human beings to be affected by this mood-enhancing food. I most crave chocolate when I am watching television or a movie in a theater. I remember going to see *Charlie and the Chocolate Factory,* directed by Tim Burton and starring Johnny Depp. Twenty minutes into the movie, I needed chocolate. I raced up the aisle to the concession stand. Others must have had those cravings, too, because there was a nice display of chocolate bars and confections next to the cash register. That made me very happy.

All these recipes come with the "happy mouth" seal of approval. There's a good variety, too, so I hope everyone finds something to like in this chapter. My true favorite is when chocolate is mixed with fruit or berries, or they are added at the end for a garnish.

The chocolate dessert I most remember from childhood was the Adams Family Black Bottom Pie. It wasn't named for the hit television show from the 1960s but rather for my grandfather's hired hand John Adams. He traveled from Texas every spring and stayed until October or November of each year. He lived on the farm and loved my grandmother's cooking. He gave her this recipe in gratitude for all she had done for him. It was very touching. So every now and then, Grandma would bake this pie and make John feel good. It was a wonderful way to grow up—on the farm and cooking.

Several of the recipes in this chapter I created to enter in the APC Crisco National Pie Championship held in Celebration, Florida, each year. My first couple of years of competition were as an amateur. As my first cookbook began to sell and I appeared on television more and more, my amateur status was taken away and I had to compete as a professional. That's okay. I was at first a bit worried, but I continued to bake and create recipes just as I have always done.

So, when it came time to enter the Chocolate category in April 2008, I entered my Chocolate Caramel Banana Pie. It's a wonderfully rich, thick, and gooey pie. The secret is truly in the sauce as you must make your own caramel. I have offered several instructions on how to make caramel, but I have noticed dulce de leche on shelves at the grocery store. You could use a can of this Mexican caramel.

Also in April 2008, I created my Chocolate McDreamy Pie. It's a recipe using my grandmother's chocolate cream pie filling and my idea of cooking up a raspberry sauce and spreading over the side and bottom of the prepared pie crust before filling. These are two of my favorite flavors—raspberry and chocolate.

So, try my chocolate pie recipes and share with friends, co-workers, your family, or neighbors. I hope each slice brings a smile to everyone's face.

"Damn good pie!"

—*TWIN PEAKS* (1990)

⸕ Chocolate Caramel Banana Pie

Crust

1¼ cups graham cracker crumbs, fine
¼ cup white sugar
¼ cup Dutch processed cocoa powder, unsweetened
⅓ cup unsalted butter, melted

1. Preheat oven to 350 degrees. Stir together the crumbs, sugar, cocoa powder, and butter until dry ingredients are uniformly moistened.
2. Press mixture on the bottom and side of a 9-inch loose-base tart or pie pan. Chill for 10 minutes. Bake for 7–10 minutes. Cool completely before adding filling.

Makes one 9-inch crust.

Filling

1 (14-ounce) can sweetened condensed milk or dulce de leche
6 ounces unsweetened chocolate, chopped
½ cup crème fraîche
1 tablespoon light corn syrup

1. To make your own dulce de leche, place the unopened can of sweetened condensed milk in a deep saucepan or stockpot. Fill pan or stockpot with water, making sure to cover the can of condensed milk with at least 1 or 2 inches of water. Bring water to boil and immediately reduce the heat to a low simmer. Low boil (a couple of bubbles rising to the top) for 2–3 hours, always making sure the water level stays 1 or 2 inches above the can (see additional instructions in the "Decorating Your Pie" chapter). If using canned dulce de leche, there is no need for cooking. Pour directly from can.
2. Remove the pan from the heat and set aside, covered, until the can has cooled completely in the water. Do not attempt to open the can until it is completely cold. ***Warning:*** Extreme pressure has built

up during the cooking process. Opening the can before it is completely cold can result in serious burns from exploding hot condensed milk.

3. Gently melt the chocolate with the crème fraîche and corn syrup in a double boiler or in a heatproof bowl over a saucepan of simmering water. Stir in the caramelized condensed milk and beat until evenly mixed. Pour the filling into the prepared chocolate graham cracker crust and spread it evenly. Refrigerate for 2–4 hours before serving.

Topping

2 bananas
Sweetened Whipped Cream (see recipe in the "Decorating Your Pie" chapter)
Chocolate Bar Curls (see instructions in the "Decorating Your Pie" chapter)

1. Slice bananas evenly and arrange them over the filling. Spoon Sweetened Whipped Cream over the bananas.
2. Cover Sweetened Whipped Cream topping with chocolate curls. Serve immediately.

Serves 8–10.

John Michael's Helpful Hint: Crème fraîche (pronounced "krem fresh") is a thick and silky heavy cream with a wonderful rich texture. Crème fraîche is widely used in France, where the cream is unpasteurized and contains the "friendly" bacteria necessary to thicken it naturally. Commercial crème fraîche is pricey, so the homemade version can save you money. Plan ahead as this process will take 8–14 hours.

Crème fraîche

1 cup whipping cream, room temperature
2 tablespoons buttermilk or ½ cup sour cream, room temperature

In a jar with a lid, place whipping cream and buttermilk (or sour cream); cover securely and shake 15 seconds. Set aside at room temperature for 24 hours or until very thick. Stir once or twice during that time. Cream will thicken faster if the room is warm. Stir thickened crème fraîche well. Refrigerate at least 6 hours before serving. Cover tightly and store in refrigerator for up to 2 weeks.

Adams Family Black Bottom Pie

John Adams was one of Grandpa's best hired men on the farm. He worked for Grandpa for more years than I can remember during the late 1960s and through the 1970s. He lived on the property in a small white house. John Adams gave Grandma this recipe. He told her that he wanted to give her one of his mother's recipes because she was such a fine cook. Grandma baked this pie for John and our family several times. One time during a picnic, John ate a piece and I believe he had tears in his eyes. I remember thinking that he missed his family and the familiar settings of home. He did tell me once that every time Grandma baked this pie, it reminded him of his family in Texas. His mother had passed away, but he still had a brother and father. He was a good man and a friend to my family.

Crust

> 1½ cups unbleached all-purpose flour
> ½ tablespoon white sugar
> ½ teaspoon kosher or sea salt, finely ground
> ¼ cup all-vegetable shortening, chilled and cut into small pieces
> ¼ cup unsalted butter, chilled and cut into small pieces
> ¼–½ cup cold water; use only as much as needed for a smooth, satiny dough ball

1. All ingredients should be cold. Combine all the dry ingredients in a large mixing bowl. Add shortening and butter. Using a pastry blender, cut in the shortening and butter until the mixture resembles coarse meal or peas.
2. Drop by drop, add the cold water. Mix in with the fingertips, not with the hands as the palms will warm the dough. Continue mixing in water until the dough begins to hold together without being crumbly yet not sticky.
3. Lightly spray a deep 9-inch pie pan or 8½-inch fluted flan pan. Roll out dough and place in pie plate, allowing the excess pastry to hang over the edge. Cut away extra, tuck under, and crimp decoratively. Prick bottom and sides with a fork. Chill in the refrigerator for at least 30 minutes.
4. Preheat the oven to 400 degrees. Line the pastry shell with parchment and baking beans or beads. Bake for 10 minutes. Remove the paper and beans or beads and return to the oven for 10 more minutes. Cool on a rack completely before filling.

Makes pastry for one 9-inch single-crust pie.

Filling

3 large eggs, separated
4 teaspoons cornstarch
6 tablespoons white sugar, divided
1⅔ cups whole milk
6 ounces unsweetened chocolate, finely chopped
1 teaspoon pure vanilla extract or paste
1 envelope unflavored gelatin
3 tablespoons water
2 tablespoons good-quality dark rum or rum extract

1. In a medium mixing bowl, stir or whisk egg yolks, cornstarch, and 2 tablespoons sugar. Set aside.

2. In a heavy-bottom saucepan over medium heat, add milk and heat until almost boiling. Remove from heat and stir or whisk in egg mixture. Return mixture to heat and continue stirring until the egg-milk mixture has thickened and is smooth. Remove from heat and pour half the custard into a mixing bowl.

3. Put the chocolate in a double boiler or a heatproof bowl placed over a saucepan of simmering water until the chocolate has melted, stirring occasionally, until smooth. Stir the melted chocolate into the custard mixture in the bowl. Add vanilla.

4. Spoon the chocolate custard over the bottom of the prepared pie crust. Cover with plastic wrap to prevent a skin from forming. Let cool and then chill in refrigerator until set.

5. Sprinkle gelatin over the water in a small bowl. Let it "bloom" for 5 minutes. Place over a pan of simmering water until the gelatin has dissolved. Fold into the remaining custard. Stir in the rum.

6. In the bowl of a standing mixer using the whisk attachment, whisk egg whites until they form soft peaks. Whisk in the remaining sugar, a little at a time, until stiff peaks form. Fold whisked egg whites into the rum-flavored custard.

7. Spoon the rum-flavored custard over the chocolate layer in the pie crust. Using a spatula or the back of a wooden spoon, level the mixture, making sure that none of the chocolate custard is visible. Return the pie to the refrigerator until the top layer has set. Garnish with Sweetened Whipped Cream (see recipe in the "Decorating Your Pie" chapter) and Chocolate Bar Curls (see instructions in the "Decorating Your Pie" chapter).

Serves 8–10.

Pie and coffee is approximately the third best social interaction a man can hope to have with a woman.

—UNKNOWN

𝑓 Chocolate Cherry Pie

Crust

  1½ cups unbleached all-purpose flour
  ½ tablespoon white sugar
  ½ teaspoon kosher or sea salt, finely ground
  ¼ cup Crisco butter-flavored all-vegetable shortening, chilled
      and cut into small pieces
  ¼ cup unsalted butter, chilled and cut into small pieces
  ¼–½ cup cold water; use only as much as needed for a smooth,
      satiny dough ball
  1 egg yolk and 1 teaspoon water for egg wash
  Crisco butter-flavored cooking spray

1. All ingredients should be cold. Combine all the dry ingredients in a large mixing bowl. Add shortening and butter. Using a pastry blender, cut in the shortening and butter until the mixture resembles coarse meal or peas.
2. Drop by drop, add the cold water. Mix in with the fingertips, not with the hands as the palms will warm the dough. Continue mixing in water until the dough begins to hold together without being crumbly yet not sticky.
3. Place dough in plastic wrap. Fold over plastic wrap and press down to form a disk. This will make rolling out easier after chilling. Finish wrapping in plastic and place in the refrigerator for at least 30 minutes.
4. Lightly spray a deep 9-inch pie pan or 8½-inch fluted flan pan with cooking spray. Roll out dough and place in pie plate, allowing the excess pastry to hang over the edge. Cut away extra, tuck under, and crimp decoratively. Prick bottom and sides with a fork. Chill in the refrigerator for at least 30 minutes.
5. Preheat the oven to 425 degrees. Line the pie crust with parchment and baking beans or beads. Bake for 10 minutes. Remove the paper and beans and cool on a wire rack. Bake an additional 10 minutes until golden. Cool on rack.

Makes pastry for one 9-inch single-crust pie.

Filling

1 (14-ounce) can sweetened
  condensed milk

1 cup semisweet chocolate
  chips

½ teaspoon sea salt

1 (21-ounce) can cherry
  pie filling

½ teaspoon pure almond
  extract

Maraschino cherries

1. In a heavy-bottom saucepan over low heat, combine milk, chocolate chips, and salt. Stir gently until chocolate melts. Fold in the cherry pie filling and almond extract.
2. Remove from heat and pour into prepared pie crust. Chill in refrigerator for at least 4 hours or until filling is firm. Garnish with Sweetened Whipped Cream (see recipe in the "Decorating Your Pie" chapter) and maraschino cherries.

Serves 8–10.

Chocolate Chip Almond Pie

Crust

1¼ cups graham cracker crumbs
¼ cup white sugar
¼ cup Dutch processed cocoa powder, unsweetened
⅓ cup unsalted butter, melted
Crisco butter-flavored cooking spray

1. Preheat oven to 350 degrees. Spray pie plate with cooking spray. Set aside.
2. Stir together the graham cracker crumbs, sugar, cocoa powder, and butter until ingredients are uniformly moistened. Press mixture on the bottom and side of prepared pie plate. Chill for 10 minutes. Bake for 7–10 minutes. Cool completely before adding filling.

Makes one 9-inch pie crust.

Filling

6 chocolate bars with almonds
17 regular size (not mini) marshmallows
½ cup whole milk
1 cup heavy cream, whipped
½ cup semisweet chocolate chips
½ cup almonds, slivered

1. Break up chocolate bars and place in a heatproof bowl over a sauce-pan of simmering water. Add marshmallows. Stir until completely melted. Remove from heat and cool completely.
2. When chocolate mixture is cool, fold in whipped cream, chocolate chips, and almonds. Gently pour into prepared pie crust and smooth with back of a wooden spoon or spatula. Chill in the refrigerator for at least 4–6 hours or until filling is set. Garnish with Chocolate Bar Curls (see instructions in the "Decorating Your Pie" chapter).

Serves 8–10.

Chocolate Coconut Cream Pie

Crust

1½ cups unbleached all-purpose flour
½ tablespoon white sugar
½ teaspoon kosher or sea salt, finely ground
¼ cup Crisco butter-flavored all-vegetable shortening, chilled and cut into small pieces
¼ cup unsalted butter, chilled and cut into small pieces
¼–½ cup cold water; use only as much as needed for a smooth, satiny dough ball
1 egg yolk and 1 teaspoon water for egg wash
Crisco butter-flavored cooking spray

1. All ingredients should be cold. Combine all the dry ingredients in a large mixing bowl. Add shortening and butter. Using a pastry blender, cut in the shortening and butter until the mixture resembles coarse meal or peas.

2. Drop by drop, add the cold water. Mix in with the fingertips, not with the hands as the palms will warm the dough. Continue mixing in water until the dough begins to hold together without being crumbly yet not sticky.

3. Place dough in plastic wrap. Fold over plastic wrap and press down to form a disk. This will make rolling out easier after chilling. Finish wrapping in plastic and place in the refrigerator for at least 30 minutes.

4. Lightly spray a deep 9-inch pie pan or 8½-inch fluted flan pan with cooking spray. Roll out dough and place in pie plate, allowing the excess pastry to hang over the edge. Cut away excess, tuck under, and crimp decoratively. Prick bottom and sides with a fork. Chill in the refrigerator for at least 30 minutes.

5. Preheat the oven to 425 degrees. Line the pie crust with parchment and baking beans or beads. Bake for 10 minutes. Remove the paper and beans or beads and cool on a wire rack. Bake an additional 10 minutes until golden. Cool on rack.

Makes pastry for one 9-inch single-crust pie.

Filling

⅔ cup white sugar, plus 3 tablespoons
⅓ cup cornstarch
¼ teaspoon kosher or sea salt
3⅛ cups whole milk, divided
3 large eggs, slightly beaten
1 tablespoon unsalted butter
2 teaspoons pure vanilla extract or paste
½ cup sweetened flaked coconut
3 tablespoons Dutch processed cocoa

1. In a medium heavy-bottom saucepan over medium heat, stir or whisk together ⅔ cup sugar, cornstarch, salt, and 3 cups milk. Mix in the eggs. Cook, stirring or whisking constantly, until the mixture begins to boil. Continue to boil for 1 minute. Remove from heat and stir in butter and vanilla. In a small mixing bowl, pour 1½ cups of the cooking filling. Fold in coconut and set aside.

2. In a mixing bowl, whisk together cocoa, 3 tablespoons sugar, and ⅛ cup milk. Pour cocoa mixture into remaining cooked filling. Return to medium heat and cook just until it begins to boil, stirring or whisking constantly. Remove from heat.

3. Pour 1 cup of cooling chocolate filling into prepared pie crust. Spoon coconut filling over chocolate layer. Top with remaining chocolate filling, using the back of a wooden spoon or spatula to smooth evenly.

4. Cover with plastic wrap so that filling does not form a skin and chill in the refrigerator for at least 4 hours or overnight until filling is set. Garnish with Sweetened Whipped Cream and Chocolate Bar Curls (see both in the "Decorating Your Pie" chapter).

Serves 8–10.

Chocolate Cream Meringue Pie

This is a yummy pie and I loved watching my grandma make it. She could always make such beautiful meringue pies. She enjoyed simply spooning the meringue on top and running swirls around the top or placing the meringue in a pastry bag and piping rosettes or puff clouds on top of the filling before browning.

Crust

1½ cups unbleached all-purpose flour
½ tablespoon white sugar
½ teaspoon kosher or sea salt, finely ground

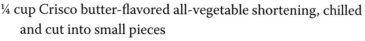

¼ cup Crisco butter-flavored all-vegetable shortening, chilled
   and cut into small pieces
¼ cup unsalted butter, chilled and cut into small pieces
¼–½ cup cold water; use only as much as needed for a smooth,
   satiny dough ball
1 egg yolk and 1 teaspoon water for egg wash
Crisco butter-flavored cooking spray

1. All ingredients should be cold. Combine all the dry ingredients in a large mixing bowl. Add shortening and butter. Using a pastry blender, cut in the shortening and butter until the mixture resembles coarse meal or peas.
2. Drop by drop, add the cold water. Mix in with the fingertips, not with the hands as the palms will warm the dough. Continue mixing in water until the dough begins to hold together without being crumbly yet not sticky.
3. Place dough in plastic wrap. Fold over plastic wrap and press down to form a disk. This will make rolling out easier after chilling. Finish wrapping in plastic and place in the refrigerator for at least 30 minutes.
4. Lightly spray a deep 9-inch pie pan or 8½-inch fluted flan pan with cooking spray. Roll out dough and place in pie plate, allowing the excess pastry to hang over the edge. Cut away excess, tuck under, and crimp decoratively. Prick bottom and sides with a fork. Chill in the refrigerator for at least 30 minutes.
5. Preheat the oven to 425 degrees. Line the pie crust with parchment and baking beans or beads. Bake the crust for 10 minutes. Remove the paper and beans or beads and cool on a wire rack. Bake an additional 10 minutes until golden. Cool on rack.

Makes pastry for one 9-inch single-crust pie.

Filling

½ cup unbleached all-purpose flour
1 cup white sugar
¼ teaspoon kosher or sea salt
3 cups whole milk
3 ounces unsweetened chocolate, coarsely chopped
3 egg yolks (save egg whites for meringue)
1½ teaspoons pure vanilla extract or paste
1 tablespoon unsalted butter

1. Preheat oven to 275 degrees. In a heavy-bottom saucepan over medium heat, add flour, sugar, and salt. Gradually add milk and stir or whisk until smooth. Continue stirring until the mixture begins to thicken. Remove from heat. Add chocolate and stir in until completely blended and smooth.
2. In a small mixing bowl, slightly beat egg yolks. Add a small amount of the cooked mixture and whisk to blend. This will help blend in the eggs and bring their temperature up so that eggs don't become scrambled. Spoon cooked mixture with the eggs into the saucepan. Return to heat source and bring to a boil, stirring constantly. Remove from heat. Stir in vanilla and butter. Cover with plastic wrap so that filling doesn't form a skin while cooling; about 20 minutes. Gently spoon cooled filling into prepared pie crust.
3. Cover top of filling with meringue (see recipe in the "Decorating Your Pie" chapter). Carefully spread meringue over the top of the filling with a spoon or spatula. Make sure to seal the edges of the pie crust with meringue to prevent shrinking (meringue will shrink inward if it doesn't touch and attach itself to crust edge). Bake for 15 minutes or until meringue is lightly browned. Cool on a rack until room temperature. Chill in refrigerator for at least 4 hours before serving.

Serves 8–10.

𝑓 Chocolate McDreamy Pie

I created this recipe for the 2008 APC Crisco National Pie Championship in Celebration, Florida. I used some of the family recipes for a creamy chocolate filling but wanted to add a twist. That twist was a layer of homemade raspberry sauce spread on the bottom and side of the prepared pie crust. You may use fruit spreads, jams, and jellies if you wish. It all makes for one lovely fruity and chocolaty pie. The name, by the way, came from the character of Doctor McDreamy. I thought it wouldn't hurt to name a pie after a character on television that women couldn't get enough of. Enjoy!

Crust

> 1½ cups unbleached all-purpose flour
> ½ tablespoon white sugar
> ½ teaspoon kosher or sea salt, finely ground
> ½ cup Crisco butter–flavored all-vegetable shortening, chilled
>   and cut into small pieces
> ¼–½ cup cold water; use only as much as needed for a smooth,
>   satiny dough ball
> 3 tablespoons white sugar
> 1 tablespoon cornstarch
> 2 cups raspberries, fresh or frozen (if frozen, thawed and drained)
> Crisco butter-flavored cooking spray

1. All ingredients should be cold. Combine all the dry ingredients in a large mixing bowl. Add shortening. Using a pastry blender, cut in the shortening until the mixture resembles coarse meal or peas.
2. Drop by drop, add the cold water. Mix in with the fingertips, not with the hands as the palms will warm the dough. Continue mixing in water until the dough begins to hold together without being crumbly yet not sticky.
3. Lightly spray a deep 9-inch pie pan or 8½-inch fluted flan pan. Roll out dough and place in pie plate, allowing the excess pastry to hang over

the edge. Cut away excess, tuck under, and crimp decoratively. Prick bottom and sides with a fork. Chill in the refrigerator for 30 minutes.

4. Preheat the oven to 400 degrees. Line the pastry shell with parchment and baking beans or beads. Bake the shell for 10 minutes. Remove the paper and beans/beads and bake for 10 more minutes or until golden. Cool on a rack.

5. In a heavy-bottom saucepan, combine sugar and cornstarch over medium heat. Stir in raspberries. Boil and stir for 2 minutes. Remove from the heat; cool for 15 minutes. Spread on bottom and side of pie crust and refrigerate while preparing filling.

Makes pastry for one 9-inch single-crust pie.

Filling

½ cup white sugar
¼ cup cornstarch
⅛ teaspoon kosher or sea salt, crushed
1 cup whole milk
6 ounces semisweet baking chocolate squares
2 egg yolks, slightly beaten
1 (3-ounce) package cream cheese, softened
1½ cups heavy whipping cream
3 tablespoons confectioner's sugar
1 teaspoon pure vanilla bean paste or extract

1. In a medium heavy-bottom saucepan, combine sugar, cornstarch, and salt; mix well. Gradually stir in milk. Add chocolate and egg yolks. Cook over medium heat, stirring mixture gently and constantly until thickened. Remove from heat; stir in cream cheese, beating until smooth. Use a whisk if necessary. Cover surface of thickened mixture with plastic wrap to keep a skin from forming while cooling. Refrigerate for about 1 hour.

2. In a large mixing bowl, beat whipping cream until soft peaks form. Add confectioner's sugar and vanilla extract. Continue beating until stiff peaks form.

3. Reserve 1 cup whipped cream for topping. Fold remaining whipped cream into cooled chocolate mixture. Spoon evenly into cooled baked shell. Spoon or pipe reserved whipped cream over filling. Refrigerate 6 hours or overnight before serving.
4. Before serving, sprinkle with Dutch processed cocoa using a decorative stencil or other pattern. Slice raspberries, blackberries, or strawberries for garnish.

Serves 8–10.

Chocolate Mousse Pie

I think you will enjoy this smooth and refreshing chocolate mousse pie. It's so light and creamy. If you prefer to bake a sweeter-tasting pie, substitute semisweet chocolate for bittersweet chocolate. Also, if you decorate with chocolate leaves on top of the Sweetened Whipped Cream, try using both white and dark chocolate for a wonderful effect.

Crust

1½ cups chocolate cookie crumbs or 30 chocolate wafers
1 tablespoon white sugar
5 tablespoons unsalted butter, melted
Crisco butter-flavored cooking spray

1. Preheat oven to 350 degrees. Spray 9-inch deep pie plate with cooking spray and set aside.
2. Add chocolate wafers or cookies to food processor or crush with mortar and pestle. Pulse until wafers or cookies are broken down. Add sugar. Mix well. Pour butter over crumb mixture and process until mixture begins to hold together.
3. Spread crumb mixture in pie plate and press into the bottom and up the side. Chill in the refrigerator for 10 minutes.
4. Bake for 10–12 minutes. Cool and place in refrigerator for 10 minutes before filling.

Filling

24 ounces bittersweet baking chocolate or chips, divided
2 large eggs
4 large eggs, separated
2 cups heavy whipping cream
6 tablespoons confectioner's sugar

1. In a heatproof mixing bowl over simmering water, melt chocolate. Remove from heat and let cool; about 15 minutes. Add 2 eggs and whisk to blend well. Whisk in 4 egg yolks and whisk until blended and smooth. Set aside.
2. In the mixing bowl of a standing mixer with a whisk attachment, whip cream and confectioner's sugar until soft peaks form. Set aside. In a clean mixing bowl with a clean whisk attachment, whisk 4 egg whites until stiff peaks form. Set aside.
3. Spoon a small amount of the whipped cream and the whisked egg whites into the chocolate mixture. Fold until well incorporated. Add remaining whipped cream and whisked egg whites into chocolate mixture, blending well.
4. Gently pour filling into prepared pie crust. Chill in refrigerator for 4–6 hours or until filling is set. Spread top of pie with Sweetened Whipped Cream and decorate top with remaining Sweetened Whipped Cream piped into rosettes and overlapping Chocolate Leaves (see both recipes in the "Decorating Your Pie" chapter).

Serves 8–10.

Note: It is suggested that caution be exercised in consuming raw and lightly cooked eggs owing to the slight risk of salmonella poisoning or other foodborne illnesses. To reduce this risk, use only fresh, properly refrigerated, clean, grade A or AA eggs with intact shells. When breaking open eggs, avoid contact between the yolks or whites and the shell.

⸙ Chocolate Peanut Butter Pie

I found this recipe years ago in our families' stack of old recipes. Chad wanted to enter the amateur division of the APC Crisco National Pie Championship with a pie containing peanut butter. Eventually he didn't choose this recipe but another called Peanut Butterfinger Pie. This is lovely pie and combines two very popular flavors of peanut butter and chocolate.

Crust

> 1¾ cups graham cracker crumbs
> 2 tablespoons light brown sugar, firmly packed
> Pinch of salt
> 6 tablespoons unsalted butter, melted
> Crisco butter-flavored cooking spray

1. Preheat oven to 350 degrees. Spray pie plate with cooking spray and set aside.
2. Combine the graham cracker crumbs, brown sugar, and salt in a large mixing bowl. Using your fingers, mix together. Add the butter and incorporate well, mixing first with a fork, then with your hands, rubbing thoroughly to form evenly moistened crumbs.
3. Spread the crumbs evenly and loosely in the pie plate, pressing them into the bottom and up the side. Refrigerate for 10 minutes.
4. Bake for 8 to 10 minutes. Cool on a rack. Refrigerate 15 minutes before filling.

Makes one 9-inch graham cracker crust.

Filling

> 12 ounces cream cheese, room temperature
> 1½ cups peanut butter, smooth or chunky
> 2 cups white sugar, divided
> 1½ cups heavy whipping cream, divided

2 ounces unsweetened baking chocolate
4 tablespoons unsalted butter
½ teaspoon pure vanilla extract or paste

1. In the mixing bowl of a standing mixer with a paddle attachment, mix together cream cheese, peanut butter, and 1½ cups sugar until well blended. In a clean bowl with a whisk attachment, whip 1 cup of heavy whipping cream until stiff peaks form. Fold the whipped cream into the peanut butter mixture. Gently spoon into the prepared pie crust and smooth with the back of a spoon or spatula.
2. In a heavy-bottom saucepan over medium heat, combine remaining sugar and cream. Bring to a boil. Reduce heat and simmer mixture without stirring for 6 minutes. Remove from heat and add the chocolate and butter; stir or whisk until melted and smooth. Add vanilla and mix well. Gently pour the topping over the peanut butter layer. Cover with plastic wrap to prevent a skin from forming. Chill in the refrigerator for at least 4 hours before serving. Garnish with Chocolate Bar Curls (see recipe in the "Decorating Your Pie" chapter).

Serves 8–10.

You'll have pie in the sky when you die.

—JOE HILL

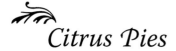

Citrus Pies

*J*UST AS CHOCOLATE INDUCES HAPPINESS in many individuals, citrus in its natural form or in a pie makes me feel terrific—almost healthy terrific. One of the very first pies I ever baked was a Lemon Meringue Pie. I remember standing on our old red vinyl step-stool kitchen chair at the stove so I could reach above the saucepan and stir the filling until it thickened. I actually cooked this all by myself after making several pies with my grandma Thelma Anderson. Mom wasn't feeling well and was sleeping in her bedroom on the second floor. I decided to bake a pie. I didn't make much of a mess and cleaned everything up when I was done. The family was surprised at how good the pie tasted, and it wasn't but a day or two before my Lemon Meringue Pie was gone. This motivated me to bake more pies, and I received encouragement from my family

Doing without has always motivated me to be creative. I grew up on a farm and learned to live with and without. If we couldn't purchase a pie or dessert at the bakery when I was young, we would make one ourselves at home. My college years were lean, so I started cooking again and began baking wonderful pies, cookies, and other confections and shared them with all my friends. I even had a little garden in plastic pots where a tree had fallen years before. I grew tomatoes, herbs, and flowers. I didn't mind doing without and found that period of my life one of the best.

At the beginning of this new century, I believed we would move into a world of science and discovery—like the Saturday morning cartoon featuring "the Jetsons." I never believed that world peace would be a problem or that the economy would collapse. No matter how negative the world gets, it motivates me to go into "emergency" mood. I can and preserve more vegetables, jams, jellies, and relishes. I bake more, freeze more, and find ways to create fun recipes to surprise our friends and neighbors. I love to can Meyer lemons to preserve their intense and complex flavors. I've also preserved limes, Key limes, grapefruit, tangerines, and clementines. One of my favorite things to do is to combine two or three of my favorite citruses and preserve them. I later will use these wonderful citruses for pies. Imagine intense citrus flavor in the middle of winter.

In some ways, I think I'm happiest when I'm in my "emergency" mood. I feel like I'm doing something worthwhile. I'm continually baking our breads and buns. Chad goes out fishing and I won't let him back in the house, or cabin at the lake, until he's caught his limit. Once the fish are cleaned (which we have someone else do), I will vacuum-pack them with my kitchen packaging system for freezing. I look for specials at the grocery store to freeze or trade my baking for pounds of wild rice, wild boar sausage, or other wonderful foods. But most important, I can everything I can get my hands on. Most canned goods will last up to two years when properly handled. Most citrus will last up to one year, so make sure you read your recipes carefully. I always date my jars so that I know when they've expired.

I hope you'll think about preserving citrus when it's in the best season. Think about how much fun you can have canning clementines when they come out around Christmastime. I also hope you'll try my citrus pie recipes topped with my Sweetened Whipped Topping. My recipe for Tropical Lime Pie calls for adding one teaspoon of dark rum to my Sweetened Whipped Cream. Experiment with my topping and add liquors you enjoy, or try my Honey Sweetened Whipped Cream, which uses honey rather than sugar or liquors.

Also, don't forget to purchase extra limes, lemons, and other citrus to slice and garnish the top of your pie or slices of pie before serving. The colors are lovely and the fragrance will please anyone who receives your beautifully baked treat.

Captain Tony's Watermelon Pie

I created this recipe after riding on Captain Tony Garcia's fishing boat through the incredible turquoise Caribbean Sea. My partner, Chad, and I host Caribe Gathering culinary vacations on the island of Isla Mujeres, Mexico, just off the coast of Cancún. One of our excursions during these vacations is to send our guests on a wonderful day of snorkeling and traditional Mayan/Yucatán cooking on a deserted island called Isla Contoy. On the return to Isla Mujeres, Captain Tony and his first mate offer watermelon to everyone on the boat. Always thinking, I was looking at the shape of my slice during one of our trips and thought it looked like a wedge of pie. That promoted more thinking about making a pie with the juice of a watermelon. As soon as I returned to the United States, I began experimenting and finally created a good solid recipe that tastes wonderful and refreshing. I hope you enjoy it.

Crust

> 1¾ cups graham cracker crumbs
> 2 tablespoons dark brown sugar, firmly packed
> ½ teaspoon ground cinnamon, preferably China cassia
> Pinch of sea salt, finely ground
> 7 tablespoons unsalted butter, melted
> Crisco butter-flavored cooking spray

1. Preheat oven to 350 degrees. Spray 9-inch pie plate or 8½-inch flan pan with cooking spray and set aside.
2. Combine the graham cracker crumbs, brown sugar, cinnamon, and salt in a large mixing bowl. Using your fingers, mix together. Add the butter and incorporate well, mixing first with a fork, then with your hands, rubbing thoroughly to form evenly moistened crumbs.
3. Spread the crumbs evenly and loosely in pie pan, pressing them into the bottom and up the side. Refrigerate for 10 minutes.
4. Bake for 10–12 minutes. Cool on a rack. Refrigerate 15 minutes before filling.

Makes one 9-inch graham cracker crust.

Filling

> 7 cups watermelon flesh with or without seeds, about
>   ¼ medium watermelon
> ⅓ cup white sugar
> 2 envelopes unflavored gelatin
> 1 tablespoon freshly squeezed lime juice
> 1 tablespoon natural watermelon extract (optional)
> 2 large egg whites, at room temperature
> 1 cup cold heavy whipping cream
> 1 cup confectioner's sugar

1. Scoop out watermelon flesh with seeds into a large mixing bowl. Add sugar. Using a potato masher or slotted spoon, mash watermelon until liquid is extracted. You may also use a blender or food processor to liquefy the watermelon pulp. Set aside for 25 minutes. Drain watermelon mixture through a fine-mesh sieve, reserving 3 cups watermelon juice. Discard the pulp and seeds.

2. Put ½ cup juice in a medium-sized bowl and sprinkle the gelatin over it. Set aside for 5 minutes to let "bloom" or dissolve. Meanwhile, heat ½ cup juice in a small heavy-bottom saucepan over medium heat. Do not boil. Whisk the hot juice into the dissolved gelatin. Pour the remaining watermelon juice into a large bowl and stir in the gelatin-watermelon juice mixture. Stir in the lime juice and natural watermelon extract (see helpful hints below). Place in the refrigerator until well set, about 45 minute to 1 hour.

3. In the bowl of a standing mixer with a whisk attachment, whisk egg whites until they form stiff peaks. Spoon into separate dish and set aside in refrigerator. Clean and dry mixing bowl and whisk attachment. Whisk heavy cream and confectioner's sugar with the mixer until it holds soft peaks. Refrigerate until gelatin mixture is set.

4. When the watermelon juice mixture is set, fold in whipped cream and, using a hand whisk, blend gently until smooth. Gently whisk in beaten egg whites until well blended. Using a spatula, spoon filling into the cooled graham cracker crust. Place in a tightly covered pie keeper or cover with plastic wrap. Refrigerate for at least 4 hours,

preferably overnight, before serving. If using flan pan, remove pie from pan and serve on a decorative serving plate or stand.

Topping

> 1¼ cups heavy whipping cream
> 2 tablespoons confectioner's sugar
> 1 teaspoon pure vanilla extract or paste
> Extra confectioner's sugar
> Star fruit, sliced
> Kiwi, sliced

Before serving, whip the heavy cream, confectioner's sugar, and vanilla extract. To serve, garnish each slice with a dusting of confectioner's sugar, a dollop of topping, and sliced exotic fruit.

Serves 8–10.

John Michael's Helpful Hint: I only use watermelon extract when watermelons are not in season and have a weaker taste, such as in the winter. During the summer months, when watermelon is robust and flavorful, a flavor boost of extract is not needed. Watermelon extracts may be found in online stores or auctions such as eBay.

Frozen Orange Pie

This is a wonderful pie to serve at a family picnic or outdoor gathering. It's like enjoying a frozen fruit bar only it's enclosed in a pie crust of graham cracker crumbs.

Crust

> 1¾ cups graham cracker crumbs
> 2 tablespoons dark brown sugar, firmly packed

½ teaspoon ground cinnamon, preferably China cassia
Pinch of sea salt, finely ground
6 tablespoons unsalted butter, melted
Crisco butter-flavored cooking spray

1. Preheat oven to 350 degrees. Spray 9-inch pie plate or 8½-inch flan pan with cooking spray and set aside.
2. Combine the graham cracker crumbs, brown sugar, cinnamon, and salt in a large mixing bowl. Using your fingers, mix together. Add the butter and incorporate well, mixing first with a fork, then with your hands, rubbing thoroughly to form evenly moistened crumbs.
3. Spread the crumbs evenly and loosely in the pan, pressing them into the bottom and up the side. Refrigerate for 10 minutes.
4. Bake for 10-12 minutes. Cool on a rack. Refrigerate 15 minutes before filling.

Makes one 9-inch graham cracker crust.

Filling

4 large eggs, separated
¾ cup white sugar
1 tablespoon orange zest
¼ cup freshly squeezed orange juice
1 cup heavy whipping cream

1. In a medium heatproof mixing bowl, lightly whisk the egg yolks. Whisk in the sugar, orange zest, and orange juice. Place over a pan of boiling water; whisk constantly until thickened. Remove from heat and let cool on a rack.
2. In a medium mixing bowl, beat egg whites with an electric mixer until stiff. Set aside. In clean medium mixing bowl with clean beaters, whip heavy cream until stiff peaks form. Set aside.
3. Fold in ¼ beaten egg whites into cooled orange mixture. Fold in remaining egg whites and whipped cream until well incorporated. Gently pour into cooled and prepared pie crust. Chill in the refrigerator for at least 2 hours.

4. Place in freezer until pie is completely frozen (about 2 hours). Tightly wrap in plastic wrap and place in a freezer bag; or use a vacuum packaging system to remove as much air as possible. Return to freezer. Let stand at room temperature for 10 minutes before serving. If using flan pan, remove pie from pan and serve on a decorative serving plate or stand. Do not thaw completely.

Serves 8–10.

Hana Hou! Daiquiri Pie—Hawaiian for "One More Time"

Winner, 2005 APC Crisco National Pie Championship; Third Place in the "Open" Category at the American Pie Festival

I love this pie and have used this recipe in many of my cooking classes featuring fun pies at the Chef's Gallery in Stillwater, Minnesota. I created this pie after visiting the Hawaiian Islands a few years ago. I fell in love with daiquiris, especially at a little bar in the town of Kapaa on the island of Kauai on Kuhio Highway. I don't remember the name of the bar, but I had just purchased groceries at the Kapaa Safeway and felt thirsty, so we stopped at a small bar in the shopping center nearby. They had a unique clock: it ran backward.

While sitting at the bar enjoying our cool and delicious daiquiris, we watched CNN on a little television on the wall. This was in January right before my birthday, which is the 17th. A report came on about the city of Bloomington, Minnesota, canceling its annual ice fishing competition because of below-zero temperatures. We howled with laughter because Bloomington is a suburb south of Minneapolis that is famous for the Mall of America. We had escaped the severe cold temperatures and were enjoying cool drinks in 90-degree tropical temperatures on an exotic island. Nothing could have been more perfect or right at that time. This pie was a result of that afternoon.

Crust

  2 cups flaked coconut
  4 tablespoons unsalted butter, melted

Combine the coconut and melted butter in a small bowl. Press into the bottom and up the side of an 8- to 9-inch pie plate. Bake at 325 degrees until the coconut is lightly browned, about 15 minutes. Cool completely while preparing filling.

Topping

  ½ cup large-flake coconut, lightly toasted

Toast at the same time as the crust to garnish the pie.

Lime Filling

  ⅔ cup white sugar
  1 envelope unflavored gelatin
  ¼ teaspoon sea salt
  ⅓ cup freshly squeezed lime juice, Key lime preferably
  ⅓ cup water
  3 large egg yolks, slightly beaten
  ½ teaspoon lime zest
  ¼ cup light rum or extract
  3 large egg whites
  6 tablespoons superfine baker's sugar

1. Combine sugar, gelatin, and salt in a medium saucepan. In a small bowl, stir together lime juice, water, and egg yolks just enough to mix. Stir into sugar-gelatin mixture. Cook on low heat, stirring constantly, until the mixture bubbles, thickens slightly, and coats a silver spoon.
2. Remove pan from heat; stir in lime zest and rum. Chill until it has the consistency of corn syrup, stirring occasionally.

3. Beat egg whites until soft peaks form; gradually beat in sugar and beat until stiff peaks form but egg whites are still glossy. Fold into thickened gelatin mixture. Chill until the mixture mounds.

Lemon Filling

¾ cup white sugar

3 tablespoons cornstarch

¼ teaspoon sea salt

¾ cup water

1 tablespoon unsalted butter

⅓ cup freshly squeezed lemon juice

1 teaspoon lemon zest

4 drops yellow food coloring or paste

1. Combine sugar, cornstarch, and salt in a medium saucepan. Gradually stir in water. Cook over medium-low heat, stirring constantly until mixture boils and thickens. Boil 1 minute.
2. Remove from heat. Add butter, stirring until it melts. Add lemon juice, zest, and food coloring and stir until smooth. Refrigerate until mixture has cooled.

ASSEMBLY

Spoon lemon filling into cooled pie shell. Cover with lime filling and sprinkle with toasted coconut. Chill several hours or overnight before serving. Decorate to look like a daiquiri cocktail with twisted lemon and lime slices and cherries skewered on paper umbrellas.

Serves 8–10.

Sing a song of sixpence, a pocket full of rye, four and twenty blackbirds, baked in a pie.

—MEDIEVAL NURSERY RHYME

🎋 John Michael's Citrus Delight Pie

I created this pie for the 2007 APC Crisco National Pie Championship. It's an "all citrus" take on my Key Lime Delight Pie from my first cookbook, *Garden County: Where Everyone Is Welcome to Sit at the Table*. I love citrus—oranges, grapefruit, lemons, Meyer lemons, limes, tangerines, and clementines. So, I decided to create a chiffon pie that would include oranges, lemons, and limes. It was wonderfully sweet and tart. After decorating with the three different types of citrus, this pie is beautiful and colorful. Not only does it taste and look great, it also will help prevent scurvy. You may also use Cookie Crust (see recipe in the "Crust" chapter).

Crust

> 1½ cups unbleached all-purpose flour
> ½ tablespoon white sugar
> ½ teaspoon kosher or sea salt, finely ground
> ¼ cup Crisco butter-flavored all-vegetable shortening, chilled and cut into small pieces
> ¼ cup unsalted butter, chilled and cut into small pieces
> ¼–½ cup cold water; use only as much as needed for a smooth, satiny dough ball
> Crisco butter-flavored cooking spray

1. All ingredients should be cold. Combine all the dry ingredients in a large mixing bowl. Add shortening and butter. Using a pastry blender, cut in the shortening and butter until the mixture resembles coarse meal or peas.
2. Drop by drop, add the cold water. Mix in with the fingertips, not with the hands as the palms will warm the dough. Continue mixing in water until the dough begins to hold together without being crumbly yet not sticky.
3. Lightly spray a 9-inch pie pan or 8½-inch fluted flan pan with cooking spray. Roll out dough and place in pie plate, allowing the excess pastry to hang over the edge. Cut away extra, tuck under, and crimp

decoratively. Prick bottom and sides with a fork. Chill for 30 minutes before baking.

4. Preheat the oven to 400 degrees. Line the pastry shell with parchment and baking beans or beads. Bake the shell for 10 minutes. Remove the paper and beans or beads and return to the oven for 10 more minutes. Cool on a rack.

Makes pastry for one 9-inch single-crust pie.

Filling

> 4 large eggs, separated
> 1 (14-ounce) can sweetened condensed milk
> Freshly squeezed juice and zest of 1 orange, 1 lemon, and 1 lime, divided
> 2 tablespoons white sugar

1. Lower the oven temperature to 325 degrees. Make the filling by beating the egg yolks in a large bowl until light and creamy. Beat in the condensed milk. Divide equally in two mixing bowls (about two cups each). Add the orange zest and juice to one bowl and add lemon and lime zest and juice to the other bowl. Mix well and continue to beat until each mixture is thick.

2. Beat egg whites until they form stiff peaks. Slowly add the sugar just until combined. Divide egg whites evenly and fold into each citrus mixture.

3. Pour each filling into the baked crust. With the back of a spoon, swirl fillings together. Bake for 20–25 minutes, or until filling is set and begins to brown. Remove and cool. Chill in refrigerator.

Topping

> 1¼ cups heavy whipping cream
> 2 tablespoons confectioner's sugar
> 1 teaspoon pure vanilla extract or paste
> 1 orange, 1 lemon, 1 lime, thinly sliced
> Citrus zest and spearmint leaves

Before serving, whip the heavy cream, confectioner's sugar, and vanilla extract. Spoon or fill pastry bag to decorate edge of pie with puffs of whipped cream. Cut citrus slices from the center to the edge and twist. Arrange the citrus slices between puffs of whipped cream. Lightly sprinkle citrus zest and delicately place mint leaves to accent the pie.

Serves 8–10.

Grandma's Lemon Chess Pie

There are many myths about the origin of the name "Chess Pie." The first mention was in a recipe published for the Fort Worth Women's Club in 1928. The name could have been derived from cheese, although no cheese is found in the recipe. The name could come from the town of Chester, England, or a piece of furniture from the Old South called a pie chest because this recipe stored well in a pie chest. Finally there is the tale of a Southern housewife who offered her recipe to her husband, who loved it. When he asked her what kind of pie it was, she replied, "I don't know. It's jus' pie."

Chess Pies have a very simple filling of eggs, sugar, butter, and a small amount of flour. Some recipes call for cornmeal and others call for vinegar. My grandma Thelma Anderson loved to add freshly squeezed lemon juice and lemon zest to her Chess Pie recipe.

As a small boy on the farm, I imagined this pie was eaten only when playing the game of chess. It wasn't until I was older that I asked where the name came from. Everyone had a different answer. No matter where you think the name originated, it's a wonderful pie to serve while playing games or sitting on the front porch with a glass of lemonade.

Crust

> 1½ cups unbleached all-purpose flour
> ½ tablespoon white sugar
> ½ teaspoon kosher or sea salt, finely ground

¼ cup Crisco butter-flavored all-vegetable shortening, chilled
  and cut into small pieces
¼ cup unsalted butter, chilled and cut into small pieces
¼–½ cup cold water; use only as much as needed for a smooth,
  satiny dough ball
1 egg yolk and 1 teaspoon water for egg wash
Crisco butter-flavored cooking spray

1. All ingredients should be cold. Combine all the dry ingredients in a large mixing bowl. Add shortening and butter. Using a pastry blender, cut in the shortening and butter until the mixture resembles coarse meal or peas.
2. Drop by drop, add the cold water. Mix in with the fingertips, not with the hands as the palms will warm the dough. Continue mixing in water until the dough begins to hold together without being crumbly yet not sticky.
3. Place dough in plastic wrap. Fold over plastic wrap and press down to form a disk. This will make rolling out easier after chilling. Finish wrapping in plastic and place in the refrigerator for at least 30 minutes.
4. Lightly spray a deep 9-inch pie pan or 8½-inch fluted flan pan with cooking spray. Roll out dough and place in pie plate, allowing the excess pastry to hang over the edge. Cut away extra, tuck under, and crimp decoratively. Brush with egg wash and return to the refrigerator until filling is ready.

Makes pastry for one 9-inch single-crust pie.

Filling

2 large eggs
4 large egg yolks
1 cup white sugar
4 tablespoons unsalted butter, melted
¼ cup heavy whipping cream
1 tablespoon unbleached all-purpose flour
1 tablespoon yellow cornmeal

    4 tablespoons freshly squeezed lemon juice
    1 tablespoon lemon zest

1. Preheat oven to 350 degrees. In the bowl of a standing mixer with the paddle attachment, beat eggs, egg yolks, and sugar at high speed for several minutes until well incorporated and pale in color. Add butter and cream. Beat again for two minutes at high speed.
2. Turn off mixer and add flour, cornmeal, lemon juice, and lemon zest. Mix on medium speed until well blended. Gently pour into prepared pie crust. Bake for 50–60 minutes or until top is medium brown. Let cool to room temperature on a rack before serving. Garnish each slice of pie with Homemade Raspberry Sauce, Sweetened Whipped Cream, and sprinkled powdered sugar (see recipes for Raspberry Sauce and Sweetened Whipped Cream in the "Decorating Your Pie" chapter).

Serves 8–10.

⸕ Lemon Honey Pie

This charming pie uses honey rather than sugar as the sweetener in the filling. Honey, unfortunately, cannot be used in place of sugar in the crust. It becomes too soggy and difficult to work with. Try different varieties of honey such as clover or buckwheat to change the flavor of this pie.

Crust

    1½ cups unbleached all-purpose flour
    ½ tablespoon dark brown sugar or white sugar
    ½ teaspoon kosher or sea salt, finely ground
    ¼ cup Crisco butter-flavored all-vegetable shortening, chilled
        and cut into small pieces
    ¼ cup unsalted butter, chilled and cut into small pieces

¼–½ cup cold water; use only as much as needed for a smooth,
    satiny dough ball
Crisco butter-flavored cooking spray

1. All ingredients should be cold. Combine all the dry ingredients in a large mixing bowl. Add shortening and butter. Using a pastry blender, cut in the shortening and butter until the mixture resembles coarse meal or peas.

2. Drop by drop, add the cold water. Mix in with the fingertips, not with the hands as the palms will warm the dough. Continue mixing in water until the dough begins to hold together without being crumbly yet not sticky. Place dough in plastic wrap. Press down to form a disk. This will make rolling out easier after chilling. Finish wrapping in plastic and place in the refrigerator for at least 30 minutes.

3. Lightly spray a deep 9-inch pie pan with cooking spray. Roll out dough and place in pie plate, allowing the excess pastry to hang over the edge. Cut away extra, tuck under, and crimp decoratively. Prick sides and bottom of pie crust with a fork. Chill in refrigerator for 30 minutes before baking.

4. Preheat the oven to 400 degrees. Line the pastry shell with parchment and baking beans or beads. Bake the shell for 10 minutes. Remove the paper and beans or beads and return to the oven for 10 more minutes. Cool.

Makes pastry for one 9-inch single-crust pie.

Filling

1½ cups water
1 cup honey, any variety
½ cup freshly squeezed lemon juice
⅓ cup cornstarch
2 tablespoons unsalted butter
1 teaspoon lemon zest
¼ teaspoon sea salt, finely ground
4 large egg yolks, lightly beaten
1½ cups heavy whipping cream, whipped to soft peaks

1. In medium heavy-bottom saucepan, combine water, honey, lemon juice, cornstarch, butter, lemon zest, and salt. Bring to a boil, stirring constantly. Boil for 2 minutes. Remove from heat.

2. Stir small amount of hot mixture into yolks to bring egg yolks to a higher temperature before incorporating into rest of mixture to prevent scrambling. Pour yolk mixture back into honey mixture; mix thoroughly. Pour into pie shell. Chill for at least 4 hours. Serve with Honey Sweetened Whipped Cream (see recipe in the "Decorating Your Pie" chapter).

Serves 8–10.

My Favorite Lemon Meringue Pie

This recipe is one of my favorites. I remember making this pie when I was about 10 years old. It was one of my very first pie-baking experiences ever, but I loved any dessert with lemon from a very young age. Almost 40 years later and I still love this recipe. When Meyer lemons are in season, I use them for an intense lemon taste. Nothing is better. You may use a shortbread crust (see recipe in the "Crust" chapter) or a Meringue Crust, which I have included at the end of this recipe. I've used all three crusts for different events and moods. The meringue crust is special for holidays, while the shortbread crust gives you a lemon cookie taste. Try all three and let me know what you think.

Crust

1½ cups unbleached all-purpose flour
½ tablespoon white sugar
½ teaspoon kosher or sea salt, finely ground
¼ cup Crisco butter-flavored all-vegetable shortening, chilled and cut into small pieces
¼ cup unsalted butter, chilled and cut into small pieces

¼–½ cup cold water; use only as much as needed for a smooth,
    satiny dough ball
Crisco butter-flavored cooking spray
1 egg yolk and 1 teaspoon water for egg wash

1. All ingredients should be cold. Combine all the dry ingredients in a large mixing bowl. Add shortening and butter. Using a pastry blender, cut in the shortening and butter until the mixture resembles coarse meal or peas.
2. Drop by drop, add the cold water. Mix in with the fingertips, not with the hands as the palms will warm the dough. Continue mixing in water until the dough begins to hold together without being crumbly yet not sticky. Place dough in plastic wrap. Press down to form a disk. This will make rolling out easier after chilling. Finish wrapping in plastic and place in the refrigerator for at least 15 minutes.
3. Lightly spray a deep 9-inch pie pan with cooking spray. Roll out dough and place in pie plate, allowing the excess pastry to hang over the edge. Cut away extra, tuck under, and crimp decoratively. Prick sides and bottom of pie crust with a fork. Chill in refrigerator for 30 minutes before baking.
4. Preheat the oven to 400 degrees. Line the pastry shell with parchment and baking beans or beads. Bake the shell for 10 minutes. Remove the paper and beans or beads and return to the oven for 10 more minutes. Cool.

Makes pastry for one 9-inch single-crust pie.

Filling

1½ cups white sugar
3 tablespoons cornstarch
3 tablespoons unbleached all-purpose flour
1½ cups hot water
3 large egg yolks, slightly beaten
2 tablespoons unsalted butter

½ teaspoon lemon zest

⅓ cup freshly squeezed lemon juice

1. Preheat oven to 350 degrees. In a medium heavy-bottom saucepan, combine sugar, cornstarch, and flour. Slowly add hot water, whisking to blend. Place saucepan over medium-high heat and bring mixture to a boil, whisking constantly. Reduce heat to simmer and cook an additional 2 minutes. Remove from heat.

2. Add a small amount of the hot mixture to the egg yolks and blend well. Pour egg yolks into hot mixture and whisk together. Return saucepan to medium-high heat and bring back to a boil. Continue cooking for 2 minutes or until thickened, whisking constantly. Remove from heat. Add butter and lemon zest. Slowly add lemon juice and whisk well to blend.

3. Gently pour hot filling into prepared pie crust. Using a spatula, smooth filling evenly. Top hot filling with meringue (see recipe in the "Decorating Your Pie" chapter). Spread meringue around edges of filling, making sure meringue touches and attaches to the inner edge of the pie crust. Fill in center and create stiff peaks or decorative swirls in the meringue. Bake for 12 to 15 minutes or until meringue becomes golden. Cool on a rack before serving.

Serves 8–10.

Construct a bullet-proof dough. Toughen it and kiln-dry it a couple of days. Fill with stewed dried apple; aggravate with cloves, lemon peel and slabs of citron; add two portions of New Orleans sugar. Then solder on the lid and set it in a safe place until it petrifies. Serve cold at breakfast and invite your enemy.

—MARK TWAIN, *A TRAMP ABROAD*

Meringue Crust (Optional)

2 large egg whites
¼ teaspoon cream of tartar
¼ teaspoon fine sea salt
½ teaspoon pure vanilla extract or paste
½ cup white sugar
Crisco cooking spray

Preheat oven to 300 degrees. Spray sides and bottom of pie dish with cooking spray. Set aside. In the bowl of a standing mixer with a whisk attachment, beat egg whites, cream of tartar, and salt until soft peaks form. Add vanilla, and slowly beat in sugar until very stiff and glossy. Spread mixture onto the sides and bottom of a 9-inch pie metal plate dish. Bake for 50 minutes. Turn oven off and leave meringue in oven for 1 hour. Cool before serving.

Makes one 9-inch meringue pie crust.

Tropical Lime Pie

As with lemon, I adore lime. I have a Key Lime Delight Pie in my first cookbook, *Garden County: Where Everyone Is Welcome to Sit at the Table,* but regular limes offer wonderful citrus flavor and a change from the usual lemon pies you find everywhere. I enjoy serving this pie with authentic Mexican Mayan/Yucatán dishes and salty margaritas.

Crust

1 cup unbleached all-purpose flour
¼ cup confectioner's sugar
¼ teaspoon sea salt, finely ground
½ cup unsalted butter, chilled and cut into small pieces
⅓ cup pecans, finely chopped
Cooking spray

1. Preheat oven to 350 degrees. Spray a 9-inch pie plate with cooking spray. Set aside. In a medium mixing bowl, stir together flour, sugar, and salt. Using a pastry blender, cut in butter until the mixture resembles coarse meal or peas. Add the pecans and mix well.
2. Evenly press the crust mixture into the bottom and side of the prepared pie plate with fingertips. Bake for 25 minutes or until crust is just beginning to turn golden. Remove and cool on a rack.

Makes one 9-inch pie crust.

Filling

1 cup white sugar
3 large eggs
5 tablespoons freshly squeezed lime juice (about 4 limes)
1 teaspoon lime zest
½ teaspoon baking powder
Pinch of fine sea salt

1. Preheat oven to 350 degrees. In a medium mixing bowl, whisk sugar, eggs, lime juice, lime zest, baking powder, and salt until well blended and smooth.
2. Gently pour filling mixture into the prepared pie crust. Bake for 25 minutes or until a knife inserted in the center comes out clean. Cool on a rack. Chill for 2 hours before serving. Garnish with confectioner's sugar sprinkled through a fine-mesh sieve. Add a dollop of Sweetened Whipped Cream (see recipe in the "Decorating Your Pie" chapter) flavored with a teaspoon of dark rum or rum extract. Sprinkle with lime zest.

Serves 8–10.

𝑓 Mango Custard Pie

I created this recipe to make for our friends on Isla Mujeres, Mexico. I have yet to present it to them, however, but at least they know now what treat lies in store for them. Just-ripe mangos make the best filling for this recipe.

Crust

> 1½ cups unbleached all-purpose flour
> ½ tablespoon white sugar
> ½ teaspoon kosher or sea salt, finely ground
> ¼ cup Crisco butter-flavored all-vegetable shortening, chilled
>   and cut into small pieces
> ¼ cup unsalted butter, chilled and cut into small pieces
> ¼–½ cup cold water; use only as much as needed for a smooth,
>   satiny dough ball
> 1 egg yolk and 1 teaspoon water for egg wash
> Crisco butter-flavored cooking spray

1. All ingredients should be cold. Combine all the dry ingredients in a large mixing bowl. Add shortening and butter. Using a pastry blender, cut in the shortening and butter until the mixture resembles coarse meal or peas.
2. Drop by drop, add the cold water. Mix in with the fingertips, not with the hands as the palms will warm the dough. Continue mixing in water until the dough begins to hold together without being crumbly yet not sticky.
3. Place dough in plastic wrap. Fold over plastic wrap and press down to form a disk. This will make rolling out easier after chilling. Finish wrapping in plastic and place in the refrigerator for at least 30 minutes.
4. Lightly spray a deep 9-inch pie pan or 8½-inch fluted flan pan. Roll out dough and place in pie plate, allowing excess to hang over the edge. Cut away extra, tuck under, and crimp decoratively. Prick sides

and bottom of pie crust with a fork. Chill in the refrigerator for at least 30 minutes.

5. Preheat oven to 400 degrees. Line the pastry shell with parchment and baking beans or beads. Bake the shell for 10 minutes. Remove the paper and beans or beads. Cool on a rack.

Makes pastry for one 9-inch single-crust pie.

Filling

2 cups mango puree, fresh or frozen
1 tablespoon freshly squeezed lime juice
¼ cup unbleached all-purpose flour
¼ cup evaporated milk
¾ cup white sugar
½ teaspoon cinnamon, preferably China cassia
2 large eggs, lightly beaten

1. Preheat oven to 350 degrees. In a medium mixing bowl, whisk together mango puree, lime juice, flour, milk, sugar, and cinnamon. Add beaten eggs and whisk until blended and smooth.
2. Gently pour filling mixture into prepared pie crust. Bake for 30 minutes or until filling is set. Cool on a rack. Chill at least 4 hours before serving. Garnish with Sweetened Whipped Cream (see recipe in the "Decorating Your Pie" chapter) and sliced fresh mango.

Serves 8–10.

Orange Meringue Pie

A funny story goes with this pie. I created this recipe to enter in the 2006 APC Crisco National Pie Championship in Celebration, Florida. The Food Network showed up and began filming me at the media event where I was preparing my Vidalia Onion Pie. They wanted to film me the next day entering my pies. If you have never baked a meringue pie in Florida, you wouldn't know that the humidity can do terrible things to a meringue topping. I made my meringue, baked it until golden, boxed up the pie, and delivered it and eight other pies to the registration site. The Food Network crew turned on their hot lights and the camera began to roll. I pulled out my Orange Meringue Pie and set it down on the registration table. All of a sudden I noticed the meringue beginning to shrink—pulling away from the pastry crust edge. As I continued talking, the meringue continued to shrink. By the end of the interview, the meringue was the size of a fried egg. The Food Network team joked that if I ever get too big for my britches, all they have to do is play the footage of the shrinking meringue. They called it my "humble pie."

Crust

> 1½ cups unbleached all-purpose flour
> ½ tablespoon white sugar
> ½ teaspoon kosher or sea salt, finely ground
> ¼ cup Crisco butter-flavored all-vegetable shortening, chilled
>   and cut into small pieces
> ¼ cup unsalted butter, chilled and cut into small pieces
> ¼–½ cup cold water; use only as much as needed for a smooth,
>   satiny dough ball
> 1 egg yolk and 1 teaspoon water for egg wash
> Crisco butter-flavored cooking spray

1. All ingredients should be cold. Combine all the dry ingredients in a large mixing bowl. Add shortening and butter. Using a pastry blender, cut in the shortening and butter until the mixture resembles coarse meal or peas.
2. Drop by drop, add the cold water. Mix in with the fingertips, not with the hands as the palms will warm the dough. Continue mixing in water until the dough begins to hold together without being crumbly yet not sticky.

3. Place dough in plastic wrap. Fold over plastic wrap and press down to form a disk. This will make rolling out easier after chilling. Finish wrapping in plastic and place in the refrigerator for at least 30 minutes.

4. Lightly spray a deep 9-inch pie pan or 8½-inch fluted flan pan. Roll out dough and place in pie plate, allowing excess to hang over the edge. Cut away extra, tuck under, and crimp decoratively. Prick sides and bottom of pie crust with a fork. Chill in the refrigerator for at least 30 minutes.

5. Preheat the oven to 400 degrees. Line the pastry shell with parchment and baking beans or beads. Bake the shell for 10 minutes. Remove the paper and beans or beads and return to the oven for 10 more minutes. Cool on a rack.

Makes pastry for one 9-inch single-crust pie.

Filling

1 cup white sugar
3 tablespoons cornstarch
3 large egg yolks, slightly beaten
1 cup freshly squeezed orange juice
½ cup water
3 tablespoons unsalted butter
1 tablespoon freshly squeezed lemon juice
1 tablespoon grated orange zest

1. Combine sugar and cornstarch in a heavy-bottom saucepan. Blend in egg yolks, orange juice, and water. Cook over medium heat, stirring constantly, until mixture thickens and just starts to boil. Boil gently for one minute and remove from heat.

2. Stir in butter, lemon juice, and orange zest. Pour into prepared pie crust. Seal pie with Meringue Topping (see recipe in the "Decorating Your Pie" chapter).

Grandma's Secret Apple Pie, see recipe on page 36.
Decorated with piemaling, see instructions on page 233.

Captain Tony's Watermelon Pie, see recipe on page 117.

John Michael's famous Vidalia Onion Pie, see recipe on page 174.

Crimping the Perfect Pie Crust, see recipe on page 13.

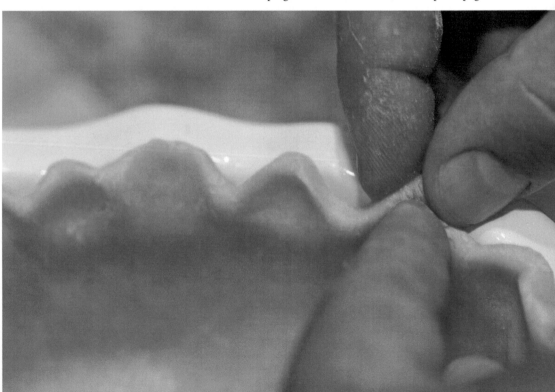

Easter Pie from John Michael Lerma's first cookbook,
Garden County: Where Everyone Is Welcome to Sit at the Table.

Many of the ribbons John Michael has won at the APC Crisco National Pie Championships.

Key Lime Delight Pie from John Michael Lerma's first cookbook,
Garden County: Where Everyone Is Welcome to Sit at the Table.

Carpe Diem Blueberry Pie, see recipe on page 44.

Rob Hudson, John Michael, and Corbin Seitz filming Showcase Minnesota
on KARE 11 during the Minnesota State Fair 2007 after John Michael won his
Food Network Medal on the Food Network Challenge.

John Michael and Keegan Gerhard during the filming of the
Food Network Challenge—National Pie Chapionship in April 2008.
John Michael is wearing his good luck Kukui Nut beads.

John Michael baking his Vidalia Onion Pie at the
APC Crisco National Pie Championship Media Event in 2006.

Rich Hoskins, Colborne Corporation; Nancy Matheison, American Pie Council;
John Michael; and Linda Hoskins, Executive Director American Pie Council awarding John
Michael 1st place Professional Division for his Coconut Cream Dream Pie in 2007.

APC National Pie Championship Brunch with pie goddesses
(from left to right) Mary Sohl, Beth Campbell, Sarah Spaugh, Patricia Lapiezo,
Phyllis Bartholomew, and John Michael in back.

John Michael, Bizarre Foods Andrew Zimmern, and Minnesota State Fair
multiple ribbon winner, cookbook writer, and television personality Marjorie Johnson.

July 4, 2007—John Michael hosting the "pie auction" in Park Rapids, MN.
It is part of the Annual 4th of July Park Rapids Pie Contest held at Beagle Books.

BT (Brian Turner), John Michael, and Lee Valsvik on the *BT and Lee Morning Show*
on Cities 97. John Michael had just won first place in the professional division for his
Coconut Cream Dream Pie at the APC Crisco National Pie Championship 2007.

Savory Pies

NOT TO SAY THAT A SAVORY PIE IS MY FAVORITE, but I adore a pie filled with cooked meats or seafood and layer after layer of vegetables baked up in a filling of dairy products and encased with a top crust. A meal in itself is what I call it.

Growing up on my grandparents' farm was a lot of fun. There was lots of hard work, but everyone made it fun and for years there were many happy occasions. Because Grandma cooked the meals for the hired men, pies fit in the equation nicely. The majority of Grandma's pies were sweet rather than savory. The hired men were astonished when Grandma would deliver a savory pie filled with leftover turkey, sausage, or pork. They ate it up and couldn't stop commenting on how they had "never seen anything like it in their lives." And, they probably never did again after they stopped working on our farm.

Today, savory pies are occasionally found in restaurants and have been raised to a new level of haute cuisine called tarts and served under a grilled meat or seafood as an embellishment. Not that I'm complaining, because I have had several wonderful meals consisting of just such an offering.

I have always loved making savory pies and enjoyed compiling the list for this chapter. I have so many wonderful recipes, but some are so far out there. My goal with this cookbook, and especially this chapter, was to make sure each recipe was basic with a bottom crust and once in a while a top crust.

The recipes listed in this chapter are my top favorites. I had to reject about 15 other recipes, but those that made it are delicious. Some might call the ones with egg custard filling quiches. If it makes you happy, call them quiches. I think of quiche as being made in a tart or flan pan with a removable bottom. You are certainly welcome to do that if you prefer. Whatever you call them, they are all still wonderful with flaky crust and a set filling. And as long as you try these recipes, I give you permission to call them whatever you choose.

Savory pies got me my start on the Food Network. In 2005 I was entering pies while the Food Network filmed everyone, but I was not featured. In 2006 I was preparing my Vidalia Onion Pie. When I first entered it in the "My Favorite Thanksgiving Pie" category to the American Pie Council, they questioned whether it was indeed a dessert pie. I wrote them that at Thanksgiving, Grandma would bake two root pies (Sweet Potato Pie and Vidalia Onion Pie). We would also have the traditional pies such as apple and pumpkin, but it was the onion pie that I loved the most. The American Pie Council let me enter my pie.

During a media event, I was preparing the filling for my Vidalia Onion Pie. The magnificent smell filled the ballroom at the Sheraton in Orlando, Florida. I had already prepared my pie crust, which was chilling in the refrigerator. I saw the Food Network crew walking over to talk to me—a television hostess, a camera man, and a sound man. I put on my happy face, tried not to be nervous, and babbled like a fool. The Food Network was intrigued by my recipe. They came back several times to check on my pie and filmed me taking it out of the oven twice (they asked if I would put it back in the oven, reopen the door, and take the pie out slowly and make a comment on what I thought it looked like).

When I arrived the next day at the Sheraton to register all my nine pies for the several different categories I had entered, the Food Network was standing right there to film each pie as I set it down. This unnerved Chad a great deal because he's camera shy and doesn't like to be filmed for television. You will usually see him in the background quickly getting out of the shot in any of the Food Network specials that I have been in.

The next day, at the awards ceremony, the Food Network filmed all of us receiving awards for our pie baking. I didn't win for my Vidalia Onion Pie, but I did for my Nesselrode Pie in the special Splenda category. Later, when I read the judges' comments, they categorized my Vidalia Onion Pie as a savory pie and didn't feel it qualified as a dessert pie. Oh my, what to do?

A month later, the Food Network called me to ask if they could fly in a crew to film me in my home and gardens in Saint Paul, Minnesota. They wanted to do a profile on me after watching me in Florida. I said yes immediately. We had a fun day filming, but it was very hot in my home. I have one word of advice: don't clean your house if the Food Network is coming to film you. They pushed my furniture to the sides of the rooms against the walls, layered thick cords everywhere, and had camera equipment covering everything. The look on Chad's face when he came home from work was amusing. I had spent two days scrubbing the house before they arrived. At least it was clean.

When all was said and done, the Food Network Challenge—The Great American Pie Challenge aired in November 2006. I was surprised at the judges' comments about my "savory" Vidalia Onion Pie. It was something new and many comments reminded me of one of my favorite films, *Strictly Ballroom.* The hero in the film wants to add new dance steps to traditional ballroom dances to please the crowds. The judges continually scold the hero with the words, "No new steps." That's how I felt that year but was delighted to start a relationship with the Food Network. As of this writing, I now have been on three Food Network Challenges because of my "savory" pie and the "new steps" I fearlessly attempted.

Hopefully, someday savory pies will be allowed at the APC Crisco National Pie Championship and get their due. Savory pies are earning respect throughout the United States at pie competitions from state fairs to small-town pie days. Try one of my savory pies in this chapter and let me know what you think. I love to hear from people who bake my pie recipes, and I love to talk pie.

A man can always accept a piece of pie. On the farm, pie is the great common denominator.

—RACHEL PEDEN, *SPEAK TO THE EARTH*

Mom's Cheesy Brunch Pie

The last time I traveled home to Grand Forks, I spent some time going through my mother's recipe box and tablets. I found this recipe on a card. I remember Mom baking this pie. Some will call it a quiche, but we always considered quiche and pie the same thing back home. The only difference was that Mom would purchase frozen pie crusts and prepare her own filling. Using ready-made crusts is not a sin. I've just made my own since I was a small boy. Mom liked to cook, but she enjoyed driving the truck in the fields more. Either way this recipe is wonderful, easy to prepare, and will please your brunch guests or family at any time.

Crust

　　1½ cups unbleached all-purpose flour
　　½ tablespoon white sugar
　　½ teaspoon kosher or sea salt, finely ground
　　¼ cup Crisco butter-flavored all-vegetable shortening, chilled
　　　　and cut into small pieces
　　¼ cup unsalted butter, chilled and cut into small pieces
　　¼–½ cup cold water; use only as much as needed for a smooth,
　　　　satiny dough ball
　　1 egg yolk and 1 teaspoon water for egg wash
　　Crisco butter-flavored cooking spray

1. All ingredients should be cold. Combine all the dry ingredients in a large mixing bowl. Add shortening and butter. Using a pastry blender, cut in the shortening and butter until the mixture resembles coarse meal or peas.
2. Drop by drop, add the cold water. Mix in with the fingertips, not with the hands as the palms will warm the dough. Continue mixing in water until the dough begins to hold together without being crumbly yet not sticky.

3. Place dough in plastic wrap. Fold over plastic wrap and press down to form a disk. This will make rolling out easier after chilling. Finish wrapping in plastic and place in the refrigerator for at least 30 minutes.

4. Lightly spray a deep 9-inch pie pan or 8½-inch fluted flan pan with cooking spray. Roll out dough and place in pie plate, allowing the excess pastry to hang over the edge. Cut away extra, tuck under, and crimp decoratively. Brush with egg wash and return to the refrigerator until filling is ready.

Makes pastry for one 9-inch single-crust pie.

Filling

4 large eggs
1 cup sour cream or crème fraîche (see crème fraîche recipe
   under Chocolate Caramel Banana Pie recipe in the
   "Chocolate Pies" chapter)
8 ounces regular or turkey bacon, cooked and crumbled
8 ounces cheddar or Swiss cheese, shredded (regular, low-fat,
   or fat-free)
2 tablespoons flat-leaf parsley, chopped

1. Preheat oven to 375 degrees. In a medium mixing bowl, stir or whisk together eggs and sour cream. Mix well. Stir in bacon, cheese, and parsley.

2. Pour mixture into prepared pie crust. Bake for 45–50 minutes until knife inserted in the center comes out clean. Cool on rack for 15 minutes before serving. Garnish with fresh chopped chives and additional sour cream.

Serves 8–10.

⨍ Cheeseburger Pie

This is another one of my favorite comfort food pies. It's a complete meal and very tasty. You may use ground turkey or Boca® ground soy crumbles to reduce fat or to serve to vegetarian friends. You may also add a variety of cheeses (for example, pepper jack) to kick the recipe up a bit. Enjoy!

Crust

    1½ cups unbleached all-purpose flour
    ½ tablespoon white sugar
    ½ teaspoon kosher or sea salt, finely ground
    ¼ cup Crisco butter-flavored all-vegetable shortening, chilled
        and cut into small pieces
    ¼ cup unsalted butter, chilled and cut into small pieces
    ¼–½ cup cold water; use only as much as needed for a smooth,
        satiny dough ball
    1 egg yolk and 1 teaspoon water for egg wash
    Crisco butter-flavored cooking spray

1. All ingredients should be cold. Combine all the dry ingredients in a large mixing bowl. Add shortening and butter. Using a pastry blender, cut in the shortening and butter until the mixture resembles coarse meal or peas.
2. Drop by drop, add the cold water. Mix in with the fingertips, not with the hands as the palms will warm the dough. Continue mixing in water until the dough begins to hold together without being crumbly yet not sticky.
3. Place dough in plastic wrap. Fold over plastic wrap and press down to form a disk. This will make rolling out easier after chilling. Finish wrapping in plastic and place in the refrigerator for at least 30 minutes.
4. Lightly spray a deep 9-inch pie pan or 8½-inch fluted flan pan. Roll out dough and place in pie plate, allowing the excess pastry to hang over the edge. Cut away extra, tuck under, and crimp decoratively.

Prick sides and bottom of pie crust with a fork. Chill in the refrigerator for at least 30 minutes.

5. Preheat the oven to 425 degrees. Line the pastry shell with parchment and baking beans or beads. Bake the shell for 10 minutes. Remove the paper and beans and cool on rack.

Makes pastry for one 9-inch single-crust pie.

Filling

1 pound ground beef, ground soy crumbles, or sausage
½ cup tomato sauce
⅓ cup red onion, chopped
⅓ cup red or green bell pepper, chopped
1 teaspoon instant beef bouillon granules
3 large eggs, beaten
2 tablespoons unbleached all-purpose flour
8 slices American, Swiss, or provolone cheese, divided

1. Preheat over to 350 degrees. In a large heavy-bottom skillet over medium-high heat, brown ground beef. Add tomato sauce, onion, bell pepper, and bouillon. Cook until the bouillon dissolves. Remove pan from heat.
2. Stir in eggs and flour; mixing well. Cut 6 slices of cheese into small pieces. Stir into beef mixture. Spoon mixture into prepared and cooled pie crust. Bake for 25 minutes or until filling is heated through.
3. Cut remaining cheese slices into wedges, triangles, and other shapes and decorate top of pie. Bake for an additional 4 minutes or until cheese has melted.

Serves 8–10.

When you die, if you get a choice between going to regular heaven or pie heaven, choose pie heaven. It might be a trick, but if it's not, ummmm, boy.

—JACK HANDEY, *DEEP THOUGHTS*

ʄ Chicken Goulash Pie

I was given this recipe by a friend back in college when I was working to obtain my master's degree in English. Back then we were all broke and would gather at my apartment to eat. Each person would bring onions, a protein (usually chicken), cans of tomatoes, oils, yogurts, and cheap bottles—or boxes—of wine. We made this recipe many times over a four-year period. I remember those years with fondness. I've embellished the recipe since those days and hope you enjoy it as much as we did.

Crust

> 1½ cups unbleached all-purpose flour
> ½ tablespoon white sugar
> ½ teaspoon kosher or sea salt, finely ground
> ¼ cup butter-flavored all-vegetable shortening, chilled and
>   cut into small pieces
> ¼ cup unsalted butter, chilled and cut into small pieces
> ¼–½ cup cold water; use only as much as needed for a smooth,
>   satiny dough ball
> 1 egg yolk and 1 teaspoon water for egg wash
> Butter-flavored cooking spray

1. All ingredients should be cold. Combine all the dry ingredients in a large mixing bowl. Add shortening and butter. Using a pastry blender, cut in the shortening and butter until the mixture resembles coarse meal or peas.
2. Drop by drop, add the cold water. Mix in with the fingertips, not with the hands as the palms will warm the dough. Continue mixing in water until the dough begins to hold together without being crumbly yet not sticky.
3. Place dough in plastic wrap. Fold over plastic wrap and press down to form a disk. This will make rolling out easier after chilling. Finish wrapping in plastic and place in the refrigerator for at least 30 minutes.
4. Lightly spray a deep 9-inch pie pan or 8½-inch fluted flan pan with cooking spray. Roll out dough and place in pie plate, allowing the

excess pastry to hang over the edge. Cut away extra, tuck under, and crimp decoratively. Brush with egg wash and return to the refrigerator until filling is ready.

Makes pastry for one 9-inch single-crust pie.

Filling

3 tablespoons extra virgin olive oil, divided
2 large red onions, chopped
3 tablespoons unbleached all-purpose flour
1½ tablespoons paprika (try smoked Spanish paprika
    for a different flavor)
½ teaspoon kosher or sea salt
¼ teaspoon freshly ground black pepper
1 pound boneless, skinless chicken breast, diced
1 tablespoon tomato paste
½ cup good-quality red wine
½ cup chicken stock
3 tablespoons plain yogurt (regular or low-fat)

1. Preheat oven to 350 degrees. In a heavy-bottom skillet over medium heat, sauté onions in 2 tablespoons of olive oil until translucent.
2. Meanwhile in a medium mixing bowl, combine flour, paprika, salt, and pepper. Add chicken, turning frequently to coat on all sides.
3. Remove cooked onions from frying pan and set aside. Add remaining olive oil to frying pan and sauté coated chicken until cooked, about 5 minutes. Return onions to pan and add tomato paste, wine, and stock. Bring to a boil. Reduce heat to low and simmer for 8 minutes. Remove pan from heat and stir in yogurt. Spoon cooked filling into prepared pie crust. Cover top of filled pie with tinfoil. Bake for 35 minutes.
4. Remove tinfoil from top of pie and bake an additional 10 minutes or until the top is golden and crusty. Cool on a rack for 10 minutes before serving. Garnish with sour cream or crème fraîche.

Serves 8–10.

ℱ Coulee Crawfish Pie

While rummaging through my grandma's recipe books and recipe boxes, I came across this interesting pie. I'm not sure if she ever prepared this for the family, as seafood was not a staple on our farm. Crawfish would have been way out there. Fish sticks were the most exotic type of fish served at our table. However, I was intrigued.

As a small boy, I used to play down the hill along a coulee that ran into the Red River next to our farm. I imagined a lot of dreams along the small streams of water and made lots of plans. I had a large rock in the middle of one stream of water where I would lie and watch the minnows and crawfish. Believe it or not, we had crawfish in Grand Forks, North Dakota. I never caught them or ate them, but I was fascinated by them. After I grew up and began to travel, I decided to order a plate of crawfish once and have loved their sweet taste ever since. They make a wonderful pie, too, and that's why I named this pie after my favorite childhood playground.

Crust

> 1½ cups unbleached all-purpose flour
> ½ tablespoon white sugar
> ½ teaspoon kosher or sea salt, finely ground
> ¼ cup Crisco all-vegetable shortening, chilled and cut
>   into small pieces
> ¼ cup unsalted butter, chilled and cut into small pieces
> ¼–½ cup cold water; use only as much as needed for a smooth,
>   satiny dough ball
> 1 egg yolk and 1 teaspoon water for egg wash
> Crisco butter-flavored cooking spray

1. All ingredients should be cold. Combine all the dry ingredients in a large mixing bowl. Add shortening and butter. Using a pastry blender, cut in the shortening and butter until the mixture resembles coarse meal or peas.

2. Drop by drop, add the cold water. Mix in with the fingertips, not with the hands as the palms will warm the dough. Continue mixing in water until the dough begins to hold together without being crumbly yet not sticky.

3. Place dough in plastic wrap. Fold over plastic wrap and press down to form a disk. This will make rolling out easier after chilling. Finish wrapping in plastic and place in the refrigerator for at least 30 minutes.

4. Lightly spray a deep 9-inch pie pan or 8½-inch fluted flan pan with cooking spray. Roll out dough and place in pie plate, allowing the excess pastry to hang over the edge. Cut away extra, tuck under, and crimp decoratively. Brush with egg wash and return to the refrigerator until filling is ready.

Makes pastry for one 9-inch single-crust pie.

Filling

1½ pounds cooked crawfish tail meat with fat (about 8–10 pounds live crawfish) or processed crawfish tail meat (about 3 cups)

4 tablespoons unsalted butter

2 cups yellow onion, chopped

1 cup green onions, white and green parts chopped

½ cup celery (including leaves), chopped

½ cup red bell pepper, chopped

3 cloves garlic, minced

¼ cup unbleached all-purpose flour

1 medium jalapeño pepper, chopped (remove seeds first)

½ teaspoon ground cayenne pepper

¼ teaspoon white pepper

½ teaspoon kosher or sea salt

1. Preheat oven to 350 degrees. If cooking your own crawfish, boil in unseasoned water. When peeling them, save as much of the fat as possible.

2. Melt butter in a large heavy-bottom skillet over medium heat. Sauté yellow and green onions, celery, and bell pepper. Cook, stir-

ring occasionally, until vegetables become tender; about 8 minutes. Stir in minced garlic last two minutes of cooking to prevent burning. Add flour and blend well. Remove from heat and gently stir in crawfish meat and fat. Add jalapeño, cayenne, white pepper, and salt. Mix well.

3. Spoon into prepared chilled pie crust. Bake for 20–30 minutes or until crust turns golden.

Serves 8–10.

John Michael's Helpful Hint: You may substitute equal measurements of shrimp or scallops for the crawfish as you desire.

⨍ That's Amore! Italian Pie

Crust

  1½ cups unbleached all-purpose flour
  ½ tablespoon white sugar
  ½ teaspoon kosher or sea salt, finely ground
  ¼ cup Crisco butter-flavored all-vegetable shortening, chilled
     and cut into small pieces
  ¼ cup unsalted butter, chilled and cut into small pieces
  ¼–½ cup cold water; use only as much as needed for a smooth,
     satiny dough ball
  1 egg yolk and 1 teaspoon water for egg wash
  Crisco butter-flavored cooking spray

1. All ingredients should be cold. Combine all the dry ingredients in a large mixing bowl. Add shortening and butter. Using a pastry blender, cut in the shortening and butter until the mixture resembles coarse meal or peas.
2. Drop by drop, add the cold water. Mix in with the fingertips, not with the hands as the palms will warm the dough. Continue mixing in

water until the dough begins to hold together without being crumbly yet not sticky.

3. Place dough in plastic wrap. Fold over plastic wrap and press down to form a disk. This will make rolling out easier after chilling. Finish wrapping in plastic and place in the refrigerator for at least 30 minutes.

4. Lightly spray a deep 9-inch pie pan or 8½-inch fluted flan pan with cooking spray. Roll out dough and place in pie plate, allowing the excess pastry to hang over the edge. Cut away extra, fold under, and crimp decoratively. Brush with egg wash and return to the refrigerator until filling is ready.

Makes pastry for one 9-inch single-crust pie.

Filling

   3 large Italian sausages, casings removed and crumbled
   3 tablespoons extra virgin olive oil
   1 cup mushrooms (Baby Bella or white button), sliced
   1 red bell pepper, diced
   3 shallots, minced
   1 garlic clove, minced
   2 tablespoons fresh basil, julienned
   ¼ teaspoon kosher or sea salt
   ¼ teaspoon freshly ground black pepper
   3 large eggs
   1 cup half-and-half
   ¾ cup mozzarella cheese, shredded

1. Preheat oven to 425 degrees. In a large heavy-bottom skillet over medium-high heat, cook crumbled sausage until brown. Remove from heat and drain. In same pan, heat olive oil. Sauté mushrooms until they release their juices. Add bell pepper, shallots, and garlic and cook until vegetables are tender, about 5 minutes. Do not burn garlic as it will become bitter. Add basil, salt, and pepper and mix well. Remove from heat.

2. In a medium mixing bowl, stir or whisk eggs until they begin to become foamy. Stir or whisk in half-and-half until well blended. Set aside.

3. Layer sausage and mushroom mixture on bottom of prepared pie crust. Cover with shredded mozzarella. Gently pour egg and half-and-half mixture in pie crust. Bake for 35–40 minutes, or until filling is set. Cool on a rack for 20 minutes before serving. Slice and serve warm with my Tuscan Tomato Sauce (see recipe in the "Decorating Your Pie" chapter).

Serves 8–10.

Love-It Meat Pie

After seeing *Sweeney Todd* on the stage and on the movie screen, I felt compelled to rename this recipe for one of the title characters (Mrs. Lovett, Sweeney's partner in crime). Chad, our good friends Stephanie Jameson, Laura McCallum, Laura's mother, Jan, and I went to see the movie version of *Sweeney Todd* on Christmas Day evening 2007. We had a blast laughing, screaming, and hiding our faces during the gruesome scenes. The rest of the audience thought we were nuts, but we had so much fun. I remembered my grandma's meat pie recipe and added it to this chapter in honor of that wonderful Christmas Day night at the movies (although I don't think Grandma would have appreciated the connection). I will never forget the looks from the audience when the lights came up. We were the ghouls rather than what we had just witnessed on the screen.

Crust

    3 cups unbleached all-purpose flour
    1 tablespoon white sugar
    1 teaspoon kosher or sea salt, finely ground
    ½ cup Crisco butter-flavored all-vegetable shortening, chilled and cut into small pieces

½ cup unsalted butter, chilled and cut into small pieces

½–¾ cup cold water; use only as much as needed for a smooth, satiny dough ball

1 egg yolk and 1 teaspoon water for egg wash

Crisco butter-flavored cooking spray

1. All ingredients should be cold. Combine all the dry ingredients in a large mixing bowl. Add shortening and butter. Using a pastry blender, cut in the shortening and butter until the mixture resembles coarse meal or peas.

2. Drop by drop, add the cold water. Mix in with the fingertips, not with the hands as the palms will warm the dough. Continue mixing in water until the dough begins to hold together without being crumbly yet not sticky.

3. Divide dough into two pieces and place each in plastic wrap. Fold over plastic wrap and press down to form a disk. This will make rolling out easier after chilling. Finish wrapping in plastic and place in the refrigerator for 30 minutes.

4. Lightly spray a 9-inch pie plate with cooking spray. Roll out dough and place in pie plate, allowing the excess pastry to hang over the edge. Cut away excess. Return to the refrigerator until filling is ready. When filling is ready, roll out top crust. Brush pie crust edge with egg wash to create a "cement" bond between bottom and top crust. Fill pie crust and carefully place top crust over filled pie. Cut away excess dough, tuck under, and crimp decoratively. Vent top crust to release steam. Protect edges of crust with a pie shield. Remove pie shield for the final 10 minutes of baking.

Makes pastry for one 9-inch double-crust pie.

Filling

1 medium yellow onion, chopped

1 pound lean ground beef, ground turkey, or ground soy crumbles

1 can tomato soup, chunky or tomato-basil

1 can French-cut green beans, drained

¼ teaspoon kosher or sea salt
¼ freshly ground black pepper

1. Preheat oven to 350 degrees. In a heavy-bottom skillet over medium-high heat, sauté onion and ground beef until the onion is translucent and the ground beef is brown. Remove from heat and drain off the excess fat. Add the can of tomato soup and mix well. Stir in the green beans, salt, and pepper. Continue to cook until well heated through. Remove from heat and set aside.

2. Gently pour the filling into the prepared and chilled pie crust. Smooth top with a spatula, brush egg wash around the edges of pie crust, and attach top crust per instructions. Bake for 25–30 minutes or until the crust is golden in color. Cool on rack for 20 minutes before serving.

Serves 8–10.

⸙ Puddin' Pork Pie

Crust

3 cups unbleached all-purpose flour
1 tablespoon white sugar
1 teaspoon kosher or sea salt, finely ground
½ cup Crisco butter-flavored all-vegetable shortening, chilled
　　and cut into small pieces
½ cup unsalted butter, chilled and cut into small pieces
½–¾ cup cold water; use only as much as needed for a smooth,
　　satiny dough ball
1 egg yolk and 1 teaspoon water for egg wash
Crisco butter-flavored cooking spray

1. All ingredients should be cold. Combine all the dry ingredients in a large mixing bowl. Add shortening and butter. Using a pastry blender, cut in the shortening and butter until the mixture resembles

coarse meal or peas. Drop by drop, add the cold water. Mix in with the fingertips, not with the hands as the palms will warm the dough. Continue mixing in water until the dough begins to hold together without being crumbly yet not sticky.

2. Divide dough into two pieces and place each in plastic wrap. Fold over plastic wrap and press down to form a disk. This will make rolling out easier after chilling. Finish wrapping in plastic and place in the refrigerator for 30 minutes.

3. Lightly spray a 9-inch pie plate with cooking spray. Roll out dough and place in pie plate, allowing excess pastry to hang over the edge. Cut away excess. Return to the refrigerator until filling is ready. When filling is ready, roll out top crust. Brush pie crust edge with egg wash to create a "cement" bond between bottom and top crust. Fill pie crust and carefully place top crust over filled pie. Cut away excess dough, tuck under, and crimp decoratively. Vent top crust to release steam. Protect edges of crust with a pie shield. Remove pie shield final 10 minutes of baking.

Makes pastry for one 9-inch double-crust pie.

Filling

> 2 pounds lean ground pork
> 2 large Italian sweet sausages, casings removed and crumbled
> 1 large yellow onion, diced
> 2 tablespoons fresh rosemary, chopped
> 1 cup bread crumbs (fresh or canned)
> 1 tablespoon flat-leaf parsley, chopped
> ½ teaspoon kosher or sea salt
> ¼ teaspoon freshly ground black pepper
> ½ cup shredded Parmesan cheese, divided

1. Preheat oven to 425 degrees. In a heavy-bottom skillet over medium-high heat, cook pork, sausage, and onion until meat is browned and onion is translucent. Remove from heat and drain off excess fat. In a medium mixing bowl, combine rosemary, bread crumbs, and parsley.

Add cooked meat mixture to bread crumb-herb mixture. Blend well and season with salt and pepper.

2. Sprinkle half the Parmesan cheese over the bottom of the prepared pie crust. Spread the pork mixture on top of the shredded cheese. Sprinkle with remaining Parmesan cheese. Brush egg wash around the edge of the pie crust and attach top crust per instructions.

3. Bake for 15 minutes. Reduce heat to 350 degrees. Bake an additional 35–40 minutes. Cool on a rack.

Serves 8–10.

⸕ A Real Pizza Pie

This is a fun way to serve pizza to your family or friends. Instead of a doughy crust, this pizza has a pastry crust that's nice and flaky. Use a combination of toppings or a single topping. I've tried browned ground beef, sautéed chicken, a variety of sausages, and vegetables. Use your imagination and hunger to dictate how you want to fill this "real pizza pie."

Crust

1½ cups unbleached all-purpose flour
½ tablespoon white sugar
½ teaspoon kosher or sea salt, finely crushed
¼ cup Crisco butter-flavored all-vegetable shortening, chilled
    and cut into small pieces
¼ cup unsalted butter, chilled and cut into small pieces
¼–½ cup cold water; use only as much as needed for a smooth,
    satiny dough ball
1 egg yolk and 1 teaspoon water for egg wash
Crisco butter-flavored cooking spray

1. All ingredients should be cold. Combine all the dry ingredients in a large mixing bowl. Add shortening and butter. Using a pastry blender,

cut in the shortening and butter until the mixture resembles coarse meal or peas.

2. Drop by drop, add the cold water. Mix in with the fingertips, not with the hands as the palms will warm the dough. Continue mixing in water until the dough begins to hold together without being crumbly yet not sticky.

3. Place dough in plastic wrap. Fold over plastic wrap and press down to form a disk. This will make rolling out easier after chilling. Finish wrapping in plastic and place in the refrigerator for at least 30 minutes.

4. Lightly spray a deep 9-inch pie pan or 8½-inch fluted flan pan with cooking spray. Roll out dough and place in pie plate, allowing the excess pastry to hang over the edge. Cut away extra, tuck under, and crimp decoratively. Brush with egg wash and return to the refrigerator until filling is ready.

Makes pastry for one 9-inch single-crust pie.

Filling

5 large eggs
One pint heavy whipping cream
½ teaspoon fresh oregano
Kosher or sea salt to taste
Freshly ground black pepper to taste
2 cups precooked and chopped pizza toppings (pepperoni, sausage, mushrooms, and onions)
2 cups pizza cheese (Parmesan, mozzarella, cheddar, Swiss, etc.), divided

1. Preheat oven to 350 degrees. In a medium mixing bowl, whisk together eggs, cream, oregano, salt, and pepper. Layer toppings on the bottom of the prepared and chilled pie crust. Sprinkle with half the cheese. Gently pour mixture over toppings and cheese. Sprinkle with remaining cheese.

2. Protect pie crust edge from excessive browning with a pie shield and remove last 10 minutes of baking. Bake for 20 minutes. Rotate pie and

continue to bake for 15–20 minutes more or until center has begun to set. Remove from oven and let cool on a rack for 15 minutes before serving.

Serves 8–10.

⸕ Sage Sausage Pie

Most local or larger grocery stores carry sage sausage. If you are unable to find it, try your local butcher. The sage offers a hearty rich flavor that blends well with sausage. You can also substitute ground lamb with fresh sage and feta or Italian sausage with mozzarella.

Crust

> 1½ cups unbleached all-purpose flour
> ½ tablespoon white sugar
> ½ teaspoon kosher or sea salt, finely ground
> ¼ cup Crisco butter-flavored all-vegetable shortening, chilled
> and cut into small pieces
> ¼ cup unsalted butter, chilled and cut into small pieces
> ¼–½ cup cold water; use only as much as needed for a smooth,
> satiny dough ball
> Crisco butter-flavored cooking spray

1. All ingredients should be cold. Combine all the dry ingredients in a large mixing bowl. Add shortening and butter. Using a pastry blender, cut in the shortening and butter until the mixture resembles coarse meal or peas.
2. Drop by drop, add the cold water. Mix in with the fingertips, not with the hands as the palms will warm the dough. Continue mixing in water until the dough begins to hold together without being crumbly yet not sticky.

3. Place dough in plastic wrap. Fold over plastic wrap and press down to form a disk. This will make rolling out easier after chilling. Finish wrapping in plastic and place in the refrigerator for at least 30 minutes.

4. Lightly spray a deep 9-inch pie pan or 8½-inch fluted flan pan. Roll out dough and place in pie plate, allowing the excess pastry to hang over the edge. Cut away extra, tuck under, and crimp decoratively. Prick sides and bottom of pie crust with a fork. Chill in the refrigerator for at least 30 minutes.

5. Preheat the oven to 400 degrees. Line the pastry shell with parchment and baking beans or beads. Bake the shell for 12 minutes. Remove the paper and beans or beads and cool on rack.

Makes pastry for one 9-inch single-crust pie.

Filling

10 ounces sage sausage, crumbled
1 small onion, finely chopped
½ cup mayonnaise (regular or low-fat)
½ cup whole milk
2 large eggs
1 tablespoon cornstarch
1½ cups grated cheese (cheddar, jack, or a combination
   of your favorite cheeses)
Garlic powder, to taste

1. Preheat oven to 350 degrees. In a heavy-bottom skillet, lightly brown the sage sausage. Add onion and cook until translucent. Remove from heat and drain off excess fat.

2. In a medium mixing bowl, stir or whisk mayonnaise, milk, eggs, and cornstarch. Stir in drained sausage, onion, cheese, and garlic powder. Pour into prepared pie crust. Protect edges of pie crust with a pie shield to prevent excessive browning. Remove final 10 minutes of baking. Bake for 30–35 minutes or until a knife inserted in the center of the pie comes out clean. Cool on a rack for 15 minutes before slicing.

Serves 8–10.

⸕ My Favorite Salmon Pie

I love salmon so much that I worked on this pie forever to get it right. I've used a simple sautéed salmon, grilled salmon, and baked salmon. Only use canned salmon if you cannot find fresh. Even frozen filets that are individually wrapped and baked are better than canned salmon. But, of course, it is a matter of taste. Also, try to use fresh dill weed if possible. The flavor is so much better. I've also substituted a fine goat cheese for the shredded Swiss cheese. The flavor completely changes but is wonderfully delicious. If you don't enjoy the earthy taste of goat cheese, by all means use Swiss cheese.

Crust

> 1½ cups unbleached all-purpose flour
> ½ tablespoon white sugar
> ½ teaspoon kosher or sea salt, finely ground
> ¼ cup Crisco butter-flavored all-vegetable shortening, chilled
>   and cut into small pieces
> ¼ cup unsalted butter, chilled and cut into small pieces
> ¼–½ cup cold water; use only as much as needed for a smooth,
>   satiny dough ball
> 1 egg yolk and 1 teaspoon water for egg wash
> ½ cup Parmesan cheese, grated
> Crisco butter-flavored cooking spray

1. All ingredients should be cold. Combine all the dry ingredients in a large mixing bowl. Add shortening and butter. Using a pastry blender, cut in the shortening and butter until the mixture resembles coarse meal or peas.
2. Drop by drop, add the cold water. Mix in with the fingertips, not with the hands as the palms will warm the dough. Continue mixing in water until the dough begins to hold together without being crumbly yet not sticky.

3. Place dough in plastic wrap. Fold over plastic wrap and press down to form a disk. This will make rolling out easier after chilling. Finish wrapping in plastic and place in the refrigerator for at least 30 minutes.

4. Lightly spray a deep 9-inch pie pan, 8½-inch fluted flan pan, or 8-inch springform pan. Roll out dough and place in pie plate, allowing the excess pastry to hang over the edge. Cut away extra, tuck under, and crimp decoratively. Sprinkle sides and bottom with grated cheese. Lightly press with fingertips and chill in the refrigerator for at least 30 minutes.

5. Preheat the oven to 375 degrees. Line the pastry shell with parchment and baking beans or beads. Bake the shell for 10 minutes. Carefully remove the paper and beans or beads from pie crust and cool on rack.

Makes pastry for one 9-inch single-crust pie.

Filling

16 ounces fresh salmon, baked or sautéed (1 large can if fresh
    is not available)
1 yellow onion, finely chopped
1 garlic clove, minced
2 tablespoons unsalted butter
2 cups sour cream
4 large eggs
1½ cups shredded Swiss cheese, divided (may also use goat cheese)
1 teaspoon fresh dill weed, finely chopped
¼ teaspoon kosher or sea salt
¼ teaspoon freshly ground black pepper

1. Preheat oven to 375 degrees. Cook fresh salmon as desired (I like to marinate and bake). Let cool to room temperature. In a heavy-bottom skillet over medium-high heat, sauté onion and garlic in butter until translucent. Do not let garlic burn or it will become bitter. Remove from heat.

2. In a medium mixing bowl, stir or whisk sour cream and eggs until well blended. Mix cooked onion and garlic into sour cream-egg mixture. Blend well. Break salmon into bite-size pieces and add to egg mixture. Stir in 1 cup cheese, dill weed, salt, and pepper. Gently pour into prepared pie crust. Sprinkle with remaining shredded cheese.

3. Protect pie crust edges with a pie shield to prevent excessive browning. Remove final 10 minutes of baking. Bake for 55–65 minutes or until a knife inserted in the center comes out clean. Cool on a rack for 15 minutes before slicing. Garnish with additional sour cream or crème fraîche and fresh dill weed or serve with my Cucumber Sauce (see recipe in the "Decorating Your Pie" chapter).

Serves 8–10.

Tuna Pie

Crust

3 cups unbleached all-purpose flour
1 tablespoon white sugar
1 teaspoon kosher or sea salt, finely ground
½ cup Crisco butter-flavored all-vegetable shortening, chilled
    and cut into small pieces
½ cup unsalted butter, chilled and cut into small pieces
½–¾ cup cold water; use only as much as needed for a smooth,
    satiny dough ball
1 egg yolk and 1 teaspoon water for egg wash
Crisco butter-flavored cooking spray

1. All ingredients should be cold. Combine all the dry ingredients in a large mixing bowl. Add shortening and butter. Using a pastry blender, cut in the shortening and butter until the mixture resembles coarse meal or peas.

2. Drop by drop, add the cold water. Mix in with the fingertips, not with the hands as the palms will warm the dough. Continue mixing in

water until the dough begins to hold together without being crumbly yet not sticky.

3. Divide dough into two pieces and place each in plastic wrap. Fold over plastic wrap and press down to form a disk. This will make rolling out easier after chilling. Finish wrapping in plastic and place in the refrigerator for 30 minutes.

4. Lightly spray a 9-inch pie plate with cooking spray. Roll out dough and place in pie plate, allowing the excess pastry to hang over the edge. Cut away excess. Return to the refrigerator until filling is ready. When filling is ready, roll out top crust. Brush pie crust edge with egg wash to create a "cement" bond between bottom and top crust. Fill pie crust and carefully place top crust over filled pie. Cut away excess dough, tuck under, and crimp decoratively. Vent top crust to release steam. Protect edges of crust with a pie shield. Remove pie shield final 10 minutes of baking.

Makes pastry for one 9-inch double-crust pie.

Filling

3 large eggs, beaten
1 tablespoon unsalted butter, melted
½ cup whole milk
1 small yellow onion, finely chopped
2 tablespoons flat-leaf parsley, chopped
¾ teaspoon fresh basil, chopped
2 cans of tuna, water-packed, drained and flaked,
    or 2 cups cooked tuna, crumbled
1 tablespoon hot sauce

1. Preheat oven to 425 degrees. In a medium mixing bowl, stir or whisk eggs, butter, milk, onion, parsley, and basil. Add tuna and hot sauce. Mix well.

2. Pour into prepared and chilled pie crust. Carefully add top crust per instructions. Bake for 25–35 minutes or until crust is golden and filling is set. Cool on a rack. Serve with my Cucumber Sauce (see recipe in the "Decorating Your Pie" chapter).

Serves 8–10.

Leftover Turkey Pie

Crust

3 cups unbleached all-purpose flour
1 tablespoon white sugar
1 teaspoon kosher or sea salt, finely ground
½ cup Crisco butter-flavored all-vegetable shortening, chilled
    and cut into small pieces
½ cup unsalted butter, chilled and cut into small pieces
½–¾ cup cold water; use only as much as needed for a smooth,
    satiny dough ball
1 egg yolk and 1 teaspoon water for egg wash
Crisco butter-flavored cooking spray

1. All ingredients should be cold. Combine all the dry ingredients in a large mixing bowl. Add shortening and butter. Using a pastry blender, cut in the shortening and butter until the mixture resembles coarse meal or peas.
2. Drop by drop, add the cold water. Mix in with the fingertips, not with the hands as the palms will warm the dough. Continue mixing in water until the dough begins to hold together without being crumbly yet not sticky.
3. Divide dough into two pieces and place each in plastic wrap. Fold over plastic wrap and press down to form a disk. This will make rolling out easier after chilling. Finish wrapping in plastic and place in the refrigerator for 30 minutes.
4. Lightly spray a 10-inch pie plate or 9-inch deep-dish pie plate with cooking spray. Roll out dough and place in pie plate, allowing excess pastry to hang over the edge. Cut away extra dough. Return to the refrigerator until filling is ready. When filling is ready, roll out top crust. Brush pie crust edge with egg wash to create a "cement" bond between bottom and top crust. Fill pie crust and carefully place top crust over filled pie. Cut away excess dough, tuck under, and crimp

decoratively. Vent top crust to release steam. Protect edges of crust with a pie shield. Remove pie shield final 10 minutes of baking.

Makes pastry for one 10-inch double-crust pie or one 9-inch deep-dish double-crust pie.

Filling

4 tablespoons unsalted butter
4 tablespoons unbleached all-purpose flour
1½ cups turkey or chicken broth
½ cup half-and-half
Kosher or sea salt, to taste
Freshly ground black pepper, to taste
5 cups cooked turkey, shredded or cut into bite-size pieces
2 teaspoons fresh sage, chopped
1½ teaspoons fresh thyme, chopped
1 cup frozen peas, thawed and dried between paper towels

1. Preheat oven to 425 degrees. In a heavy-bottom saucepan over medium heat, melt butter. Add flour and blend well. Cook for 2 minutes, stirring constantly. Stir or whisk in broth and continue to stir or whisk until sauce begins to thicken. Mix in half-and-half. Turn heat to lowest setting and continue to cook, stirring occasionally, for 15 minutes. Season with salt and pepper to taste.
2. Add turkey, herbs, and peas. Mix gently. Spoon turkey mixture into prepared and chilled pie crust. Add top crust per instructions. If you have extra pie crust dough, use turkey cutouts or other fun and decorative cutouts to adorn the top of your pie. Brush with egg wash before baking.
3. Bake for 10 minutes, then lower oven heat to 325 and continue baking for 30 minutes or until the crust is golden and filling is bubbling through vents. Cool on a rack for at least 30 minutes before slicing.

Serves 8–10.

⸫ Thelma Anderson's Flexible Pie

One of Grandma's most versatile pies, this recipe can help any cook use leftover meats or seafood. When I was young, Grandma would use leftover hamburgers that she would crumble along with any breakfast sausage. I've used a variety of seafood and cheese that were left in my refrigerator to create a wonderful "flexible" pie. Use any combination of meats, vegetables, cheeses, and herbs. Use your imagination to create a one-of-a-kind pie for your family and friends.

Crust

> 1½ cups unbleached all-purpose flour
> ½ tablespoon white sugar
> ½ teaspoon kosher or sea salt, finely ground
> ¼ cup Crisco butter-flavored all-vegetable shortening, chilled and cut into small pieces
> ¼ cup unsalted butter, chilled and cut into small pieces
> ¼–½ cup cold water; use only as much as needed for a smooth, satiny dough ball

There is a story about Prince Philip, Duke of Edinburgh, the Queen's husband, visiting a small town in northern Canada. During the . . . visit, he had lunch at the local diner. He was accompanied by his entourage and members of the local and national press, who crowded into the adjacent booths and tables. It is easy to imagine the attention lavished on a member of the Royal Family dining at the local establishment. Of course all eyes were on [Prince Philip's] booth when the restaurant's proprietress came to the table to clear the plates and, while gently lifting it from his plate, smiled warmly and advised, "Keep your fork, Duke, there's pie."

—AUTHOR UNKNOWN

1 egg yolk and 1 teaspoon water for egg wash
Crisco butter-flavored cooking spray

1. All ingredients should be cold. Combine all the dry ingredients in a large mixing bowl. Add shortening and butter. Using a pastry blender, cut in the shortening and butter until the mixture resembles coarse meal or peas.
2. Drop by drop, add the cold water. Mix in with the fingertips, not with the hands as the palms will warm the dough. Continue mixing in water until the dough begins to hold together without being crumbly yet not sticky.
3. Place dough in plastic wrap. Fold over plastic wrap and press down to form a disk. This will make rolling out easier after chilling. Finish wrapping in plastic and place in the refrigerator for at least 1 hour.
4. Lightly spray a deep 9-inch pie pan, 8½-inch fluted flan pan, or 8-inch springform pan. Roll out dough and place in pie plate, allowing the excess pastry to hang over the edge. Cut away extra, tuck under, and crimp decoratively. Chill in the refrigerator for at least 30 minutes.
5. Preheat the oven to 375 degrees. Line the pastry shell with parchment and baking beans or beads. Bake the shell for 10 minutes. Remove the paper and beans or beads and cool on rack.

Makes pastry for one 9-inch single-crust pie.

Filling

2 cups of cooked meat cut up or shredded or 2 cups of seafood, in bite-size pieces
1½ cups cheese (such as cheddar, Swiss, or jack), shredded
⅓ cup Parmesan cheese, grated
¾ cup vegetables (onions, green onions, broccoli, carrots, etc.), chopped
3 large eggs
1 cup whole milk
1 tablespoon fresh herbs (basil, thyme, oregano, dill weed, etc.), chopped

Kosher or sea salt, to taste
Freshly ground black pepper, to taste

1. Preheat oven to 350 degrees. Arrange meats or seafood in an even layer on the bottom of the prepared and cooled pie crust. Next add shredded cheese, Parmesan, and chopped vegetables.
2. In a medium mixing bowl, beat or whisk eggs until they begin to foam. Stir or whisk in milk, herbs, salt, and pepper. Gently pour over layers of filling in pie crust. Protect pie crust edges with a pie shield to prevent excessive browning. Remove final 10 minutes of baking. Bake for 45 minutes or until a knife inserted in the center comes out clean. Cool on a rack for 15 minutes before slicing.

Serves 8–10.

Vegetable Pies

W HEN PREPARING A VEGETABLE PIE you must begin with the freshest ingredients. Just because the first savory pies recorded in history were called "coffins" or "coffyns" in medieval England, that does not give you license to use inferior produce or products. You can use your wilted or dried-up vegetables for soup stocks—maybe—but you want to use the best-quality and freshest ingredients for all your pies. That includes herbs and spices.

I grew up in the Red River Valley of North Dakota, one of the richest agricultural areas in the world. I often joke that one can drop a seed anywhere in the Red River Valley and it will grow regardless of the conditions. My statement is not far from the truth. Due to overland flooding by the Red River, the silt and sediment left behind create a nutrient-rich black soil that resembles chocolate cake. It is ideal for growing wheat, barley, corn, and potatoes on a large scale and tomatoes, pumpkins, radishes, berries, and other produce for the home gardener.

When I was a young boy, I enjoyed helping my grandma care for the five-acre garden west of the farmyard. Grandma Thelma Anderson and I would pull all of our equipment in my Radio Flyer classic red wagon through a windbreak of small trees and bushes. It was so exciting because each day we would work on a different section of the garden. It could be a couple of days or up to one week since we had weeded or cultivated that area. The corn may have grown another five inches, the peas could be ready for picking, the pumpkin or squash may have fattened up a couple more inches. Every section of the garden was always working and always a surprise. I was especially anxious after a couple of days of rain and the time that it would take to dry the soil. So much would happen in the garden in just those few days. But along with all the beauty of the produce came weeds—tons of weeds. My grandpa Julian Anderson made me a small wooden square stool to sit upon and pick weeds. I would set it on a large piece of cardboard so the legs wouldn't sink into the soft soil. I would pick weeds and talk with Grandma or we might listen to KNOX-AM on her little transistor radio. I believe the tuning dial on Grandma's radio had rusted in place to 1310. We never listened to any other station. We would listen to the farm report, country and contemporary music, along with their daily call-in show on which people would discuss the issues affecting their daily lives.

I remember us picking several wooden buckets full of corn, radishes, onions, bright purplish red beets, green beans, carrots, parsnips, and squash. We would load everything in my red wagon and, together, pull the fresh produce back to the farmhouse about a quarter of a mile away. Maneuvering this heavy load through the brush and over the gravel road took both our strength and plenty of rest stops. For a refreshing snack, Grandma and I would pull out a couple of carrots that we had just picked, wipe the black dirt off with our gardening gloves or shirttails, and enjoy a cool, sweet nibble. I still enjoy planting carrots in my backyard and eating them directly out of the ground. They are so sweet!

Once we got the produce to the house, Grandma and I would rinse everything with fresh water from the outdoor hose, and then we prepared to preserve our daily harvest. Corn was shucked and blanched. After an ice bath, the corn was dried, wrapped in foil, and packed in freezer bags. Enough corn was kept aside for that evening's supper. Nothing is better than fresh corn right from the garden. The sugar in corn begins to turn to starch the minute it is picked. Immediate refrigeration slows this process, but nothing beats growing your own, picking your own, and cooking your own. However, most home gardens in the United States are unable to grow corn. I have been fortunate to grow it in my own backyard in Saint Paul, Minnesota, but it has taken years to amend the soil to support a 10-foot-by-10-foot patch. It certainly makes a wonderful conversation piece when we entertain in the backyard.

The preservation of fresh produce on the farm or in my current home takes a great deal of planning. One rule is not to rush the process. Grandma and I would plan the week by what was ready in the garden or what we could obtain at the local farmers' market in nearby Grand Forks, North Dakota. During the summer and fall months, Grandma's water bath canner and pressure canner were never removed from the stove top. They were constantly in use. So, what we didn't freeze was canned and stored in a root cellar under the house. It had been built out from the basement so that it was not under the house but under the dirt—surrounded by ground except for the door from the main basement. This was an actual room with well-built shelves and a light in the center; it was not a hole in the ground like most root cellars. This room was cold, black as night, and perfect for storing root vegetables and canned goods. I wish I could re-create this room. Perhaps when we build a new home someday we will have this perfect food storage space. One of my favorite devices of Grandma's for storing carrots and parsnips was a couple of large pails of sand. After picking, cleaning, and drying the carrots and parsnips, we would remove the greens and push the vegetables down into the sand with only their tops showing. This method helped preserve these root crops through the winter and into the spring. They never dried out. Whenever we needed carrots or parsnips, we would go into the root cellar and simply pick them out of the sand buckets. How perfect.

All the recipes that appear in this chapter represent the pies that we would bake on the farm, as well as pies that I have introduced on television and radio. Savory pies, especially vegetable pies, hold a special place on my table, along with meat entrées and during holidays. One of the biggest surprises in the pie world has been my Vidalia Onion Pie recipe. Many have been taken aback by the sweetness and consistency of this pie. Served as a dessert pie along with apple and pumpkin pie at Thanksgiving, it helps our family enjoy the rewards of gardening and preserving.

If you don't can or preserve, do visit your local farmers' market. Fresh vegetables are best, but using frozen is not a crime. Whatever works for your schedule and household, please try making one of these wonderful recipes for your family. These vegetable pies are also magnificent to bring to potlucks or gatherings of family and friends. I guarantee there will be no competition as yours will be the only vegetable pie on the buffet table.

John Michael's Helpful Hint: Make pie pastry ahead of time, wrap flattened disks in plastic, and freeze.

⸕ Parsnip Pie

Parsnips are related to and resemble carrots, except they are paler and have a stronger flavor. In this recipe, parsnips can be either boiled or roasted. Roasting parsnips makes them sweeter than they already are. Preheat your oven to 400 degrees, cut parsnips into sticks, and toss with extra virgin olive oil or vegetable oil. Arrange in a single layer on a baking sheet and roast for approximately 30 minutes.

Crust

> 1½ cups unbleached all-purpose flour
> ½ tablespoon white sugar
> ½ teaspoon kosher or sea salt, finely ground
> ¼ cup Crisco butter-flavored all-vegetable shortening, chilled
>   and cut into small pieces
> ¼ cup unsalted butter, chilled and cut into small pieces
> ¼–½ cup cold water; use only as much as needed for a smooth,
>   satiny dough ball
> Crisco butter-flavored cooking spray
> 1 egg yolk and 1 teaspoon water for egg wash

1. All ingredients should be cold. Combine all the dry ingredients in a large mixing bowl. Add shortening and butter. Using a pastry blender, cut in the shortening and butter until the mixture resembles coarse meal or peas.

2. Drop by drop, add the cold water. Mix in with the fingertips, not with the hands as the palms will warm the dough. Continue mixing in water until the dough begins to hold together without being crumbly yet not sticky.

3. Place dough in plastic wrap. Fold over plastic wrap and press down to form a disk. This will make rolling out easier after chilling. Finish wrapping in plastic and place in the refrigerator for at least 30 minutes.

4. Lightly spray a deep 9-inch pie pan or 8½-inch fluted flan pan with cooking spray. Roll out dough and place in pie plate, allowing the excess pastry to hang over the edge. Cut away extra, tuck under, and crimp decoratively. Brush with egg wash and return to the refrigerator until filling is ready.

Makes pastry for one 9-inch single-crust pie.

Filling

>   1 cup boiled or roasted parsnips
>   2 tablespoons unsalted butter
>   ¼ teaspoon sea salt
>   2 large eggs
>   ¾ cup white sugar
>   ½ teaspoon freshly ground nutmeg
>   1 cup whole milk

1. Preheat oven to 400 degrees. Place hot parsnips in a mixing bowl and mash with a wire masher or large fork until smooth. Strain through a fine-mesh sieve if desired. While still warm, add butter and salt.

2. Lightly beat eggs. Stir into parsnip mixture. Add sugar, nutmeg, and milk to the parsnip mixture and blend well. Pour mixture into chilled pie crust. Sprinkle with nutmeg and bake for 30 minutes or until the custard filling is thick and nicely browned.

Serves 6–8.

Vidalia Onion Pie

I baked my signature Vidalia Onion Pie at the APC Crisco National Pie Championship in Celebration, Florida, for the Open category in 2006. It caught the attention of the Food Network and many other media representatives. The APC judges questioned whether it was a dessert pie or a savory pie. I explained that at Thanksgiving our family served two root pies (a sweet potato pie and an onion pie), along with the traditional fruit pies of the season. I was allowed to enter, but this recipe met with mixed reviews from the judges. My readers and "foodies" have cherished the appealing flavors and luscious taste of this pie, both for dessert and as an entrée. I hope you enjoy it.

Crust

1½ cups unbleached all-purpose flour
½ tablespoon white sugar
½ teaspoon kosher or sea salt, finely ground
¼ cup Crisco butter-flavored all-vegetable shortening, chilled
    and cut into small pieces
¼ cup unsalted butter, chilled and cut into small pieces
¼–½ cup cold water; use only as much as needed for a smooth,
    satiny dough ball
Crisco butter-flavored cooking spary
1 egg yolk and 1 teaspoon water for egg wash

1. All ingredients should be cold. Combine all the dry ingredients in a large mixing bowl. Add shortening and butter. Using a pastry blender, cut in the shortening and butter until the mixture resembles coarse meal or peas.
2. Drop by drop, add the cold water. Mix in with the fingertips, not with the hands as the palms will warm the dough. Continue mixing in water until the dough begins to hold together without being crumbly yet not sticky.

3. Place dough in plastic wrap. Fold over plastic wrap and press down to form a disk. This will make rolling out easier after chilling. Finish wrapping in plastic and place in the refrigerator for at least 30 minutes.

4. Lightly spray a deep 9-inch pie pan or 8½-inch fluted flan pan with cooking spray. Roll out dough and place in pie plate, allowing the excess pastry to hang over the edge. Cut away excess dough, tuck under, and crimp decoratively. Brush with egg wash and return to the refrigerator until filling is ready.

Makes pastry for one 9-inch single-crust pie.

Filling

2 pounds Vidalia onions, cut in half and thinly sliced
½ cup unsalted butter
3 large eggs, beaten
1 cup sour cream
3 tablespoons unbleached all-purpose flour
¼ teaspoon sea salt
½ teaspoon freshly ground black pepper
Freshly grated Parmesan and Asiago cheese

1. Preheat oven to 450 degrees. Over medium heat, melt butter. Add onions and sauté until translucent. Do not brown. Combine eggs, sour cream, and flour. Add to onion mixture. Season with salt and pepper and pour into chilled piecrust. Top with grated cheese.

2. Bake for 20 minutes. Reduce oven temperature to 325 degrees for the last 20 minutes or until center is set.

Serves 6–8.

Yes, in the poor man's garden grow far more than herbs and flowers— kind thoughts, contentment, peace of mind, and joy for weary hours.

—AUTHOR UNKNOWN

⸙ Green Tomato Pie

Ever wonder what to do with all your extra green tomatoes? Make this yummy pie. A great leftover, it is better the second day. Reheat using a conventional or toaster oven. Reheating in a microwave makes this pie soggy.

Crust

> 3 cups unbleached all-purpose flour
> 1 tablespoon white sugar
> 1 teaspoon kosher or sea salt, finely ground
> ½ cup butter-flavored all-vegetable shortening, chilled and
>   cut into small pieces
> ½ cup unsalted butter, chilled and cut into small pieces
> ½–¾ cup cold water; use only as much as needed for a smooth,
>   satiny dough ball
> Butter-flavored cooking spray
> 1 egg yolk and 1 teaspoon water for egg wash

1. All ingredients should be cold. Combine all the dry ingredients in a large mixing bowl. Add shortening and butter. Using a pastry blender, cut in the shortening and butter until the mixture resembles coarse meal or peas.
2. Drop by drop, add the cold water. Mix in with the fingertips, not with the hands as the palms will warm the dough. Continue mixing in water until the dough begins to hold together without being crumbly yet not sticky.
3. Divide dough into two pieces and place each piece in plastic wrap. Fold over plastic wrap and press down to form a disk. This will make rolling out easier after chilling. Finish wrapping in plastic and place in the refrigerator for at least 30 minutes.
4. Lightly spray a deep 9-inch pie plate with cooking spray. Roll out one dough disk and place in pie plate, allowing the excess pastry to hang over the edge. Cut away excess dough. Brush bottom and sides of crust with egg wash and refrigerate until filling is ready.

Makes pastry for one 9-inch double-crust pie.

Filling

> 1 large yellow onion
> 4 tablespoons unsalted butter
> 4 medium green tomatoes
> ¼ pound Swiss cheese (regular or low-fat)
> ¼ pound mild cheddar cheese (regular or low-fat)
> ½ cup Panko Japanese or whole wheat bread crumbs
> Sea salt and freshly ground black pepper to taste
> 1 tablespoon brown sugar
> Red wine vinegar

1. Preheat oven to 375 degrees. Slice onion into ¼-inch rounds. In a heavy-bottom frying pan over medium heat, melt butter and sauté onion until golden and translucent.
2. Meanwhile, cut out stem ends and thickly slice the green tomatoes. Set aside. Using a cheese plane or slicer, slice both cheeses as thinly as possible. Set aside.
3. Remove bottom crust from refrigerator and sprinkle with bread crumbs. Layer tomato slices, cheeses, and sautéed onion over crumbs. Sprinkle with salt, pepper, and brown sugar. Repeat layers until all ingredients are used up, or until pie crust is full but not overflowing. Top with more bread crumbs and a generous sprinkling of red wine vinegar.
4. Before applying top crust, brush bottom crust edge with egg wash (this will create a cement bond between the top and bottom crusts). Roll out top crust and carefully attach bottom and top crusts; tuck under and crimp decoratively. Cut vents in the top to release steam. Brush top with remaining egg wash. If you have small cookie cutters in the shape of vegetables, get creative and cut out remaining dough and paste on top of crust with egg wash.
5. Bake for 50 to 60 minutes or until golden brown and filling begins to bubble.

Serves 6–8.

*Grandma Thelma's Zucchini Pie

Crust

1½ cups unbleached all-purpose flour
½ tablespoon white sugar
½ teaspoon kosher or sea salt, finely ground
¼ cup Crisco butter-flavored all-vegetable shortening, chilled
    and cut into small pieces
¼ cup unsalted butter, chilled and cut into small pieces
¼–½ cup cold water; use only as much as needed for a smooth,
    satiny dough ball
Crisco butter-flavored cooking spray
1 egg yolk and 1 teaspoon water for egg wash

1. All ingredients should be cold. Combine all the dry ingredients in a large mixing bowl. Add shortening and butter. Using a pastry blender, cut in the shortening and butter until the mixture resembles coarse meal or peas.
2. Drop by drop, add the cold water. Mix in with the fingertips, not with the hands as the palms will warm the dough. Continue mixing in water until the dough begins to hold together without being crumbly yet not sticky.
3. Place dough in plastic wrap. Fold over plastic wrap and press down to form a disk. This will make rolling out easier after chilling. Finish wrapping in plastic and place in the refrigerator for at least 30 minutes.
4. Lightly spray a 9-inch pie plate with cooking spray. Roll out dough and place in pie plate, allowing excess pastry to hang over the edge. Cut away excess dough, tuck under, and crimp. Brush bottom and sides of crust with egg wash. Return to the refrigerator until filling is ready.

Makes pastry for one 9-inch single-crust pie.

Filling

4 cups sliced zucchini
1½ teaspoons cream of tartar

⅛ teaspoon sea salt

2 tablespoons unbleached all-purpose flour

1 tablespoon freshly squeezed lemon juice

⅛ teaspoon freshly ground nutmeg

1¼ cups white sugar

1½ teaspoons cinnamon, preferably China cassia

1 teaspoon unsalted butter

Topping

½ cup unsalted butter

½ cup white sugar

1 cup unbleached all-purpose flour

1. Preheat oven to 375 degrees. Peel zucchini and cut lengthwise. Scoop out seeds and slice as you would apples. In a heavy-bottom saucepan, cook zucchini slices in a small amount of water, enough to cover the bottom of the pan, for 10 minutes. Drain.
2. Mix the cream of tartar, salt, flour, lemon juice, nutmeg, sugar, and cinnamon with the zucchini. Pour into prepared pie crust. Dot with butter.
3. Mix all ingredients for the topping. Crumble over the pie filling. Bake for 45 minutes. Remove from oven and cool before slicing.

Serves 6–8.

Leek Pie

I love the interesting taste of leeks in this recipe. As a matter of fact, I enjoy leeks in just about any of my recipes, from soups to pies. My grandma Thelma Anderson used grated Swiss cheese in her recipe. I've tested several different types of cheese and find the tang of Gruyère compliments the cooked leeks. I hope you enjoy this special pie as much as I do.

Crust

> 1½ cups unbleached all-purpose flour
> ½ tablespoon white sugar
> ½ teaspoon kosher or sea salt, finely ground
> ¼ cup Crisco butter-flavored all-vegetable shortening, chilled
>   and cut into small pieces
> ¼ cup unsalted butter, chilled and cut into small pieces
> ¼–½ cup cold water; use only as much as needed for a smooth,
>   satiny dough ball
> Crisco butter-flavored cooking spray
> 1 egg yolk and 1 teaspoon water for egg wash

1. All ingredients should be cold. Combine all the dry ingredients in a large mixing bowl. Add shortening and butter. Using a pastry blender, cut in the shortening and butter until the mixture resembles coarse meal or peas.
2. Drop by drop, add the cold water. Mix in with the fingertips, not with the hands as the palms will warm the dough. Continue mixing in water until the dough begins to hold together without being crumbly yet not sticky.
3. Place dough in plastic wrap. Fold over plastic wrap and press down to form a disk. This will make rolling out easier after chilling. Finish wrapping in plastic and place in the refrigerator for at least 30 minutes.
4. Lightly spray a 9-inch pie plate with cooking spray. Roll out dough and place in pie plate, allowing the excess pastry to hang over the edge. Cut away extra, tuck under, and crimp decoratively. Brush bottom and sides of crust with egg wash. Return to the refrigerator until filling is ready.

Makes pastry for one 9-inch single-crust pie.

Filling

> 3 pounds fresh leeks
> 3 tablespoons unsalted butter

1 teaspoon fresh thyme, chopped
2 large eggs, lightly beaten
⅓ cup heavy cream
1 cup grated Gruyère cheese, divided

1. Preheat oven to 425 degrees. Rinse leeks to remove sand or dirt. Dry and trim. Julienne (cut into thin long strips) leeks, using only the white parts.
2. In a large heavy-bottom skillet, melt butter over medium heat. Add leeks and cook for about 20 minutes until softened. Remove from heat and cool.
3. When leeks are cool, add thyme, eggs, and cream. Mix well. Fold in ¾ cup of cheese. Pour into prepared pie crust. Top with remaining cheese. Bake for 40 minutes. Remove from oven and cool before serving.

Serves 6–8.

⨍ Mom's Mashed Potato Pie

Don't let the name of this pie deceive you. It was not my mother's recipe but rather her mother's, Thelma Anderson. My mother, Judy Kay Lerma, would announce that she was making meatloaf or hamburger and "Mom's Mashed Potato Pie." My older sister and I couldn't wait. I would cut a large serving for myself and smother it in tomato catsup. It's that good!

Crust

3 cups unbleached all-purpose flour
1 tablespoon white sugar
1 teaspoon kosher or sea salt, finely ground
1 teaspoon garlic powder (optional)
½ cup Crisco butter-flavored all-vegetable shortening, chilled and cut into small pieces
½ cup unsalted butter, chilled and cut into small pieces

½–¾ cup cold water; use only as much as needed for a smooth, satiny dough ball
Crisco butter-flavored cooking spray
1 egg yolk and 1 teaspoon water for egg wash

1. All ingredients should be cold. Combine all the dry ingredients in a large mixing bowl. Add shortening and butter. Using a pastry blender, cut in the shortening and butter until the mixture resembles coarse meal or peas.
2. Drop by drop, add the cold water. Mix in with the fingertips, not with the hands as the palms will warm the dough. Continue mixing in water until the dough begins to hold together without being crumbly yet not sticky.
3. Divide dough into two pieces and place each piece in plastic wrap. Fold over plastic wrap and press down to form a disk. This will make rolling out easier after chilling. Finish wrapping in plastic and place in the refrigerator for at least 30 minutes.
4. Lightly spray a deep 9-inch pie plate with cooking spray. Roll out one dough disk and place in pie plate, allowing the excess pastry to hang over the edge. Cut away excess and refrigerate until filling is ready. When filling is ready, roll out top crust. Brush pie crust edge with egg wash to create a cement bond between bottom and top crust. Fill pie crust and carefully place top crust over filled pie. Cut away excess dough, tuck under, and crimp decoratively. Vent top crust to release steam. Protect edges of crust with a pie shield. Remove pie shield for the final 10 minutes of baking.

Makes pastry for one 9-inch double-crust pie.

Every garden, great and small, starts with a plot of ground and willing hands to accomplish numerous tasks from situating the garden to harvesting its bounty.

—AUTHOR UNKNOWN

Filling

4 tablespoons unsalted butter or extra virgin olive oil

3 large russet potatoes, peeled, cooked, and mashed

1 medium yellow onion, finely chopped

3 green onions, finely chopped

1½ cups sour cream or plain yogurt (regular or fat-free)

1 (10½-ounce) can cream of chicken soup (regular or fat-free)

1 cup cheddar cheese, shredded (regular, low-fat, or fat-free)

½ teaspoon sea salt

1 teaspoon freshly ground black pepper

1. Preheat oven to 425 degrees. Melt butter in a heavy-bottom sauce-pan over medium heat. Add yellow onion and cook until translucent, about 5 minutes. Remove from heat.
2. Using a large mixing bowl, blend potatoes, cooked yellow onion, and green onions. Add the sour cream and soup and mix well. Stir in cheese, salt, and pepper. Continue to stir until velvety.
3. Spoon filling into prepared pie crust. Add top crust per instructions. Brush top with remaining egg wash. If you have small cookie cutters that resemble vegetables, get creative and cut out remaining dough and paste on top of crust with egg wash.
4. Bake for 30–35 minutes, or until crust turns a golden brown. Serve warm or at room temperature with a garnish of fresh chives.

Serves 6–8.

Ratatouille Pie

Every summer Chad, our daughter, Heather, and I vacation at Beauty Bay Lodge near Nevis, Minnesota. We rent a two-bedroom log cabin built in the 1940s or 1950s. The largest nearby city is Park Rapids, Minnesota. In the summer of 2007, Chad and I took our daughter, Heather, her cousin Kaylie, and Beauty Bay Lodge owner's daughter

Marie to see the animated film *Ratatouille*. Afterward I began thinking about creating a pie based on the recipe that inspired the film. This is my recipe.

Crust

> 1½ cups unbleached all-purpose flour
> ½ tablespoon white sugar
> ½ teaspoon kosher or sea salt, finely ground
> ¼ cup Crisco butter-flavored all-vegetable shortening, chilled
>   and cut into small pieces
> ¼ cup unsalted butter, chilled and cut into small pieces
> ¼–½ cup cold water; use only as much as needed for a smooth,
>   satiny dough ball
> Crisco butter-flavored cooking spray
> 1 egg yolk and 1 teaspoon water for egg wash

1. All ingredients should be cold. Combine all the dry ingredients in a large mixing bowl. Add shortening and butter. Using a pastry blender, cut in the shortening and butter until the mixture resembles coarse meal or peas.
2. Drop by drop, add the cold water. Mix in with the fingertips, not with the hands as the palms will warm the dough. Continue mixing in water until the dough begins to hold together without being crumbly yet not sticky.
3. Place dough in plastic wrap. Fold over plastic wrap and press down to form a disk. This will make rolling out easier after chilling. Finish wrapping in plastic and place in the refrigerator for at least 30 minutes.
4. Lightly spray a 9-inch pie plate with cooking spray. Roll out dough and place in pie plate, allowing excess to hang over the edge. Cut away extra, tuck under, and crimp decoratively. Brush bottom and sides of crust with egg wash. Return to the refrigerator until filling is ready.

Makes pastry for one 9-inch single-crust pie.

Filling

2 tablespoons extra virgin olive oil and more for drizzling

2 tablespoons unsalted butter

2 small zucchini, diced

2 medium eggplant, divided, 1 diced and 1 sliced into ¼-inch slices

½ cup roma tomatoes, diced

1 cup red bell pepper, diced

½ cup yellow onion, diced

2 cloves garlic, finely minced

¾ teaspoon sea salt

¼ teaspoon freshly ground black pepper

1 teaspoon freshly chopped basil or ½ teaspoon dried basil

½ teaspoon fresh thyme or ¼ teaspoon dried thyme

1 cup Italian-style tomato sauce (see the Tuscan Tomato Sauce recipe in the "Decorating Your Pie" chapter)

3 large eggs, lightly beaten

½ cup cream

½ cup Parmesan cheese, grated or curls

¼ cup sliced ripe black olives

1. Preheat oven to 375 degrees. In a large heavy-bottom skillet over medium heat, add oil and butter. When butter has melted, add zucchini, diced eggplant, tomato, red pepper, onion, and garlic. Season with salt and pepper. Stirring occasionally, cook until the vegetables are tender but still crisp. Sprinkle vegetable mixture with basil and thyme. Remove from heat.

2. Pour tomato sauce over cooked vegetable mixture and stir in. Carefully spoon mixture into prepared pie crust. Beat together eggs and cream. Pour over vegetables. Top with eggplant slices, placing in a decorative circle on top of mixture. Sprinkle grated cheese over eggplant and top with black olives. Lightly drizzle with additional olive oil.

3. Bake for 30–35 minutes or until the tomato sauce bubbles and the grated cheese begins to turn golden. Serve warm or at room temperature with additional Italian-style tomato sauce ladled on top.

Serves 6–8.

⸙ Potato, Leek, and Spinach Pie

Crust

1½ cups unbleached all-purpose flour
½ tablespoon white sugar
½ teaspoon kosher or sea salt, finely ground
¼ cup Crisco butter-flavored all-vegetable shortening, chilled
    and cut into small pieces
¼ cup unsalted butter, chilled and cut into small pieces
¼–½ cup cold water; use only as much as needed for a smooth,
    satiny dough ball
Crisco butter-flavored cooking spray

1. All ingredients should be cold. Combine all the dry ingredients in a large mixing bowl. Add shortening and butter. Using a pastry blender, cut in the shortening and butter until the mixture resembles coarse meal or peas.
2. Drop by drop, add the cold water. Mix in with the fingertips, not with the hands as the palms will warm the dough. Continue mixing in water until the dough begins to hold together without being crumbly yet not sticky.
3. Lightly spray a deep 9-inch pie pan or 8½-inch fluted flan pan with cooking spray. Roll out dough and place in pie plate, allowing the excess pastry to hang over the edge. Cut away extra, fold under, and crimp decoratively. Prick the side and bottom of the pie crust with a fork and refrigerate for at least 30 minutes.
4. Preheat oven to 400 degrees. Remove chilled pie crust from refrigerator. Line the bottom and side of crust with parchment paper weighted down by baking beans or beads. Blind bake (see the "Crust" chapter) for 10 minutes. Remove parchment paper and beans or beads. Remove from oven, cool, and set aside until filling is ready.

Makes pastry for one 9-inch single-crust pie.

Filling

  3 medium russet potatoes, peeled and sliced
  2 tablespoons extra virgin olive oil
  2 tablespoons unsalted butter
  2 garlic cloves, finely minced
  2 leeks, washed and sliced (use the white parts and some of the green portion)
  1 pound (16 ounces) spinach, cooked and chopped (may use frozen, drained of liquid)
  1 cup shredded cheddar cheese, divided
  4 large eggs
  ½ cup heavy cream
  ½ cup whole milk

1. Preheat oven to 350 degrees. In a large heavy-bottom frying pan or skillet over medium heat, add olive oil and butter. When butter has melted, add the garlic and sliced potatoes. Gently coat potatoes with oil and butter. Continue cooking for 8 minutes. Remove from pan and drain on paper towels. Set aside.

2. Place leeks in frying pan or skillet, add more olive oil as needed, and cook until tender. Remove from heat. Add spinach to frying pan or skillet and cook until wilted. If using frozen spinach, cook until additional moisture has evaporated. Remove from heat and spread out on paper towels to dry.

3. Spread ½ cup cheese over the bottom of prepared pie crust. Top with half of the potatoes, half of the leeks, and half of the spinach. Repeat the layers.

4. In a mixing bowl, add eggs, cream, and milk; whisk until eggs are lightly beaten and mixture is slightly foamy. Pour over the layered cooked vegetables. Place in oven and bake for 1 hour and 10 minutes, or until filling is firm and top is turning golden brown. Serve warm or at room temperature.

Serves 6–8.

❦ Parsnip with Blue Cheese Pie

Crust

1½ cups unbleached all-purpose flour
½ tablespoon white sugar
½ teaspoon kosher or sea salt, finely ground
¼ cup Crisco butter-flavored all-vegetable shortening, chilled
    and cut into small pieces
¼ cup unsalted butter, chilled and cut into small pieces
¼–½ cup cold water; use only as much as needed for a smooth,
    satiny dough ball

1. All ingredients should be cold. Combine all the dry ingredients in a large mixing bowl. Add shortening and butter. Using a pastry blender, cut in the shortening and butter until the mixture resembles coarse meal or peas.
2. Drop by drop, add the cold water. Mix in with the fingertips, not with the hands as the palms will warm the dough. Continue mixing in water until the dough begins to hold together without being crumbly yet not sticky.
3. Lightly spray a deep 9-inch pie pan or 8½-inch fluted flan pan with cooking spray. Roll out dough and place in pie plate, allowing the excess pastry to hang over the edge. Cut away extra dough, tuck under, and crimp. Prick the side and bottom of the pie crust with a fork and refrigerate for at least 30 minutes.
4. Preheat oven to 400 degrees. Remove chilled pie crust from refrigerator. Line the bottom and side of crust with parchment paper weighted down by baking beans or beads. Blind bake (see the "Crust" chapter) for 10 minutes. Remove parchment paper and beans or beads. Remove from oven, cool, and set aside until filling is ready.

Makes pastry for one 9-inch single-crust pie.

Filling

 2 tablespoons extra virgin olive oil
 1 medium yellow onion, chopped
 2 carrots, diced
 2 parsnips, diced
 2 teaspoons cumin seeds
 ¼ teaspoon sea salt
 2 tablespoons chopped coriander leaves/cilantro or
    1 tablespoon dried coriander leaves/cilantro
 ¾ cup Gorgonzola cheese, crumbled
 2 large eggs, beaten
 ⅔ cup heavy cream
 Freshly ground black pepper

1. Preheat oven to 350 degrees. In a large heavy-bottom skillet, heat oil. Add onion, carrots, and parsnips. Stir until the onion becomes translucent and soft, the carrots and parsnips crisp-tender. Stir in cumin seeds, coriander/cilantro, and salt. Remove from heat and cool.
2. Spread crumbled cheese over the bottom of prepared pie crust. Spoon the cooked vegetable mixture over the cheese.
3. In a mixing bowl whisk together eggs and cream. Pour over the vegetable mixture. Sprinkle filling with pepper. Bake for 45 minutes, or until the filling is firm and the top and turning a golden brown. Serve warm or at room temperature.

Serves 6–8.

A mother is a person who, seeing there are only four pieces of pie for five people, promptly announces she never did care for pie.

—TENNEVA JORDAN

Pie It Forward
and Celebrate National Pie Day
on January 23

Share pie. Whether you make a pie or buy one, share it. By its very nature, pie is meant to be eaten with others.

Pay it forward. Hand out pie slices to strangers and encourage them to do the same for others. It could spread the peace on earth and goodwill to mankind that we all hope for.

Be a good Samaritan. Buy an extra pie at your local grocery store and give it to the person behind you in line. You may just change their life!

Take care of Mom. Return the favor for all those pies Mom baked for you while you were growing up. Bake her favorite pie and surprise her with it.

Reach out to new neighbors you haven't met and bring them some pecan pie—it says you're thoughtful. Stay awhile to get to know each other over pie and fill them in on the neighborhood.

Indulge your co-workers. Bring some pie to work—you'll create a lot of good rapport and maybe even get a raise.

Surprise your significant other at work and bring him or her a pie to share with co-workers.

Say thank you. Know a special someone who deserves some thanks? Maybe it's a friend who did you a favor, your child's teacher, or your postal worker. What better way to say thanks than with a warm hug wrapped in a delicious crust?

Got a crush? Invite the "apple pie of your eye" for some pie and get to know each other better. But make it chocolate—most Americans believe it's the most romantic pie. Before long, you may be calling each other "sweetie pie."

Delight your family. Share the love and share your favorite memories together over a warm, fresh pie. Have older family members talk about the history behind the family favorites. Start a new tradition and publish pie memories and recipes, then send them to family members.

Spend time with your kids and make a pie together. Let them pick their favorite pie and show them how it's done. They'll be proud of their creation and have fond memories of you as the best parent ever for years to come!

Get caught up with friends and invite them over for some afternoon pumpkin pie. You can dish on all their latest news.

Throw a pie potluck get-together. Have everyone bring a favorite pie and exchange recipes. We've heard of events where more than a hundred folks come with a hundred pies. Have a contest to see who can come up with the most pie songs. The winning prize? A pie!

Deliver pies to a local homeless or women's shelter. Share the warmth and goodness of pie with someone who could use a treat.

Hold a pie-making contest. Invite the best pie makers in town to compete for prizes in various categories. Ask cooking teachers, pastry chefs, and pie lovers to be judges. Be sure the kids are involved—you can include pie poetry and pie art contests for them.

Go to piecouncil.org. It's a great resource—you can register for the American Pie Council (APC)/Crisco National Pie Championships being held every April in Orlando, Florida. You can also find the winning recipes from past championships, and you can sign up to become an APC member—they're the only national organization devoted to eating, making, selling, and enjoying pie!

Eat pie. Whether you make it yourself, buy it at a supermarket or bakery, or order it at a restaurant, "pie it forward" and enjoy some pie on National Pie Day—it's great with lunch or dinner, or as a late-night snack.

Holiday and Nut Pies

*T*HE TITLE "HOLIDAY AND NUT PIES" SAYS TO ME that guests are coming over. I've always set aside a select number of recipes that I consider "just right" for holidays. And I honestly don't know why a nut pie is considered a holiday pie. It's something completely ingrained in my head from birth. However, at holidays both my grandma and my mother would bring out fancy dishes with assorted nuts. Cheese balls and cheese logs contained nuts. Specialty breads had dried cranberries, raisins, and nuts. Confections such as divinity had nuts. So it stood to reason that the majority of our holiday pies contained nuts. Maybe it's a Norwegian thing. Being both half-Norwegian and half-Mexican, I know it's not a Mexican thing.

One of my fondest memories of preparing pumpkin for the coming holidays was picking pumpkins with Grandma in the garden, slicing them in half, and scooping out the stringy stuff and seeds. We would keep the seeds for roasting later. We would take the pumpkin halves into the kitchen and place them sliced side down on a baking sheet. We baked them until they were a beautiful brown. Once they cooled, Grandma and I would put the baked pumpkin meat in the KitchenAid mixer to produce a smooth pureed pumpkin filling. We would then freeze the puree in plastic bags to use during the holidays and for other recipes such as cookies and bars.

I also have to share a story about baking with pumpkin and a holiday contest offered by KNOX-AM radio during the 1960s. The contest was called "Don't Say Hello, Say Merry Christmas." Many times throughout each day a radio host would randomly pick a name and telephone number from the Grand Forks directory. The radio host would call the number and those who answered saying "Merry Christmas" instead of "hello" won $25.00, which was a lot of money then, especially during the holidays. Anyway, Grandma and I were baking pumpkin bars and cookies one afternoon following Thanksgiving. The telephone rang and she answered with "Merry Christmas." Grandma won the money and couldn't thank the radio host enough. She then spent the next hour calling all the relatives to tell them she had won.

Years later, Grandma received a beautiful blender for Christmas. We used it to process the pumpkin instead of her KitchenAid mixer. We roasted the pumpkin, peeled off the skins, and scooped the hot pumpkin meat into the blender. Grandma forgot to put the top on, however, and when she switched the blender on high, hot pumpkin flew all over the kitchen—on the ceiling, the cupboards, the countertops, and the floor. Grandma and I couldn't stop laughing. Not only was the kitchen a mess, but we were covered with pumpkin as well. It is still one of my favorite memories of spending an afternoon with Grandma.

Now among all these recipes for pies to serve during holidays, you will not find a single one for a sweet potato pie. I have several I could have included here, but I tasted a sweet potato pie a couple years ago and I haven't been the same since.

I was hosting one of our culinary vacations called Tuscan Gathering in the eastern edge of Tuscany near Cortona, Italy. We arrived back in the United States the day before Thanksgiving. There was no way I could unpack, clean house, and still make a Thanksgiving dinner for guests *and* bake pie, so I called in the troops. There are two women that I have met in the Twin Cities of Minnesota who make wonderful pie: Rose McGee and Cynthia Sutter. Rose McGee is an educator/writer/goddess with the voice and presence of Maya Angelou. She joined me in Celebration, Florida, in 2007 at the APC Crisco National Pie Championship. We had a wonderful time and she witnessed something really cool right before the awards ceremony. She witnessed a *gathering*. I know I'm digressing, but I have to tell this story.

We were sitting at the Market Street Café in Celebration, enjoying a class of wine, when former APC Crisco National Pie Championship Best of Show winner Phyllis Bartholomew and her sister Mary walked up. Of course, we beckoned them to sit with us. Moments later, we were joined by Hector, Grace, and Collin, three young people from New York City who were there to videotape the championship for Young United Professionals for Pie in New York. We had all became friends, and we titled them "the kids." We had a blast. Wine was flowing and the laughter was so loud we couldn't hear the traffic. Rose was observing the table of friends and she leaned over to me.

"I'm actually witnessing it happening," she said.

"What?" I asked.

"What you wrote about in your last book. Gathering—it's happening right here before me. This is what you wrote about."

I couldn't have been more touched. That was one of the most special things anyone has said to me because she saw it: gathering to laugh, to be happy, to socialize, and to enjoy. What could define a holiday more than that?

Okay, back to my original story. Rose McGee owns Deep Roots Desserts and has the most wonderful sweet potato pie. Her branding for her company and even the scarf she wears on her head replicate the color of a sweet potato. She is amazing.

We had just returned from Italy. I needed pies, so I called Cynthia Sutter, who owns Sugar Pie and produces the most incredible sugar pie I have ever tasted. She was out of pies and so were her distributors. A friend of mine was at the Global Market on Lake Street in Minneapolis, where Rose sells her pies. She had one sweet potato pie left, and my friend brought it home for me. I heard later that Rose had to go home that night and bake another. Bless her heart

I made dinner for Chad and our guests. I sliced the pie and we ate. I about died. It was the finest sweet potato pie I had ever tasted. Really! I ate another piece and another. I was floored. I make so many pies (approximately 200 a year, practicing for competitions, television, and for fund-raisers), I can't seem to find pies that live up to the standard of a good homemade pie. Well, Rose did it. So I have retired all my sweet potato pie recipes and tell everyone to simply purchase a pie from Rose. They don't get any better than hers.

Whatever the holiday I hope you enjoy these recipes as much as my family, friends, and guests have over the decades. And remember, don't say hello, say Merry Christmas.

🍯 Honey Surprise Pecan Pie

Winner, 2006 Minnesota State Fair Third Place "Honey Pastries"
Pecan Pie category in the Honey and Bee Division

Crust

> 1½ cups unbleached all-purpose flour
> ½ tablespoon white sugar
> ½ teaspoon kosher or sea salt, finely ground
> ¼ cup Crisco butter-flavored all-vegetable shortening, chilled
> and cut into small pieces
> ¼ cup unsalted butter, chilled and cut into small pieces
> ¼–½ cup cold water; use only as much as needed for a smooth,
> satiny dough ball
> Crisco butter-flavored cooking spray
> 1 egg yolk and 1 teaspoon water for egg wash

1. All ingredients should be cold. Combine all the dry ingredients in a large mixing bowl. Add shortening and butter. Using a pastry blender, cut in the shortening and butter until the mixture resembles coarse meal or peas.
2. Drop by drop, add the cold water. Mix in with the fingertips, not with the hands as the palms will warm the dough. Continue mixing in water until the dough begins to hold together without being crumbly yet not sticky.
3. Place dough in plastic wrap. Fold over plastic wrap and press down to form a disk. This will make rolling out easier after chilling. Finish wrapping in plastic and place in the refrigerator for at least 30 minutes.
4. Lightly spray a deep 9-inch pie pan or 8½-inch fluted flan pan with cooking spray. Roll out dough and place in pie plate, allowing the excess pastry to hang over the edge. Cut away extra, tuck under, and crimp decoratively. Brush with egg wash and return to the refrigerator until filling is ready.

Makes pastry for one 9-inch single-crust pie.

Filling

1½ cups pecans, chopped

6 ounces semisweet chocolate chips or swirl chips (dark and
white chocolate)

3 large eggs

1 cup honey, any variety

½ teaspoon pure vanilla extract or paste

¼ cup unsalted butter, melted and cooled to room temperature

1. Preheat oven to 325 degrees. Distribute pecans and chocolate chips
over the bottom of prepared and chilled pie crust. In a medium mixing bowl, whisk eggs until well beaten. Add honey and vanilla. Whisk
to blend well. Add butter, whisk, and gently pour mixture into pie
crust. Cover pie crust edges with a pie shield to prevent excessive
browning or burning.
2. Bake for 50–60 minutes or until center is firm. Remove pie shield for
the final 10 minutes of baking. Cool on a rack. Garnish with Honey-
Sweetened Whipped Cream (see recipe in the "Decorating Your Pie"
chapter).

Serves 8–10.

Wet Bottom Shoofly Pie

Crust

1½ cups unbleached all-purpose flour

½ tablespoon white sugar

½ teaspoon kosher or sea salt, finely ground

¼ cup Crisco butter-flavored all-vegetable shortening, chilled
and cut into small pieces

¼ cup unsalted butter, chilled and cut into small pieces

¼–½ cup cold water; use only as much as needed for a smooth,
satiny dough ball

Crisco butter-flavored cooking spray
1 egg yolk and 1 teaspoon water for egg wash

1. All ingredients should be cold. Combine all the dry ingredients in a large mixing bowl. Add shortening and butter. Using a pastry blender, cut in the shortening and butter until the mixture resembles coarse meal or peas.
2. Drop by drop, add the cold water. Mix in with the fingertips, not with the hands as the palms will warm the dough. Continue mixing in water until the dough begins to hold together without being crumbly yet not sticky.
3. Place dough in plastic wrap. Fold over plastic wrap and press down to form a disk. This will make rolling out easier after chilling. Finish wrapping in plastic and place in the refrigerator for at least 30 minutes.
4. Lightly spray a deep 9-inch pie pan or 8½-inch fluted flan pan with cooking spray. Roll out dough and place in pie plate, allowing the excess pastry to hang over the edge. Cut away extra, tuck under, and crimp decoratively. Brush with egg wash and return to the refrigerator until filling is ready.

Makes pastry for one 9-inch single-crust pie.

Filling

3 tablespoons unsalted butter
1½ cups unbleached all-purpose flour
⅔ cup dark brown sugar, packed
¼ teaspoon fine sea salt
1 teaspoon baking soda
1 cup hot water
1 cup dark molasses
1 large egg

1. Preheat oven to 400 degrees. In a medium mixing bowl, combine butter, flour, brown sugar, and salt. Using a pastry blender, cut in

and crumble the mixture until it resembles coarse meal or peas. Set aside.

2. In a large mixing bowl, add baking soda and hot water. Whisk until soda dissolves. Add molasses and egg. Whisk vigorously until well blended. Pour molasses mixture into prepared pie crust.

3. Sprinkle crumb mixture evenly over pie filling. Some crumbs will sink and some will float. That's okay. Cover pie crust edges with a pie shield to prevent excessive browning or burning. Bake 10 minutes. Reduce oven temperature to 350 degrees and bake an additional 35–40 minutes or until a knife inserted in the center comes out clean. Remove pie shield for the final 10 minutes of baking. Cool on a rack to room temperature before serving.

Serves 8–10.

⸔ Pecan Dream Pie

This is my typical Thanksgiving pie that I serve to guests each year. This wonderful recipe has been in the family for generations, and it's irresistible.

Crust

> 1½ cups unbleached all-purpose flour
> ½ tablespoon white sugar
> ½ teaspoon kosher or sea salt, finely ground
> ¼ cup Crisco butter-flavored all-vegetable shortening, chilled
>   and cut into small pieces
> ¼ cup unsalted butter, chilled and cut into small pieces
> ¼–½ cup cold water; use only as much as needed for a smooth,
>   satiny dough ball
> Crisco butter-flavored cooking spray
> 1 egg yolk and 1 teaspoon water for egg wash

1. All ingredients should be cold. Combine all the dry ingredients in a large mixing bowl. Add shortening and butter. Using a pastry blender, cut in the shortening and butter until the mixture resembles coarse meal or peas.

2. Drop by drop, add the cold water. Mix in with the fingertips, not with the hands as the palms will warm the dough. Continue mixing in water until the dough begins to hold together without being crumbly yet not sticky.

3. Place dough in plastic wrap. Fold over plastic wrap and press down to form a disk. This will make rolling out easier after chilling. Finish wrapping in plastic and place in the refrigerator for at least 30 minutes.

4. Lightly spray a 9-inch pie plate with cooking spray. Roll out dough and place in pie plate, allowing the excess pastry to hang over the edge. Trim extra, tuck under, and crimp decoratively. Brush side and bottom with egg wash. Return to the refrigerator until filling is ready.

Makes pastry for one 9-inch single-crust pie.

Filling

4 large eggs, well beaten
¾ cup white sugar
⅓ cup pure maple syrup
½ cup light corn syrup
½ cup dark corn syrup
2½ teaspoons pure vanilla extract or paste
¼ teaspoon sea salt
1 cup pecans, broken
⅓ cup melted unsalted butter
Pecan halves to decorate pie
2 tablespoons maple syrup to glaze pie

1. Preheat oven to 375 degrees. In a medium mixing bowl, combine eggs, sugar, maple syrup, both corn syrups, vanilla, and salt; stir until well blended. Stir in pecans and melted butter.

2. Brush pastry with egg wash and pour filling into pastry-lined pie plate. Place pecan halves decoratively on top of filling. Protect edge of pie with a pie shield to prevent excessive browning. Carefully transfer to oven.

3. Bake 20 minutes. Reduce oven temperature to 350 and bake 30–40 minutes or until center is set. Remove pie shield for the final 10 minutes of baking. Brush hot pie with maple syrup after removing from oven for a bronze glaze. Cool and store in refrigerator.

Serves 8–10.

Pears and Pecans in Chocolate Pie

Oh, what a lovely treat is this pie. I have prepared it two different ways. One is baked in a regular pie plate and served at the table with a choice of Sweetened Whipped Cream or Honey-Sweetened Whipped Cream. Another is to bake it in a flan pan with a removable bottom. Once the pie has cooled, I remove the pie from the pan and set it on a decorative cake plate or cake stand. One of my hobbies is collecting antique cake plates and stands. Of course, the holidays are the time to shine and bring out all your favorite serving pieces to share with your guests.

Crust

1½ cups unbleached all-purpose flour
½ tablespoon white sugar
½ teaspoon kosher or sea salt, finely ground
¼ cup Crisco butter-flavored all-vegetable shortening, chilled
     and cut into small pieces
¼ cup unsalted butter, chilled and cut into small pieces
¼–½ cup cold water; use only as much as needed for a smooth,
     satiny dough ball
Crisco butter-flavored cooking spray

1. All ingredients should be cold. Combine all the dry ingredients in a large mixing bowl. Add shortening and butter. Using a pastry blender, cut in the shortening and butter until the mixture resembles coarse meal or peas.
2. Drop by drop, add the cold water. Mix in with the fingertips, not with the hands as the palms will warm the dough. Continue mixing in water until the dough begins to hold together without being crumbly yet not sticky.
3. Place dough in plastic wrap. Fold over plastic wrap and press down to form a disk. This will make rolling out easier after chilling. Finish wrapping in plastic and place in the refrigerator for at least 30 minutes.
4. Lightly spray a deep 9-inch pie pan or 8½-inch fluted flan pan with cooking spray. Roll out dough and place in pie plate, allowing the excess pastry to hang over the edge. Cut away extra, tuck under, and crimp decoratively. Chill in the refrigerator for at least 30 minutes.
5. Preheat the oven to 400 degrees. Line the pastry shell with parchment and baking beans or beads (see instructions for Blind Baking in the "Crust" chapter). Bake the shell for 10 minutes. Remove the paper and beans or beads and return to the oven for 10 more minutes or until golden. Cool.

Makes pastry for one 9-inch single-crust pie.

Filling

3 pears (not fully ripe), peeled, cored, and cut in half
¾ cup white sugar, divided
⅔ cup water
Zest of 1 lemon
2 ounces semisweet chocolate
4 tablespoons unsalted butter, diced
¾ cup light corn syrup
3 large eggs, slightly beaten
1 teaspoon pure vanilla extract or paste
1¼ cup pecans, coarsely chopped
2 tablespoons good-quality pure maple syrup

1. Preheat oven to 400 degrees. In a heavy-bottom saucepan, add ¼ cup sugar, water, and lemon zest. Over medium-high heat, bring to a boil. Add sliced pears. Cover and lower heat to simmer. Continue cooking for 10 minutes. Remove pan from heat and take out the pears with a slotted spoon. Let pears cool. Discard the cooking liquid.

2. In a heat-proof bowl over simmering water, melt chocolate. Add butter and whisk until well blended. Remove from heat and set aside.

3. In another heavy-bottom saucepan over low heat, add remaining sugar and corn syrup. Cook, stirring occasionally, until the sugar has dissolved. Increase heat to medium high and bring mixture to a boil. Lower heat to a simmer and continue cooking for 2 more minutes. Remove from heat.

4. Add the beaten eggs to the melted chocolate. Whisk together until well blended. Add vanilla and pecans.

5. Place pears flat side down on cutting board. Using a shape knife, cut lengthwise along each pear 3 to 4 times; do not cut all the way through. Carefully lift the pear half and place on bottom of prepared pie crust. You will have six pears halves, so place decoratively along the outer edge of the pie crust. Fan out pear halves as much as possible without splitting or breaking.

6. Gently pour the pecan-chocolate mixture into the pie crust. Pears should be visible through the mixture.

7. Bake for 25–30 minutes or until the center of the filling is set. Remove from oven and place on a rack. Using a pastry brush, immediately brush maple syrup on pie crust edges and top of filling for a bronze glaze. Let cool to room temperature before serving. Garnish with Sweetened or Honey-Sweetened Whipped Cream (see both recipes in the "Decorating Your Pie" chapter).

Serves 8–10.

I have nibbled at Utterly Deadly Southern Pecan Pie, and have served it to those on whose welfare I took no interest.

—MARJORIE KINNAN RAWLINGS, *CROSS CREEK COOKERY*

⨏ Pumpkin Pecan Pie

This recipe combines two of my favorite holiday flavors: pumpkin and pecans. Top it with my Sweetened Whipped Cream or Honey-Sweetened Whipped Cream and you'll be in heaven. The fragrance in your home while this pie is baking is phenomenal. Grandma found this recipe in a 1960s *Farm Journal.* Grandpa subscribed to the magazine for decades. Grandma got so many wonderful recipes that other farm wives shared through the *Farm Journal.* As with all things, I've updated the recipe a bit by specifying some definitive spices and changing the crust recipe, but that doesn't mean you can't use what you have in your pantry. These are only suggestions. Whatever the case, I just want you to try this recipe and delight your family and guests.

Crust

> 1½ cups unbleached all-purpose flour
> ½ tablespoon white sugar
> ½ teaspoon kosher or sea salt, finely ground
> ¼ cup Crisco butter-flavored all-vegetable shortening, chilled
>   and cut into small pieces
> ¼ cup unsalted butter, chilled and cut into small pieces
> ¼–½ cup cold water; use only as much as needed for a smooth,
>   satiny dough ball
> Crisco butter-flavored cooking spray
> 1 egg yolk and 1 teaspoon water for egg wash

1. All ingredients should be cold. Combine all the dry ingredients in a large mixing bowl. Add shortening and butter. Using a pastry blender, cut in the shortening and butter until the mixture resembles coarse meal or peas.
2. Drop by drop, add the cold water. Mix in with the fingertips, not with the hands as the palms will warm the dough. Continue mixing in water until the dough begins to hold together without being crumbly yet not sticky.

3. Place dough in plastic wrap. Fold over plastic wrap and press down to form a disk. This will make rolling out easier after chilling. Finish wrapping in plastic and place in the refrigerator for at least 30 minutes.

4. Lightly spray a deep 9-inch pie pan or 8½-inch fluted flan pan with cooking spray. Roll out dough and place in pie plate, allowing the excess pastry to hang over the edge. Cut away extra, tuck under, and crimp decoratively. Brush with egg wash and return to the refrigerator until filling is ready.

Makes pastry for one 9-inch single-crust pie.

Filling

2 large eggs, beaten until foamy
2 cups fresh pumpkin puree or 1 (16-ounce) can of solid-pack pumpkin
¾ cup white sugar
½ teaspoon fine sea salt
1 teaspoon cinnamon, preferably China cassia
¼ teaspoon ground ginger, preferably China powdered
¼ teaspoon ground cloves
2 tablespoons good-quality pure maple syrup
1 (12-ounce) can evaporated milk
½ cup unbleached all-purpose flour
½ cup pecans, coarsely chopped
¼ cup dark brown sugar, packed
3 tablespoons unsalted butter, room temperature

1. Preheat oven to 375 degrees. In a large mixing bowl, combine eggs, pumpkin, sugar, salt, cinnamon, ginger, cloves, syrup, and milk. Whisk until well blended. Gently pour into prepared pie crust. Cover pie crust edges with a pie shield to prevent excessive browning or burning.

2. Bake for 30 minutes. Meanwhile, in a small mixing bowl, combine flour, pecans, brown sugar, and butter. Mix well with a fork. Remove pie from oven and carefully sprinkle topping over the pie. Return

to oven and bake an additional 20–25 minutes or until a knife inserted in the center comes out clean. Remove pie shield for the last 10 minutes of baking. Cool on a rack to room temperature before serving. Garnish with Sweetened Whipped Cream (see recipe in the "Decorating Your Pie" chapter).

Serves 8–10.

✟ Wolf Pack Trail Mix Pie

Winner, 2008 APC Crisco American Pie Championship, Honorable Mention Professional Division in the Nut Category

There is a wonderful and sad story behind this pie. My good friend Lee Valsvik, who appears on Minneapolis television *KARE 11 Saturday Morning Show* and cohosts Cities 97's *BT* (Brian Turner) *and Lee in the Morning* show on radio, has a sister named Mary Wolf. Mary was diagnosed with breast cancer in 2007. She has had an incredible fight, and Lee and many others have been there to help her along the way. In early spring of 2008, Lee told me that she, her sister, and many others had formed a team named "The Wolf Pack" to walk in the 60-mile Breast Cancer 3-Day Walk. Their team goal was to raise $26,400.00. Lee asked if there was anything I could do to help. So, I created a pie using their name with the idea of walking in mind. I used the basic structure of a pecan pie, filled it with trail mix (for the walking), and topped it with whipped cream (sugar high). The pie was wonderful. The first couple of experiments were okay, though nothing to write home about. Then I added real coconut cream to the filling—not milk. That did it! It was perfect.

During a fund-raiser in Stillwater, Minnesota, we auctioned off two Wolf Pack Trail Mix Pies, including the Emile Henry "Pink" Ceramic Pie Dish. The Emile Henry Company donates 10 percent of the retail price from the sale of their "pink" pie dish to fight breast cancer. I've used Emile Henry pie dishes exclusively, and this was a perfect combination: a pie and a pie dish that both worked for something good.

Crust

> 1½ cups unbleached all-purpose flour
> ½ tablespoon white sugar
> ½ teaspoon kosher or sea salt, finely ground
> ¼ cup Crisco butter-flavored all-vegetable shortening, chilled
>   and cut into small pieces
> ¼ cup unsalted butter, chilled and cut into small pieces
> ¼–½ cup cold water; use only as much as needed for a smooth,
>   satiny dough ball
> Crisco butter-flavored cooking spray
> 1 egg yolk and 1 teaspoon water for egg wash

1. All ingredients should be cold. Combine all the dry ingredients in a large mixing bowl. Add shortening and butter. Using a pastry blender, cut in the shortening and butter until the mixture resembles coarse meal or peas.
2. Drop by drop, add the cold water. Mix in with the fingertips, not with the hands as the palms will warm the dough. Continue mixing in water until the dough begins to hold together without being crumbly yet not sticky.
3. Place dough in plastic wrap. Fold over plastic wrap and press down to form a disk. This will make rolling out easier after chilling. Finish wrapping in plastic and place in the refrigerator for at least 30 minutes.
4. Lightly spray a deep 9-inch pie pan or 8½-inch fluted flan pan. Roll out dough and place in pie plate, allowing the excess pastry to hang over the edge. Cut away excess dough, tuck under, and crimp decoratively. Brush with egg wash. Chill in the refrigerator while preparing filling.

Makes pastry for one 9-inch single-crust pie.

Filling

> 3 large eggs
> ½ cup dark brown sugar, firmly packed
> 1 cup cream of coconut

2 tablespoons unsalted butter, melted

¼ cup heavy whipping cream

1½ teaspoons pure vanilla extract or paste

1 teaspoon freshly squeezed lemon juice

1½ cups homemade or store-bought trail mix (cashews, pecans, dried cranberries, dried blueberries, etc.—do not use peanuts as many people are allergic, plus peanuts change the taste of this pie in a negative way)

1. Preheat oven to 350 degrees. In a medium mixing bowl, whisk eggs and brown sugar together until smooth. Add cream of coconut, butter, cream, vanilla, and lemon juice. Stir in trail mix. Carefully spoon or pour mixture into prepared pie crust. Using a fork or spatula, redistribute the nuts evenly throughout the filling before baking. Cover pie crust edges with a pie shield to prevent excessive browning or burning.
2. Bake for 20 minutes and turn pie 180 degrees. Continue to bake an additional 20 minutes or until the filling has puffed slightly around the edges and the center is set. The filling should wiggle but not seem liquid or wavy. Remove pie shield for the final 10 minutes of baking.
3. Let pie cool on a wire rack. Refrigerate at least 4 hours before serving. Add topping.

Topping

1 cup heavy whipping cream

3 tablespoons confectioner's sugar

1 teaspoon pure vanilla bean paste or extract

½ cups homemade or store-bought (no peanuts) trail mix for garnish

Whisk or beat heavy cream until it begins to thicken. Gradually add confectioner's sugar and vanilla. Continue beating until stiff peaks form. Pipe or spoon whipped topping over top of pie. Sprinkle with trail mix.

Serves 8–10.

⸙ Honey Pumpkin Pie

This is another one of my recipes using honey as a sweetener rather than sugar in the filling. I just wish I could come up with something to replace sugar in the pie crust, but any type of liquid simply makes it soggy. I really enjoy the change of taste from sugar to honey. Also, try different types of honey—sunflower honey, wildflower honey, and so on. A wonderful place to see all the varieties of honey is the Honey and Bee exhibits in the Agriculture-Horticulture Building at the Minnesota State Fair. My partner, Chad, has won many awards for his photographs of bees. As a matter of fact, Chad took home First Place and Sweepstakes Ribbons in 2005 from the Honey and Bee Association at the Minnesota State Fair for his extraordinary photographs of honeybees. I was with him when he took the photos at a farm in Wisconsin and got a bee stuck in my hair. I got stung on the top of my head. One must suffer for someone else's art.

Crust

1½ cups unbleached all-purpose flour
½ tablespoon dark brown or white sugar
½ teaspoon kosher or sea salt, finely ground
¼ cup butter-flavored all-vegetable shortening, chilled and
    cut into small pieces
¼ cup unsalted butter, chilled and cut into small pieces
¼–½ cup cold water; use only as much as needed for a smooth,
    satiny dough ball
Butter-flavored cooking spray
1 egg yolk and 1 teaspoon water for egg wash

1. All ingredients should be cold. Combine all the dry ingredients in a large mixing bowl. Add shortening and butter. Using a pastry blender, cut in the shortening and butter until the mixture resembles coarse meal or peas.

2. Drop by drop, add the cold water. Mix in with the fingertips, not with the hands as the palms will warm the dough. Continue mixing in water until the dough begins to hold together without being crumbly yet not sticky.

3. Place dough in plastic wrap. Fold over plastic wrap and press down to form a disk. This will make rolling out easier after chilling. Finish wrapping in plastic and place in the refrigerator for at least 30 minutes.

4. Lightly spray a deep 9-inch pie pan with cooking spray. Roll out dough and place in pie plate, allowing the excess pastry to hang over the edge. Cut away extra, tuck under, and crimp decoratively. Lightly brush sides and bottom of crust with egg wash. Chill in refrigerator for 30 minutes before filling and baking.

Filling

2 cups fresh pureed pumpkin or 1 (16-ounce) can of
    solid-pack pumpkin
1 cup evaporated milk
¾ cup honey, any variety
3 large eggs, slightly beaten
2 tablespoons unbleached all-purpose flour
1 teaspoon ground cinnamon, preferably China cassia
½ teaspoon ground ginger
½ teaspoon rum or rum extract

1. Preheat oven to 400 degrees. Combine all ingredients in a mixing bowl. Beat until well blended.

2. Pour into prepared pie crust. Cover pie crust edges with a pie shield to prevent excessive browning or burning. Bake for 45 minutes or until knife inserted near center comes out clean. Remove pie shield for the final 10 minutes of baking. Cool on a rack. Chill at least 4 hours or overnight before serving. Garnish with Honey-Sweetened Whipped Cream (see recipe in the "Decorating Your Pie" chapter).

Serves 8–10.

ʃ Praline Pecan Pumpkin Pie

I remember the morning I baked this pie for the 2007 APC Crisco National Pie Championship in Celebration, Florida, a southern suburb of Orlando. Chad and I had rented a condo for one week. I planned this contest like an athlete—I was in training to bake the best six pies of my life. Each morning we would walk about four miles along a beautiful paved path, have a breakfast of oatmeal, and then I would begin my day baking for the championship. One morning Chad and I took off on our morning walk; I had brought along a large stick because of all the reports of alligators leaving their ditches, ponds, and other usual habitat. The drought conditions in central Florida were taking their toll on the reptiles. We were walking in the sun, and it was hot for April—about 85. We were almost to the 2.5-mile mark when I noticed something on the sidewalk. I let out a scream (probably shattering the windows of nearby retail stores) and tried to crawl my way to the top of Chad's bald head. There in front of us was a snake. I have to tell you that I have the most horrible phobia of snakes. An alligator I could have handled, but this was my limit.

Chad actually got angry with me because I frightened him with my behavior. I turned around and tried to make a mad dash in the opposite direction, but my legs felt like I was stuck in thick mud. Then I couldn't breathe and everything was becoming dark. I was starting to faint. Chad grabbed hold of my arm and said loudly, "This isn't the time to pass out with snakes on the sidewalk." That did it! I was up in a second and walking the fastest I have ever walked in my life.

Of course, to this day Chad teases me about the size of the snake. He tells all our friends and anyone who will listen that it was a little garden snake. As I recall, it was large, coiling madly, and spitting venom. We will never agree.

Crust

> 1½ cups unbleached all-purpose flour
> ½ tablespoon white sugar
> ½ teaspoon kosher or sea salt, finely ground
> ¼ cup all-vegetable shortening, chilled and cut into small pieces
> ¼ cup unsalted butter, chilled and cut into small pieces
> ¼–½ cup cold water; use only as much as needed for a smooth, satiny dough ball
> ½ cup pecan pralines, finely chopped
> Butter-flavored cooking spray
> 1 egg yolk and 1 teaspoon water for egg wash

1. All ingredients should be cold. Combine all the dry ingredients in a large mixing bowl. Add shortening and butter. Using a pastry blender, cut in the shortening and butter until the mixture resembles coarse meal or peas.
2. Drop by drop, add the cold water. Mix in with the fingertips, not with the hands as the palms will warm the dough. Continue mixing in water until the dough begins to hold together without being crumbly yet not sticky.
3. Lightly spray a 9-inch pie pan with cooking spray. Roll out dough and place in pie plate, allowing the excess pastry to hang over the edge. Trim extra, tuck under, and crimp decoratively. Sprinkle pralines around crust and gently press into dough with fingertips. Prick bottom and sides with a fork. Chill for 1 hour before baking.
4. Preheat oven to 400 degrees. Line the pastry shell with parchment and baking beans or beads. Bake the shell for 10 minutes. Remove the paper and beans or beads and return to the oven for 10 more minutes. Cool.

Makes pastry for one 9-inch single-crust pie.

Filling

> 3 large eggs, slightly beaten
> 2 cups freshly pureed pumpkin or 1 (16-ounce) can
>   solid-pack pumpkin
> 1 cup dark brown sugar, firmly packed, divided
> 1½ cups half-and-half
> ¼ cup and 3 tablespoons bourbon, divided
> 1 teaspoon cinnamon
> ½ teaspoon ginger
> ¼ teaspoon salt
> 2 tablespoons unsalted butter
> 1 cup pecan praline halves

1. Preheat oven to 425 degrees. Combine eggs, pumpkin, ¾ cup brown sugar, half-and-half, 3 tablespoons bourbon, cinnamon, ginger, and salt. Whisk ingredients well.
2. Pour mixture into pie shell. Cover pie crust edges with a pie shield to prevent excessive browning or burning. Bake for 10 minutes. Reduce heat to 350 degrees and bake an additional 45 minutes or until set. Set aside to cool.
3. Combine butter and ¼ cup brown sugar in a saucepan, cook over medium heat, stirring until sugar dissolves. Add pecan pralines and 2 tablespoons bourbon, stirring to coat. Spoon mixture over the pie.
4. **Optional garnish:** Heat the remaining bourbon in a saucepan just long enough to produce fumes (do not boil), remove from heat, ignite, and pour over pie. Serve pie when flames die down.

Serves 8-10.

Pumpkin pie! There's a chemical released when you eat pumpkin pie that produces the hysterical adrenaline necessary for decision-making in gift-buying. People think it's the DEADLINE that makes them start buying after Thanksgiving, but it's not! It's the pie enzyme.

—CATHY GUISEWHITE

⨍ John Michael's Basic Pumpkin Pie

Some people have told me, "I don't need a pumpkin pie recipe with all the bells and whistles." Well, here is that recipe—simple and easy. Try my pie crust recipe, but if that intimidates you, using a store-brought or ready-made crust is not a sin. I just want my readers to make, eat, and enjoy pie.

Crust

1½ cups unbleached all-purpose flour
½ tablespoon white sugar
½ teaspoon kosher or sea salt, finely ground
¼ cup Crisco butter-flavored all-vegetable shortening, chilled
    and cut into small pieces
¼ cup unsalted butter, chilled and cut into small pieces
¼–½ cup cold water; use only as much as needed for a smooth,
    satiny dough ball
Crisco butter-flavored cooking spray
1 egg yolk and 1 teaspoon water for egg wash

1. All ingredients should be cold. Combine all the dry ingredients in a large mixing bowl. Add shortening and butter. Using a pastry blender, cut in the shortening and butter until the mixture resembles coarse meal or peas.
2. Drop by drop, add the cold water. Mix in with the fingertips, not with the hands as the palms will warm the dough. Continue mixing in water until the dough begins to hold together without being crumbly yet not sticky.
3. Place dough in plastic wrap. Fold over plastic wrap and press down to form a disk. This will make rolling out easier after chilling. Finish wrapping in plastic and place in the refrigerator for at least 30 minutes.
4. Lightly spray a deep 9-inch pie pan or 8½-inch fluted flan pan. Roll out dough and place in pie plate, allowing the excess pastry to hang over the edge. Remove extra, tuck under, and crimp decoratively. Brush with egg wash. Chill in the refrigerator while preparing filling.

Makes pastry for one 9-inch single-crust pie.

Filling

2 cups fresh pumpkin puree or 1 (16-ounce) can
   solid-pack pumpkin
1 cup sour cream
½ cup heavy whipping cream
½ cup dark brown sugar, firmly packed
2 large eggs
1 teaspoon cinnamon
1 teaspoon ground ginger
¼ teaspoon freshly grated nutmeg
¼ teaspoon ground cloves
¼ teaspoon fine sea salt
½ cup white sugar

1. Preheat oven to 400 degrees. In a large mixing bowl, whisk pumpkin, sour cream, whipping cream, brown sugar, eggs, cinnamon, ginger, nutmeg, cloves, salt, and white sugar. Blend well.
2. Gently pour into prepared pie crust. Cover pie crust edges with a pie shield to prevent excessive browning or burning. Bake for 50–60 minutes or until the center is almost set and not jiggly. Remove pie shield for the final 10 minutes of baking. Cool on a rack until room temperature.
3. Decorate with pumpkin cutouts or other holiday cutouts (see instructions in the "Decorating Your Pie" chapter introduction). Garnish with Sweetened Whipped Cream (see recipe in the "Decorating Your Pie" chapter).

Serves 8–10.

Vidalia Onion and Mushroom Pie

You thought my Vidalia Onion Pie was wonderful. In this newest update to my classic "claim to fame" pie, I've added mushrooms. Try a variety of mushrooms from white button to dried porcini—the "shroomier," the better. Any day you make this pie for your guests and family is a holiday.

Crust

1½ cups unbleached all-purpose flour
½ tablespoon white sugar
½ teaspoon kosher or sea salt, finely ground
¼ cup Crisco butter-flavored all-vegetable shortening, chilled
    and cut into small pieces
¼ cup unsalted butter, chilled and cut into small pieces
¼–½ cup cold water; use only as much as needed for a smooth,
    satiny dough ball
Crisco butter-flavored cooking spray
1 egg yolk and 1 teaspoon water for egg wash

1. All ingredients should be cold. Combine all the dry ingredients in a large mixing bowl. Add shortening and butter. Using a pastry blender, cut in the shortening and butter until the mixture resembles coarse meal or peas.
2. Drop by drop, add the cold water. Mix in with the fingertips, not with the hands as the palms will warm the dough. Continue mixing in water until the dough begins to hold together without being crumbly yet not sticky.
3. Place dough in plastic wrap. Fold over plastic wrap and press down to form a disk. This will make rolling out easier after chilling. Finish wrapping in plastic and place in the refrigerator for at least 10 minutes.
4. Lightly spray a deep 9-inch pie pan or 8½-inch fluted flan pan. Roll out dough and place in pie plate, allowing the excess pastry to hang over the edge. Remove extra, tuck under, and crimp decoratively. Brush with egg wash. Chill in the refrigerator while preparing filling.

Makes pastry for one 9-inch single-crust pie.

Filling

4 tablespoons unsalted butter
1 tablespoon extra virgin olive oil
2 medium (1 pound) Vidalia onions, sliced in half and thinly sliced
8 ounces (about 3 cups) mushrooms, any variety, sliced

2 garlic cloves, minced

4 large eggs

1 cup heavy whipping cream

¼ cup freshly grated Parmesan cheese, plus some for sprinkling
   on top of pie

1 tablespoon fresh thyme, chopped

1½ teaspoons sea salt

½ teaspoon freshly ground black pepper

⅛ teaspoon freshly grated nutmeg

1. Preheat oven to 350 degrees. In a large heavy-bottom skillet over medium heat, melt butter and heat the olive oil. Add onions and mushrooms. The onions will come apart during cooking. Sauté for about 8–10 minutes or until onions become translucent and somewhat milky and mushrooms release their juices. Add garlic last 3 minutes of cooking. Remove from heat and set aside.

2. In a large mixing bowl, whisk eggs until foamy. Blend in the whipping cream, cheese, thyme, salt, pepper, and nutmeg. Spoon onion mixture into mixing bowl and stir to blend well. Gently pour filling into prepared pie crust. Sprinkle with additional Parmesan cheese. Cover pie crust edges with a pie shield to prevent excessive browning or burning. Remove pie shield for the final 10 minutes of baking. Bake for 45–55 minutes or until center is set. Cool on a rack until room temperature. Serve with dollop of sour cream and chives.

Serves 8–10.

⸙ My Grandma's Mincemeat Pie

I have always loved mincemeat pies. Grandma and I used to can mincemeat in quart jars and store it in the basement. I haven't canned mincemeat for years. If you do can your own mincemeat, prepare my pie crust and use 1 quart of mincemeat. Follow the instructions for applying a top crust and baking. That's it. You'll have a wonderful holiday pie.

Traditionally more people associate mincemeat pie with Thanksgiving, but I've served it on both winter holidays.

If you're not familiar with suet, it is the solid white fat from around the kidneys; the connective tissue, blood, and other nonfat items are removed by a butcher. They coarsely grind the fat and make it ready for use. It must be kept refrigerated and used within a few days of purchase like any meat product. Ask your butcher for suet as it is not usually offered in the refrigerated section. You can also check with your meat dealers at local farmers' markets. Do not use the suet sold in stores for feeding birds.

This recipe makes a good deal of filling. If you're using 9-inch frozen pie crusts or ready-made pie crusts, this recipe will make two pies. If using 9-inch or 10-inch deep dish pie crusts, this will make one full pie.

Crust

    3 cups unbleached all-purpose flour
    1 tablespoon dark brown sugar
    1 teaspoon kosher or sea salt, finely ground
    ½ cup butter-flavored all-vegetable shortening, chilled and
        cut into small pieces
    ½ cup unsalted butter, chilled and cut into small pieces
    ½–¾ cup cold water; use only as much as needed for a smooth,
        satiny dough ball
    Butter-flavored cooking spray
    1 egg yolk and 1 teaspoon water for egg wash

1. Combine all the dry ingredients in a large mixing bowl. Add shortening and butter. Using a pastry blender, cut in the shortening and butter until the mixture resembles coarse meal or peas.
2. Drop by drop, add the cold water. Mix in with the fingertips, not with the hands as the palms will warm the dough. Continue mixing in water until the dough begins to hold together without being crumbly yet not sticky.
3. Divide dough into two pieces and place one piece of dough in plastic wrap. Fold over plastic wrap and press down to form a disk. This will

make rolling out easier after chilling. Finish wrapping in plastic and place in the refrigerator for at least 30 minutes.

4. Lightly spray a deep 9-inch pie pan with cooking spray. Roll out one dough disk and place in pie plate, allowing the excess pastry to hang over the edge. Cut away excess dough, and lightly brush sides and bottom of crust with egg wash. Chill in refrigerator until filling is ready. When filling is ready, roll out top crust. Brush pie crust edge with egg wash to create a "cement" bond between bottom and top crust. Fill pie crust and carefully place top crust over filled pie. Cut away excess dough, tuck under, and crimp decoratively. Vent top crust to release steam.

Makes pastry for one 9-inch double-crust pie.

Filling

1¼ pounds beef round or leftover roast
¼ pound suet
1½ pounds (about 3 cups) apples (Cortland, Granny Smith, or other cooking apples), peeled, cored, and chopped
1 cup raisins
½ cup white sugar
½ cup brown sugar, firmly packed
⅛ teaspoon freshly ground black pepper
½ teaspoon fine sea salt
2 teaspoons cinnamon, preferably China cassia
1 teaspoon ground cloves
2 teaspoons freshly grated nutmeg
¼ cup good-quality brandy
2 cups good-quality apple cider

1. If meat is uncooked, simmer for 2–3 hours or until extremely tender. Add suet during the last 30 minutes of cooking. When cooking is complete, or if using cooked meat, chop beef and suet very fine or pulse in a food processor until ¼-inch pieces are produced.

2. Add apples to food processor bowl and pulse until meat, suet, and apples are well chopped. If not using a food processor, mix meat, suet,

and chopped apples on a cutting board. Rocking knife back and forth, finely chop and blend together.

3. In a large mixing bowl, add beef, suet, apples, raisins, white sugar, brown sugar, pepper, salt, cinnamon, cloves, nutmeg, brandy, and apple cider. Stir well to blend. Let sit 30 minutes tightly covered for flavors to mix.

4. Preheat oven to 425 degrees. Gently pour meat filling into prepared pie crust. Cover with top crust per instructions. Cover pie edges with pie shield to prevent excessive browning or burning. Remove pie shield for the final 10 minutes of baking.

5. Bake for 45–55 minutes or until steam is rising from open slits in crust and crust is turning a golden brown. Cool on a rack until room temperature.

Serves 8–10.

Buttermilk Pie

This is one of my choice pies during any holiday. And, everyday is a holiday in my world. I usually associate Buttermilk Pie with Crazy Days in Grand Forks, North Dakota. It seems that Grandma always made this the first couple weeks of August for the hired men on the farm, but we also would have a piece when we came home from shopping at Crazy Days, which was also always held in August—right before school started. It was a big holiday in downtown Grand Forks. I remember Ferris wheels and other rides for kids, plus lots of treats like cotton candy and popcorn. Mom and Grandma would plan their attack on several of the stores. The majority of stores would line the sidewalks with tons of products marked down to "ridiculous" prices. I would save every penny for months so that I could buy really cool toys. One year I purchased a children's soda fountain machine. I always hated trying on clothes because the fitting rooms were packed and the stores were hot. Sometimes Mom would make us change in the store aisle because the fitting rooms had such long lines. That was not fun. Lunch, however, was. We always ate at the Palace Café, a large 1950s–1960s diner with high ceilings. It was like something out of the movie *Mildred Pierce.* I loved the open-faced roast beef sandwiches with mashed potatoes and gravy. It was the place to be at noon during Crazy Day in Grand Forks. Oh, and by the way, they offered tremendous pies. My love of coconut cream pie started there.

Crust

> 1½ cups unbleached all-purpose flour
> ½ tablespoon white sugar
> ½ teaspoon kosher or sea salt, finely ground
> ¼ cup Crisco butter-flavored all-vegetable shortening, chilled
>   and cut into small pieces
> ¼ cup unsalted butter, chilled and cut into small pieces
> ¼–½ cup cold water; use only as much as needed for a smooth,
>   satiny dough ball
> Crisco butter-flavored cooking spray
> 1 egg yolk and 1 teaspoon water for egg wash

1. All ingredients should be cold. Combine all the dry ingredients in a large mixing bowl. Add shortening and butter. Using a pastry blender, cut in the shortening and butter until the mixture resembles coarse meal or peas.
2. Drop by drop, add the cold water. Mix in with the fingertips, not with the hands as the palms will warm the dough. Continue mixing in water until the dough begins to hold together without being crumbly yet not sticky.
3. Place dough in plastic wrap. Fold over plastic wrap and press down to form a disk. This will make rolling out easier after chilling. Finish wrapping in plastic and place in the refrigerator for at least thirty minutes.
4. Lightly spray a deep 9-inch pie pan or 8½-inch fluted flan pan. Roll out dough and place in pie plate, allowing the excess pastry to hang over the edge. Remove extra, tuck under, and crimp decoratively. Brush with egg wash. Chill in the refrigerator while preparing filling.

Makes pastry for one 9-inch single-crust pie.

Filling

> 1½ cups white sugar
> 3 tablespoons unbleached all-purpose flour
> 1 cup buttermilk, divided
> 3 large eggs, slightly beaten
> ¼ cup unsalted butter, melted
> 1 teaspoon pure vanilla extract or paste
> ½ cup pecans, coarsely chopped

1. Preheat oven to 425 degrees. In a large mixing bowl, whisk to combine sugar, flour, and ½ cup buttermilk. Add beaten eggs and the remaining buttermilk. Whisk vigorously until well blended. Add the butter and vanilla.
2. Gently pour into prepared pie crust. Carefully sprinkle pecans over the filling. Cover pie edges with pie shield to prevent excessive browning or burning. Bake 10 minutes and then reduce oven temperature to 350F degrees. Bake for an additional 25–30 minutes or until a knife inserted in the center comes out clean. Remove pie shield for the final 10 minutes of baking. Cool on a rack until room temperature. Garnish with Sweetened Whipped Cream (see recipe in the "Decorating Your Pie" chapter).

Serves 8–10.

"Bye bye, Miss American pie."

—DON MCLEAN

Decorating Your Pie

THE LAST THING MOST BAKERS THINK ABOUT IS "how am I going to decorate my pie?" Some bakers do, though, and I for one am continually on the quest to make the tops of my pies as attractive as possible through miniature cutouts, braided dough, and, my newest technique, a form of stenciling that I call "piemaling." I use cinnamon sugar, cocoa, or other toppings such as dried dill on Tuna Pie or My Favorite Salmon Pie. The most extensive piemaling technique involves using nontoxic food coloring dusting powders to create decorative flowers or a clock face on my top crusts. I've worked tirelessly to simplify this technique for the home cook. Most bakers hardly have time to bake a pie, let alone decorate it. So through lots of practice and experimentation, I have found that most stenciling with a dusting of cinnamon sugar, cocoa, or other products takes about 25 seconds. Not bad. Painting the top crust with nontoxic food coloring dusting powders takes about 15 minutes. Both produce satisfying results. In most cases, my guests moan when I cut into the pies and destroy the design. But it's worth it and more pies can be made.

Decorating pies doesn't always have to mean my piemaling technique or using miniature cutouts. Placing Chocolate Bar Curls on top of a pie or pie slice is a beautiful way to display your finished pie; drizzling with my Raspberry Sauce is another fantastic way to offer your guests a slice of dessert with a little extra something to make their eating experience just a bit more elegant.

For savory and vegetable pies I offer my Cucumber Sauce and Tuscan Tomato Sauce. These both keep extremely well if covered tightly and stored in the refrigerator. They also have more uses than just embellishing slices of pie. Either sauce can be used with pasta or seafood. Being brought up on a farm taught me to be frugal and use everything.

Before making your pie, decide whether you want to decorate it or if you even have the time. I tell my students, readers, and television viewers to allow at least two hours from beginning to end to prepare a pie. Hurrying the process will only cause frustration and stress. Plan to bake your pie when you have a little extra time. Turn on your favorite radio station, pour yourself a glass of your favorite beverage—nonalcoholic if you're using knives—and take your time to create something you'll be proud of. But also take some time to decide whether you want to make a double crust and add a piemaling design or apply a lattice crust. Perhaps you will decide on simply using miniature cookie cutters to cut out the shape of the type of fruit you have in your filling. Maybe you'll cut slits in the top crust to release steam. No matter what you choose, I hope you'll take your time and enjoy the act of creation. Once the pie is baked and cooling on a rack in your home, you can't resist the urge to bend down and inhale its sweet fragrance. There is no better perfume.

One of the simplest ways to decorate your pie is with Sweetened Whipped Cream. I have added two of my recipes. One uses confectioner's sugar (powdered sugar) and one uses honey. Experiment with flavored extracts or stop by your local herb and spice shop for rose water or orange water. We are very fortunate to have Penzeys Spices near our home in Saint Paul. I love riding my bike over to their store and spending a good hour browsing through all their herbs and spices. They offer recipes cards using their products and testing jars so that customers can smell or taste the variety of goods they offer. They sell the best pure vanilla and almond extracts (www.penzeys.com)

When enhancing whipped cream, try using rum or other flavors. You might need to experiment a little to decide how much to add per your taste. If you choose nonalcoholic, there are many brands of rum and bourbon extract. I found an extract company on eBay called Faerie's Finest (www.faeriesfinest.com). They offer the best cherry extract I have ever tasted. I used it in my Triple Crown Cherry Pie, which won a ribbon at the 2008 APC Crisco National Pie Championship. All their extracts are natural and add wonderful flavor.

One more word about miniature cutouts: I love them and use them all the time to designate the type of fruit filling I have under my top crust. I have miniature apples, strawberries, and blueberries, plus many others. Since I've started decorating with nontoxic food coloring dusting powders, I have also begun painting the cutout apples red or the blueberries a bluish purple. The cutout releases the steam as well as providing simple and easy decoration.

I've also used extra pie dough to create large maple leaves or pumpkins. I recently purchased large butterfly and harvest moon cookie cutters. I put the cutout on parchment paper placed on a baking sheet. I bake it at 375 degrees for 10–12 minutes or until golden brown and let it cool. I will arrange the baked cutout on top of a cooling custard, pumpkin, or pecan pie. It's just one more way to decorate your baked treasure.

I hope you will try some of my suggestions. Once you do, it's fun to sit back and see your creative work. Cooking is not supposed to be simply a job or something you have to do. Bring out your creative forces and make your pie a work of art.

At once impressive and unremarkable, pie can be complicated and challenging or simple and homey. Whether ordinary or elegant, though, a pie is not something to eat by yourself. It should be made to share, preferably while fresh and warm.

—LISA CHERKASKY, *THE ARTFUL PIE*

⸕ Lattice Crust

◈ On a 15- x 11-inch sheet of parchment paper roll out chilled pie dough into a rectangle that is slightly larger than 14 x 9 inches. Trim the dough to an exact 14- x 9-inch rectangle. Cut 12 strips that are 14 inches long and ¾ inch wide. If the dough gets soft, slide the parchment and dough onto a baking sheet or cutting board and chill briefly before continuing. On a parchment-lined baking sheet, arrange 6 strips horizontally, setting them ¾ inch apart; these will be the "bottom" strips. Set the rest aside on a separate piece of parchment; these will be the "top" strips. This recipe calls for 5 horizontal and 5 vertical strips, but I like to make extra in case of an accident.

◈ Beginning from the middle:
1. Lay down five horizontal strips, making sure that they're evenly spaced.
2. Working from the right side, fold back every other horizontal strip (numbers 1, 3, and 5).
3. Lay down a vertical strip in the center, next to the fold.
4. Fold horizontal strips 1, 3, and 5 back over the vertical strip.
5. Working again from the right, fold back horizontal strips 2 and 4 by one-third.
6. Lay down a second vertical strip next to this fold. Fold strips 2 and 4 back over the vertical strip.
7. Again, from the right, fold back horizontal strips 1, 3, and 5, about a quarter of the way over. Lay your third vertical strip next to this fold and fold the horizontal strips back over it.
8. Repeat this process with two strips on the other side, working from the center.

◈ Slide parchment paper with completed lattice crust on to a baking sheet. Place in the freezer for 40–45 minutes until well chilled. Remove from freezer, turn parchment paper and lattice over and place on top of filled pie crust. Carefully peel parchment paper from lattice crust. Lattice crust will begin to soften as it warms. Crimp together with bottom crust and apply egg wash before baking. You can also sprinkle regular or vanilla sugar after applying egg wash.

ᶠ Meringue

4 large egg whites
¼ teaspoon cream of tartar
½ cup white sugar
¾ teaspoon pure vanilla extract or paste

In the bowl of an electric mixer using the whisk attachment, beat egg whites and cream of tartar on high speed until foamy. Turn speed to low and slowly add sugar. Turn speed back up to high and continue beating until egg whites and sugar become stiff and glossy. Stop mixer and add vanilla. Beat in vanilla on low speed until incorporated.

This recipe makes enough meringue for up to one 10-inch pie.

John Michael's Helpful Hints: You may also use meringue powder to create a meringue topping. Using meringue powder will give you more stability in humid climates. Dissolve ¾ cup white sugar in ½ cup boiling water. Let cool. Add ¼ cup meringue powder and beat to stiff and glossy peaks. Meringue powder can be found at most cooking and craft stores.

Substitute packed brown sugar for regular sugar to create a Brown Sugar Meringue.

ᶠ Sweetened Whipped Cream

1 cup heavy or gourmet whipping cream
4 tablespoons confectioner's sugar
1 teaspoon pure vanilla extract or paste

1. In a mixing bowl, whisk or beat cream on high until it begins to thicken.
2. Gradually add confectioner's sugar. Continue until stiff peaks form. Add vanilla and beat until incorporated into whipped cream.

Makes about 2 cups.

Honey-Sweetened Whipped Cream

1 cup heavy whipping cream
3 tablespoons honey
1 teaspoon pure vanilla extract or paste

In medium mixing bowl, beat cream with electric mixer until soft peaks form. Fold in honey and vanilla.

Makes about 2 cups.

Chocolate Bar Curls

1 regular white or dark chocolate candy bar

Microwave chocolate bar for 5 seconds and no longer. Using a vegetable peeler, carefully run blade lengthwise along chocolate bar edge to create chocolate curls. Sprinkle chocolate curls on whipped cream topping, meringue topping, or to decorate pies.

Chocolate Leaves

8 ounces bittersweet chocolate; also may use white chocolate
1 tablespoon Crisco all-purpose vegetable shortening
Lemon, camellia, or other waxy leaves, cleaned

In a heat-proof mixing bowl over simmering water, melt chocolate and shortening, stirring constantly. Remove from heat and stir until smooth. Using a pastry brush or spoon, coat underside of leaves to bring out more details of veins and stem. Place on baking dish or tray and freeze until firm. Carefully separate chocolate from leaves starting at the stem end of the leaf.

∮ Pecan Brittle

Crisco butter-flavored cooking spray
1½ teaspoons baking soda
1 teaspoon water
1 teaspoon pure vanilla extract or paste
1½ cups white sugar
1 cup water
1 cup light corn syrup
3 tablespoons unsalted butter
1 pound pecan halves

1. Spray two baking sheets, each 15½ x 12 inches, with Crisco butter-flavored cooking spray, or rub baking sheets with unsalted butter; keep warm. Combine soda, 1 teaspoon water, and vanilla; set aside.
2. Combine sugar, 1 cup water, and corn syrup in a large heavy-bottom saucepan. Cook over medium heat, stirring occasionally, to 240 degrees on a candy thermometer (or until a small amount of syrup dropped into very cold water forms a soft ball that flattens when removed from water).
3. Stir in butter and pecans. Cook, stirring constantly, to 300 degrees (or until a small amount of mixture dropped into very cold water separates into threads that are hard and brittle). Watch mixture carefully so that it does not burn.
4. Immediately remove mixture from heat; stir in soda mixture thoroughly. Pour half the candy mixture onto each warm baking sheet and quickly spread evenly, about ¼ inch thick. Cool; break candy into pieces.

Makes about 2 pounds.

John Michael's Helpful Hint: The key to "brittleness" is "thinness." To ensure this quality, be sure to spread the candy mixture carefully and thinly. Make sure your baking sheets are warm as well as the utensil you use to spread the candy mixture.

ƒ Caramel or Dulce de Leche

Dulce de leche means "milk candy." It's a wonderful Latin American caramel that is not difficult to make. It just needs your attention. The majority of recipes begin with a can of sweetened condensed milk. The first method I describe is how my grandmother showed me to make caramel with condensed milk. Whatever method you use, following the instructions is extremely important.

In the can. This is the classic way my grandmother taught me and it's quite simple. Place an unopened can (you may do two or three at a time) of sweetened condensed milk in a stockpot or deep saucepan. Fill stockpot or saucepan with water, making sure to cover the can(s) of condensed milk with at least 1 or 2 inches of water. Bring water to a boil and immediately reduce the heat to a low simmer. Low boil (a couple of bubbles rising to the top) for 2–3 hours, always making sure the water level stays 1 or 2 inches above the can. **If the can of condensed milk is not completely submerged it can explode.** The longer it cooks, the thicker the caramel will be. Two hours of cooking produces a thick pourable caramel. Three hours produces a thick candy. When the desired cooking time is complete, turn off heat source, leave the pot on the stove top, and let the can(s) cool in the water. Leave for several hours until *completely* cool or at room temperature before opening. I usually do this process the day before I need caramel for my pies.

In a pressure cooker. You also can caramelize condensed milk in a pressure cooker. Place can(s) of sweetened condensed milk in the pressure cooker and fill with water, making sure there is one or two inches of water covering the can(s). Cover and pressure cook for 20–30 minutes.

In a saucepan. This method requires constant attention but produces the same results. In a heavy-bottom saucepan over low heat pour in can of condensed milk. Stir or whisk constantly until the milk becomes a thick caramel.

In the oven. Preheat oven to 350 degrees. Pour can of condensed milk into a shallow baking dish. Cover tightly with foil. Create a water bath by placing the shallow baking dish in a larger baking dish or pan. Fill with hot water only halfway up the side of the baking dish. Place in oven and stir every 30 minutes for a couple of hours or until you have the desired consistency. Remove from the oven and stir or whisk to remove lumps.

In the microwave. Use a large microwavable bowl that can hold twice the volume of the can of condensed milk. Pour the condensed milk into the bowl and microwave on medium for five 5-minute intervals, stirring each time. The contents will foam up quickly as the milk cooks, so do watch carefully. Cook to desired consistency in 5-minute intervals.

Cucumber Sauce

> 4 large cucumbers
> 1 small yellow onion
> ½ cup mayonnaise (regular, low-fat, or fat-free)
> 3 teaspoons white vinegar
> 2 cups sour cream (regular, low-fat, or fat-free)

1. Using a vegetable peeler, remove cucumber skin. Slice cucumber lengthwise and scoop out any seeds. Peel onion and cut into quarters. Place onions and cucumber in the bowl of a food processor. Pulse until completed pureed. Pour into a fine-mesh sieve and drain. Press to release as much liquid as possible.
2. In a medium mixing bowl combine mayonnaise, vinegar, and sour cream. Add processed cucumber and onion. Cover tightly and refrigerate for at least two hours to let flavors blend.

Makes about 3 cups of sauce.

✝ Raspberry Sauce

I love this sauce. When my raspberries are in season, you will probably find me pouring this sauce not only over my favorite pies but also over pancakes, chocolate chip cookies, my Chocolate Truffle Cheesecake, Chambord cheesecake, and pound cake. Try it over ice cream or a warm brownie. You're only limited by your imagination and taste buds.

½ cup white sugar
½ cup water

2 cups fresh raspberries or frozen, completely thawed and drained

1. In a heavy-bottom saucepan over medium heat, bring sugar and water to a boil, stirring occasionally. Reduce heat to low and simmer until sugar is completely dissolved.
2. Remove from heat. Cool to room temperature
3. In a blender or food processor, combine sugar mixture and raspberries. Process until smooth. Strain through a fine-mesh sieve or strainer. Use the back of a spoon to push juice through if needed. Discard solids. Store in jars for up to one week in the refrigerator.

Makes about 2 cups.

✝ Tuscan Tomato Sauce

I cannot recommend this recipe enough. It is so fresh and full of flavor, especially if you use your own homegrown tomatoes. I "put up" around 50 pounds of meaty roma tomatoes each year. If you don't have the desire to can your own, by all means use the best-quality canned tomatoes you can find. With all the interest in Italian foods, you should have no difficulty finding roma tomatoes at your local grocery store.

12 cups canned roma tomatoes
¼ cup extra virgin olive oil
4 large garlic cloves, minced

1 teaspoon red pepper flakes
1 cup Chianti or other good-quality red wine
1 tablespoon fresh oregano, chopped
¼ teaspoon kosher or sea salt
⅓ teaspoon freshly ground black pepper
½ cup fresh basil leaves, torn into thin strips
½ teaspoon fresh English or French thyme leaves

1. In batches, puree tomatoes in a blender. You want your tomatoes somewhat chunky, so pulse the blender to prevent them from liquefying. You may also add your tomatoes and mash with a potato masher after adding to stockpot or dutch oven.
2. Using a medium-size stockpot or dutch oven, heat the olive oil over medium heat. Add the garlic and cook until golden but not brown as garlic will become bitter. Add red pepper flakes, tomatoes, and wine and reduce heat to low. While mixture is simmering, add oregano, salt, and pepper. Simmer uncovered until the sauce thickens, about ½ to 2 hours, stirring occasionally.
3. Before serving, add basil and combine. This sauce may be kept in the refrigerator for up to 5 days in an airtight container. You may also freeze for up to 2 months. I use a food vacuum and store in mason jars or freezer bags for optimal storage and freshness.

Makes 4–5 quarts.

Piemaling—Pie Art

1 top crust dough, rolled out
Stencil
Cinnamon sugar
Assorted spices
Cocoa
Sanding sugar, assorted colors
Food color dusting powder
1 egg yolk and 1 teaspoon water for egg wash

For Sprinkling over Stencil

Prepare crust for a two-crust pie. Before attaching top crust, place stencil on top of rolled-out dough. Slowly roll over the stencil with rolling pin to adhere stencil to dough. Brush over stencil with egg wash. Sprinkle sugars, spices, and/or cocoa over open areas of the stencil. If dough becomes too warm, place in refrigerator to chill. Carefully remove stencil, being mindful not to spill excess sprinkling items outside of stencil. Attach top crust, vent, crimp, and bake per recipe instructions.

For Applying Nontoxic Food Coloring Dusting Powder

Prepare crust for two-crust pie. Before attaching top crust, place stencil on top of rolled-out dough. Slowly roll over the stencil with rolling pin to adhere stencil to dough. Using a dry brush, apply dusting powder to open areas of stencil. You may need to apply a small amount of water or egg wash to open area first if pie dough is too dry. Be creative with your color choices and blend for realistic effects. Dusting powder will adhere to the oils in the dough. If dough becomes too warm, place in refrigerator to chill. Carefully remove stencil, being mindful not to spill excess dusting powders outside of stencil. Attach top crust, vent, crimp, and bake per instructions.

Pie Competitions

𝑓 Minnesota State Fair

At the end of August each year the Great Minnesota Get-Together takes place in the city of Falcon Heights, Minnesota. Falcon Heights is a small community wedged between the behemoths of Minneapolis and Saint Paul. Attendance in 2008 reached 1,693,533 for an all-time record. Over 500,000 corn dogs are consumed each year in 12 days of fairgoing, but you can still find pies among all the food fads.

Creative Activities

The Creative Activities Building is my favorite spot on the fairgrounds to visit each year. Walls of canned goods, baked goods, handicrafts, and woodwork are displayed for the public along with any ribbons entries received during the judging before opening day of the fair. Between 1999 and 2006, I entered up to 35 categories in the canned goods and baked goods. I can and preserve jams, jellies, relishes, and pickles all year long, but the baking has to be at its freshest, so I would plan a schedule to meet the entry date for baked goods. The first couple of years of baking preparation took three days. Pound cake can be made ahead of the

---

"This is Food Network Challenge—Great Pie Cook-Off"

—JOHN MICHAEL LERMA, INTRODUCING THE SHOW, NOVEMBER 2007

---

entry date because it actually tastes better. Pies are different. And the Minnesota State Fair Creative Activities only allows fruit pies to be entered. They usually have three categories: apple, a berry or berry combination, peach, fruit, or pecan—basic pies that must be done right.

Each year I would end my preparation days of baking for the fair by baking the pies. I would prepare the perfect crust; use only the freshest apples, fruits, berries, or nuts; and bake carefully to prevent burning, spillage, or a runny filling.

Removing each pie carefully, I would inspect it for imperfections and quickly wipe away any filling that had bubbled over. While the pie was extremely hot, I sprinkled regular or vanilla sugar over the top and let it slowly melt into the crust or topping. Everything seemed perfect, and I was usually pleased with the outcome.

Entry day is always the Sunday morning before opening day of the fair. Chad and I would rise very early. The day before entry day, I would borrow Wyatt Miller's (the little boy across the street) red wagon to haul all my entries to the registration area from the car. After much strong coffee, I would begin boxing my cakes and pies, and packing my cookies in accordance with the instructions in the Creative Activities catalog (I could write an entire chapter on the rules of entering canned and baked goods to the fair and making sure they are not disqualified). Chad would pack everything into the car—including Wyatt's red wagon—and we were off to the State Fair grounds.

After 9/11, security became extremely tight. Following preregistration, people are given instructions on entering exhibits. Once through the security gates the rush was on. Only those entering exhibits understand the importance of arriving early. I liked to arrive as soon as the gates opened because the lines only get longer with each hour.

Each year entry was a trial, and after dropping off all the exhibits and completing registration, the feeling was anticlimactic. Chad and I would find a quiet restaurant for breakfast and talk about which items were sure winners. Of course our predictions were never right, and my pies, no matter how well baked and prepared, never won a single ribbon in the pie competition.

I did, however, win a second-place ribbon in the Pillsbury Refrigerated Pie Crust Baking competition for my Key Lime Delight Pie using Pills-

bury Refrigerated Pie Crust with a lattice top. It was beautiful presentation and I was thrilled to win. My pie was displayed with all the other
winners in a refrigerated case. However, by day twelve of the fair, my Key
Lime Delight didn't look so delightful even in its refrigerated state.

I cannot encourage anyone more to enter a pie at your county fair as
well as your state fair. There is nothing as exciting as opening day at the
fair and pushing through the crowds to see if a ribbon is lying next to
your creation. Go ahead and bake your best. Even if you don't win a ribbon, you've won by simply entering. You will feel wonderful and have a
fine time at your state's "great get-together."

Honey and Bee

Another pie competition held at the Minnesota State Fair is in the Honey
and Bee Division in the Horticulture and Agriculture Building. I have
always been fascinated by this wing of the building because they have
hourly demonstrations of honey and beeswax extraction, a large glass
hive with bees, and an enclosed glass booth where candle making, cooking, and other honey crafts are demonstrated.

I was asked to offer a couple of "Making Pies with Honey" demonstrations in that glass booth. I'm happy to report it is air-conditioned and
very comfortable—and I don't like enclosed areas. I had a fun time and
was enormously honored to be asked. The audiences love information
on baking techniques they are not familiar with. I demonstrated making
pie filling using honey as the sweetener. Many asked about using honey
in the pie crust, but unfortunately that would make it too soggy and unable to be worked properly.

For several years I entered my pies using honey as a sweetener and
only won in 2006 for my Honey Pecan Dream Pie. I was so excited because it was my one and only true Minnesota State Fair ribbon for pie
baking outside of the Pillsbury Refrigerated Pie Crust Baking Contest.

Many people don't understand why that was important to me, since
I had won several awards nationally for my pie baking, but for someone
who grew up on a farm in North Dakota, winning ribbons at your county
or state fair meant everything. I guess you can't take the farm out of the
boy or off the farm.

✦ Park Rapids Annual 4th of July Pie-Baking Contest

In 2007, I was asked by the owner of Beagle Books in Park Rapids, Minnesota, if I could assist them in finding ways to help the Park Rapids Library raise money. The library's public funds had been drastically cut, resulting in reduced hours, jobs cuts, and materials cuts. I told them I would help.

It was difficult, growing up in Grand Forks, North Dakota, during the 1970s to obtain accurate information. Television was awash with family comedies that solved their problems by the end of the half hour. Open family discussions hadn't caught on yet because Oprah hadn't arrived on the scene. Phil Donahue was the main talk show of the day, but his subjects were controversial and we didn't speak about them in our household—yet. I found my answers at the Grand Forks Public Library. It held a wealth of information with thousands of books, antique to popular music albums, and a wonderful periodicals department. I lived at the library on weekends and would research a variety of topics, and it helped me become who I was growing into. I found my answers there. I read about current events, listened to new and old music (and developed an appreciation for both), and checked out as many items as I could carry in my backpack home on my bicycle.

Back home I read the magazines and books while listening to music. I dreamed of becoming a playwright and worked on script ideas at age 13. I also dreamed of writing classical music or at least playing some of the wonderful pieces I was listening to. This prompted me to take piano lessons and, eventually, play the music I loved. But mainly I understood what was happening to me physically and mentally. It still didn't make that part of life easy, but at least I knew what was happening to me and simply moved on to the things of life that excited me, such as music and writing. It was an exhilarating time because I had too many interests and not enough time to make all my dreams come true. It was a blissful time and I still feel like that now, and I'm still visiting the library in Saint Paul, Minnesota, on a regular basis and still dreaming of things I can become.

So when this call to arms came from Jennifer Wills Geraedts, manager of Beagle Books, I thought about what we could do.

Park Rapids is where Chad, our daughter, Heather, and I travel each summer for our family vacation. We go to Beauty Bay Lodge and Resort near Nevis on Lake Belle Taine. We have stayed in cabin number 4 overlooking the lake north for several years. Chad's parents took their family for their summer vacation to Beauty Bay Lodge and Resort until their children were grown. I love it there and find total peace and relaxation—ten minutes after we leave the resort, I long to return as soon as possible. It really is that perfect. It's mostly thanks to owners Tim and Jennifer Meyer. Beauty Bay Lodge is about 10 minutes from Park Rapids.

Jennifer of Beagle Books and I put our heads together, and I suggested holding a pie contest on the 4th of July at Beagle Books. I told her that nothing brings people together like pie. So we set up a strategy and got to work. Park Rapids celebrates the 4th of July with parades and a large firework display. We created judging forms, devised a contest with ribbons and cash prizes, and decided we would auction all the judged pies after the awards ceremony and right before the parade. Beagle Books worked on enlisting some local celebrities to help in the judging, and press releases were sent to local and regional newspapers. I had an interview with Jean Ruzicka from the Park Rapids *Enterprise* and she promised great coverage. We were excited.

I spoke with Nancy Mathieson from the American Pie Council. She told me to expect about 10 pie entries for the first year. She thought it was great what we were doing and said the APC would donate an Amateur Membership to the Best of Show winner. Chad, Heather and I drove up for our weeklong summer vacation, but the pie contest was on my mind. Chad said everything would be fine, but I started to worry. What if no one showed up?

We got to our cabin. Chad and Heather unpacked the car, and I began putting everything away in its place. Chad and Heather call this "John Michael's nesting." Once the car is unpacked, they both head down to the beach and leave me to the "nesting." I don't blame them. I drive myself crazy setting up a temporary home.

Chad and I drove into Park Rapids for a few groceries. As we were standing at the checkout counter, I looked down and saw a five-by-seven-inch color photo—one of my favorites—of me sitting at a café table in Cortona, Italy. "That's me!" I exclaimed. The woman at the checkout looked down and agreed. "Yep, that's you." She shared that everyone was reading about the pie contest and asked if I was a celebrity or something. Chad proudly told her I was the celebrity judge and that she should enter a pie (I should hire him as a PR person).

After that encounter I felt more confident that our pie contest would be all right. And it was. The morning of the 4th of July at nine o'clock, I was at Beagle Books when our first entries began to arrive. The pie bakers were nervous and excited. We charged a five-dollar entry fee, which would go to the library. We told everyone to return at 2:00 that afternoon for the awards announcement.

Pie after pie continued to arrive. We had 20 pies entered in two hours. The former owners of Beagle Books, Jill and Deane Johnson, and their beagle, Kallie, were asked to judge along with Jennifer's husband, Wonewok chef Tom Geraedts. We had four categories of pie: Fruit and Cream, Single Crust, Double Crust, and Children's (ages 8–12). We had a blast. It was a judging party. In three hours we were ready to announce the winners.

At 2:00 P.M., a sizable crowd had gathered outside Beagle Books. We announced the winners to some very surprised pie bakers. Our first Best of Show winner was stunned. Afterward I auctioned off all the pies we had judged as only one small piece had been removed from each pie. I had also baked my famous Vidalia Onion Pie in a beautiful Emile Henry pie dish. We received a final bid of $75 for it, and the grand total for all the pies and entry fees was around $500. Not bad for our first year. The Park Rapids Library was thrilled.

On the 4th of July 2008, we held our Second Annual Park Rapids 4th of July Pie Contest. We had the same amount of entries, but the proceeds came to more than $1,100, more than double the first year's amount. At the writing of this book we are eagerly planning for 2009 with expanded entries, single pie slice sales, and much more. If you're in the neighborhood, enter a pie. This contest is open to everyone who loves baking or eating pies. And, the money goes to a great cause.

One of the reasons the Park Rapids Library had its funding pulled was because some people feel libraries are "liberal think tanks." Another radical view expressed on radio talk shows urges listeners to keep their children away from the library because they will become sick from all the germs on books, periodicals, and media. I find these opinions disturbing because many listeners believe them, but they demonstrate all the more strongly why we need libraries, especially in small communities like Park Rapids. Libraries are not liberal (or conservative) think tanks but venues to give community residents new ways to dream.

∮ Braham Pie Day

In 1990, Governor Rudy Perpich named Braham, Minnesota, the "Homemade Pie Capital" of the state. Since then Braham's Pie Day event has grown to include a pie-baking contest, pie-eating contests, an art fair, pie art show, hourly performances and demonstrations, a pie auction for charity, and, at the end of the day, a pie relay race. Thousands of people attend each year in this rural town of approximately 1,276 people. Over 150 volunteers serve over 500 baked fruit pies in the park, and thousands of dollars are raised for charity efforts that benefit the young people of this community. Braham Pie Day is held the first Friday of August each year.

Braham is located one hour north of Minneapolis–Saint Paul. During the 1930s and 1940s, families would drive to their summer lake homes and stop in Braham for a cup of coffee and a piece of pie. It was the halfway mark between Minneapolis–Saint Paul and Duluth, Minnesota.

I started competing in the pie-baking competition at Braham in 2005. My first year, I received a First Place ceramic medallion for Best Single Crust Pie for my Vidalia Onion Pie. It was the first "savory" pie to win in Braham. My example actually set up a flood of savory entries in the following year (to my delight). I also received another First Place ceramic medallion for Best Cream or Custard Pie for my Coconut Cream Dream Pie. I didn't receive Best of Show because no savory pie had ever been given that award. The Best of Show went to the second place winner instead. Ahh, the trials and tribulations I've been through because of my Vidalia Onion Pie.

After I had entered my pie for competition, Chad and I went for a long bike ride around the rural areas and through town. The weather couldn't have been better. The beginning of August in east-central Minnesota is perfect. Wild flowers are blooming everywhere, temperatures are in the low 90s, the skies are clear, and everything is so green. The fields are just starting to turn their color before the harvest. It's a time each year that I look forward to with much anticipation for both the weather and Braham Pie Day.

In 2006, I was asked to serve as a "celebrity" judge and eagerly said yes. I arrived at the Lutheran church around 10:00 a.m. and prepared to judge pie. That year 41 pies were entered for five categories. I was the only judge, so I ate a great deal of pie. After three and a half hours, I had the winners. I was whisked down to the park, a five-minute drive including parking, to help hand out prizes to the winners.

After the awards, Chad and I walked around the art and crafts fair and purchased fair foods. Corn dogs were not the best idea after all the pie I had consumed, but I ate them anyway.

The following year, I was asked back to be a celebrity judge along with representatives from General Mills in Minneapolis. We had a wonderful time tasting pies, and it was fun to have companions to discuss the pies and what made the recipes work or not.

I also baked my Coconut Cream Dream Pie in an Emile Henry pie dish to be part of the pie auction for charity. Four months before Pie Day, I had filmed the Food Network Challenge—The Great American Pie Cook-Off and won a Bronze Food Network medal. One of the highest-rated pies during that challenge was my Coconut Cream Dream Pie.

The pie auction started and I assisted by walking assorted pies up and down the aisles for all the attendees under a large white and yellow striped canopy tent to see. Most pies were going for $25 to $75. The prize-winning pies were bringing in around $125 each. It came time for my Coconut Cream Dream Pie. I explained it was one of the three pies I had baked during the challenge on Food Network and that it would come with the Emile Henry ceramic pie dish that retailed for at least $40. I thought I would try and bring up the bid as much as possible.

A Smith Auction House representative started the bidding. I wasn't paying attention until I heard the auctioneer yell "$600!" I did a double take because I couldn't believe I had heard him correctly.

"I have $700! Do I hear $750? $800?"

Several people were bidding and the numbers continued to rise. The final bid was for $1,250. I almost fell off the stage in Freedom Park. I quickly delivered my pie to a woman named Phyllis Londgren. I thanked her for her incredible bid and told her that for $1,250, I would have come to her home and baked the pie.

Phyllis Londgren is a long-time resident of the Braham community. She taught school in Braham and after retiring researched and wrote a large book about the first 100 years of the town, from 1899 through 1999. Her bid, she told me, was to give back to the youth of her wonderful community. What a beautiful woman. She also found me later in the park and gave me a copy of her book, *Braham, Minnesota—100 Years.* I asked her to autograph it for me. She wrote, "I love you, John! Phyllis Londgren." I was extremely touched by her generosity.

In 2008, I was asked back to act as judge along with author and Minneapolis *Star Tribune* writer Anne Gillespie Lewis. We had a wonderful time tasting pies and coming up with winners in each category. I prefer to have someone to judge with and we are usually surprised at how close our scores are afterward.

For the 2008 auction, I baked my Captain Tony's Watermelon Pie in an Emile Henry pie dish. I told the audience under the white and yellow canopy that because I was in the process of editing my next cookbook, which just happened to be all pie recipes, I would up the ante. Whoever won the bid would not only get my Watermelon Pie baked in the Emile Henry ceramic pie dish, but I would also print their name in my cookbook in the chapter about pie competitions.

So the bidding began and my Watermelon Pie brought in $150 from Don Moulton and Jerry Moses of East Central Sanitation. They added, "Friendliest Sanitation in East Central Minnesota." I love it. Don had several pie boxes stacked in his arms as he and a friend were running them to a vehicle. He told me the team at East Central Sanitation love arriving to work on the Monday morning after Pie Day because Don bids for and wins about 10 pies each year and brings all of them to work to share. Talk about a good guy and great sponsor of the Braham Pie Day.

The 2008 winner for Best of Show was Beverly Johnson from Crookston, Minnesota, for her Caramel Apple-Pecan Pie. Beverly was so excited and shocked. I visited with her afterward to obtain some information because she also was awarded a membership with the American Pie Council as Best of Show.

Braham Pie Day may be rural and small town, but I cannot imagine not being a part of it each year. Perhaps it brings me back to my roots in North Dakota, but I truly enjoy the people, the food, and their quiet life. But boy, when they throw a party they know how to throw a party. Drive up the first Friday of August and join the fun. Stop at the Park Café on Main Street and have a cup of coffee and a piece of pie anytime you're in town.

ʄ APC Crisco National Pie Championship

In early 2005, I had no idea that the American Pie Council or a National Pie Championship existed. This was after I had become ill in 2003 after surgery for a large tumor in my throat. After a tracheotomy was performed to keep me alive, complications occurred and I was bedridden for months.

While staring at the television from my bed, I unintentionally watched the APC Crisco National Pie Championship from Celebration, Florida, on the Food Network. I had been baking pies since I was about 10 years old. It was an interesting program and entertaining.

Contestants looked as if they were having the time of their lives. They showed the Never-Ending Pie Buffet, the pie competitions, profiling bakers like Raine Gottess (2003 Best of Show), Marles Riessland and her daughter Karen Hall, Beth Campbell, Sarah Spaugh, Dionna Hurt, and Phyllis Bartholomew (2004 Best of Show). The pies themselves looked amazing. When the program was over, I thought, Wow, if only my life were different.

Ultimately, my life did become different.

In April 2005, Chad and I traveled to Orlando, Florida, so that we could attend the American Pie Festival in Celebration and I could enter my pies in the APC Crisco National Pie Championship. We stayed at a Residence Inn near Sea World, and they provided me with a large toaster oven to bake my pies. I knew this was going to be a challenge, but I worked on my recipes and set up house to bake over three days. I also agreed to bake at the resort that hosted the championship during a media event.

The day of my first media event was chaotic. I couldn't stop shaking all morning as I was getting ready. I was shaking in the shower, while shaving, while packing items for baking. Chad told me to have a glass of wine before leaving, but I didn't think it would be a good idea to show up with alcohol on my breath.

I literally thought I was going to pass out as I walked into the resort and registered. I couldn't breathe. And then, I was escorted into the large ballroom set up for the media event. There was Dionna Hurt, Sarah Spaugh, and Phyllis Bartholomew. I wanted to run. You may have heard me refer to these three as the "Pie Goddesses," and I mean it. I watched the Food Network specials from 2003 and 2004, and here I was in the middle of all of this national pie excitement.

I found my station, set up my utensils, and greeted people as they walked by. Dionna Hurt was at the station next to mine. She immediately came over and introduced herself. She was friendly and fashionable. My nervousness was easing up a bit. Since that first meeting Dionna and I have become good friends.

The media event went very well and I was proud of my baking performance. As soon as it was over, Chad and I returned to the Residence Inn. We took a break at the pool before I went back to baking. I had entered six pies that year and needed to bake through most of the night.

After supper, I began baking wildly. During the media event, I had baked two pies. This left four before the next morning to be completed. I was working on my Hana Hou! Daiquiri Pie. Using the toaster oven for my crust was an adventure, but that was only the beginning. Chad was in the bedroom and had ordered a Hollywood movie through the room's pay-per-view system. Chad knows that when I'm baking, especially for a contest, it's best to make yourself scarce.

Just as the filling was beginning to thicken, the fire alarms sounded throughout the building. Chad walked out into the hallway to check and returned saying that we should evacuate as all the other guests were. I looked at him and responded that my filling was at a certain stage of perfection and that if I evacuated it would be ruined. I told Chad we were not leaving the suite until I smelled or saw smoke. At that time, I would have Chad go out into the parking lot below our suite and I would throw down my completed pies. I would also throw down my completed pie crust for my Daiquiri Pie and the filling that I was cooking.

Chad looked worried and bewildered.

Fortunately it was a false alarm, but it showed me how determined—or stupid—I was to compete in this contest. This was no longer the Minnesota State Fair but a national competition.

That first year I won second place in the Fruit and Berry category for my Razzle Dazzle Berry Pie. I ran to the stage so excited that I could hardly breathe. The audience was very generous with their applause and happy for me. I felt like one of the gang now and was so honored. A couple of categories later, my name was called again. I had won third place in the Open category for my Hana Hou! Daiquiri Pie. Thank goodness I hadn't left the filling on the stove when the fire alarm had sounded.

The following year, 2006, I entered nine pies. Chad and I rented a condo with a full kitchen. We also arrived a day early to accommodate the extra baking. I had an hour-to-hour schedule. That was also the year I entered my Vidalia Onion Pie. During the media event, cameras from Food Network stopped by to film me preparing the filling. They later stopped back to film me removing the pie from the oven.

The next morning the Food Network cameras filmed each of my pies arriving for registration. It was so exciting except that the meringue for my Orange Meringue Pie had begun to shrink. The humidity of Florida and the hot lights on the cameras were creating a disastrous situation for my pie. By the time the filming was over, the meringue top was the size of a fried egg. Since that day I have called it my "humble pie."

My Vidalia Onion Pie didn't win that year, but one month later the Food Network called to ask if they could fly up to my home in Saint Paul to film a profile. This was better than a ribbon and started a wonderful relationship with the Food Network.

In 2007, I was moved from the amateur division to the professional division owing to my cookbook sales, teaching at various cooking schools throughout the Twin Cities, and hosting culinary vacations to Tuscany. I didn't mind because, yes, I was now a professional. However, I was a bit worried about my competition. I was going up against pastry chefs, bakery owners, restaurant owners, and others.

Chad and I had also agreed to assist in judging commercial pies during the festival. We volunteered to judge Pumpkin Pie. Thirty-four pumpkin pies later, our judging table picked the best of the bunch: Hill and Valley Family Pumpkin Crème Pie, J. Horner's Premium Pumpkin Pie, Bakers Square Gourmet Pumpkin Cream Pie, and Bakers Square Super Gourmet Pumpkin Praline Pie.

During the judging, I met the most remarkable man. He was a young twenty-something from Houston, Texas, and his name was Hector. Extremely handsome with wavy black hair and exceptionally articulate,

Hector was fresh out of college and full of vinegar (pun intended for pie bakers).

Hector and his friends from New York City, Grace and Collin, head up a group called Young United Professionals for Pie (YUPP). Hector explained they already have 267 members and are setting up a Web site for their organization. Collin documented the entire weekend with his digital camcorder while Hector and Grace volunteered to be judges in every division. Over the weekend we christened them "the kids."

Check out their videos on YouTube.com from the 2007 American Pie Festival:

Pie Storm: www.youtube.com/watch?v=I_CrB_hWmbU

YUPP at the Pie Festival (Episode 1): www.youtube.com/watch?v=waWP43heSa8

YUPP at the Pie Festival (Episode 2): www.youtube.com/watch?v=CE6DgF1lUdU

When my name was announced as the first prize winner in the professional division for my Coconut Cream Dream Pie, I jumped in the air, ran up to the stage, and gave a bear hug to Linda Hoskins, the executive director of the American Pie Council. Chad said he could see everyone on stage brace themselves when my name was called. I don't win awards gracefully.

My Coconut Cream Dream Pie's secret is to use real coconut cream, not coconut milk as most recipes specify. It's covered with my grandma's whipped cream topping that's filled with toasted coconut; it's a mile high and full of creamy righteousness.

After bounding to the stage and my spirited assault on the American Pie Council members, I was greeted by pie bakers I had watched when I was bedridden, the women who inspired me with their fantastic pie recipes and energy on the Food Network so many years ago. I cherished each of the hugs from Phyllis, Sarah, Dionna, Marles, Karen, Jeannie, and many others.

I was in a very nice place in my life. I couldn't have imagined it five or six years before but there I was in Celebration, Florida winning the grandest accolade of my cooking career and being honored by the people I admired most. Could any confection be any sweeter or more savory?

⸙ Food Network Challenge

In the preceding section I touched on how the Food Network filmed me in 2006 preparing my Vidalia Onion Pie. They also flew a film crew and television host to film my home and gardens in Saint Paul, Minnesota. Thanks to that special, I received hundreds of requests for my recipe and interest in my cookbook after it was televised in November 2006. I started wonderful dialogues with many bakers from around the world. It was a very exciting time, but I found it difficult to respond to so many e-mails. You see, at the time, Chad and I were in Tuscany hosting our culinary vacations titled "A Gathering in Tuscany." The Food Network is not shown in Italy or at least not in Tuscany. I forgot about the showing and woke the next day to over 300 e-mails. At the time, the speed of Internet in the hills of Tuscany was that of "dial up." It took days, if not months, to reply to everyone. I returned to the United States and spent most of the month of December replying to e-mails. I enjoyed it, however.

The following year, in March 2007, I received a telephone call from a producer at the Food Network. Her name was Jen Adducci. She asked if I would be interested in appearing in a Food Network Challenge for pie. I screamed yes as my response. Chad and I were on our way to the Mall of America for a morning walk. The temperature in the Mall of America is a perfect 70 year round. We like to walk each floor at a brisk pace. Each floor at the Mall is exactly half a mile. So by walking each of the three floors we can walk a mile and a half no matter what time of year. That morning, after the call from the Food Network, my walk was extra brisk as I could hardly contain myself. I must have driven Chad crazy with my ranting about which pies to make during the challenge.

The trip to the Food Network Challenge began with a panic attack on the flight to the studios in Denver. After 30 minutes of not being able to breathe, I got up and stood at the back of the airplane. Two backrubs later, from separate flight attendants, and a great deal of red wine, and I was panic free and ready to rumble with the best of them in the Food Network kitchens.

I arrived late at the Denver airport, obtained my really cool white PT Cruiser that the Food Network rented for me, and drove to the hotel. My suite was large, large enough to sleep a family of eight.

After a restless night and five *Sopranos* episodes later, I prepared to appear at the studios for a couple of hours of pre-interviews with an assistant producer and film crew. Then I could set up for mise en place. Even though I have cooked for many years and call myself a chef, I had to look up this French phrase that means "to put in place, to organize" (i.e., to have the ingredients for a dish prepared and ready to combine when the recipe calls for them).

The pre-interview was enjoyable, but we did a lot of retakes. I was asked to repeat my answers but "with more enthusiasm" or to "smile more" or to "take more time to reflect before answering." I did everything as asked and had fun with the crew. After an hour and a half, it was off to the studio where the challenge would take place.

About the American Pie Council

The American Pie Council° (APC) is the only organization committed to preserving America's pie heritage and promoting Americans love affair with pies. Designed to raise awareness, enjoyment, and consumption of pies, the APC offers both Personal and Commercial Memberships.

While the consumer member benefits from the exchange of recipes, in-store coupons, and ideas from other pie lovers, the commercial member can participate in a variety of network and promotional opportunities provided by the American Pie Council. Important to the commercial member is the combined effort of the members of the American Pie Council to grow and improve the pie industry. The Pie Marketing Committee is actively focused on promoting programs that will help grow the pie industry.

As a member of the APC, you will have access to all information that we have available for the pie-baking industry. In addition, the APC will help you research any information that we do not have immediately available. Each year the American Pie Council hosts the National Pie Championships at which amateur, professional, and commercial pie bakers can compete in their categories for the best pies in the country. The quarterly newsletter, *Pie Times*, will keep you up to date on what's new in the "pie world." The APC even designated and registered National Pie Day . . . January 23rd. All of this is yours with your membership to the American Pie Council. We invite you to discover all the benefits we have to offer. Joining is as easy as pie (www.piecouncil.org).

I was escorted to the large studio where the Food Network challenges are filmed. There were five kitchen stations set up with appliances. Everything was shiny metal and had a high-tech look. Before we arrived we had been instructed to bring our own utensils and to provide a shopping list of all the ingredients we needed for the competition.

When I walked over to my station I found my two large boxes of utensils, equipment, and decorative presentation plates waiting for me. The producers placed name tags at each of our stations along with specially designed aprons with our names on them that we were to wear during filming. I unpacked and organized my station. When I attempted to pull out one of my antique decorative cake plates, I found it shattered into a million pieces. I quietly asked myself if the post office workers had played volleyball with my box.

During a small meeting the producers told us our morning call was to be at 5:30 and that once filming began, each round would be 90 minutes to complete a pie—three rounds altogether. Everything must be made from scratch—no canned goods. We then met the judges. I was happy to know Linda Hoskins from the American Pie Council. It felt good in this unfamiliar world to at least know someone. I hugged Linda tightly.

Chad didn't make the trip with me. We had been vacationing on Isla Mujeres, Mexico, one of the first vacations we had taken outside of our culinary vacations, which are really for my work. We were waiting for a boat to take us across the Bay of Mujeres when my cell telephone rang. I answered it and it was Jen Adducci from the Food Network. She was calling to inform me that they had moved the dates of the filming. It would take place earlier than planned. She said they would fly me from Saint Paul to Denver on Sunday rather than Tuesday of the following week. I explained that I was waiting for a boat in Mexico to a tiny island in the Caribbean and we were not returning to the U.S. until the Tuesday morning I was to fly to Denver.

Move ahead a couple of hours and Food Network's travel agency contacted me to say everything was set for me to fly from Cancún, Mexico, to Denver on Sunday. My vacation would be cut short by three days, but at least I would be able to make the filming. I told Chad to stay on the island and enjoy the rest of our vacation rather than coming with me. Let's not waste it, I said. So we enjoyed the time we had on the island before the challenge.

After a second restless night and several false starts, Food Network host Keegan Gerhard announced our names and the Food Network clock was started. The audience of 200 clapped wildly. The five of us were each assigned a field producer asking questions captured by a camera and a sound person. Above our head was a camera on a large crane. During every round, the judges approached us and asked questions or challenged our baking techniques and preparation methods.

At the end of round one, I tied for fourth place with my Grandma's Secret Apple Pie. My filling didn't cook and the judges could taste flour. This was not a good thing. I needed to pull a trick out of my chef's hat for round two. And, with my Coconut Cream Dream Pie, I did. After the announcement of scores for round two, I was in first place. I was in shock. I needed to shake it off, though, because I couldn't bake my last pie without a great deal of concentration. It needed several steps before it was completed. As I began, I was simply working through the paces and I needed to bake the perfect Key Lime Delight Pie.

I blind baked the crust, completed the filling, and put the two together. I was done after adding the whipped topping. With 20 seconds on the clock, I realized that I had not garnished my pie. I ran to the refrigerator and grabbed my mint leaves and lime zest. I sprinkled the zest over the pie and carefully, but quickly, placed the mint leaves atop each puff of whipped cream. I placed the last leaf, dropped the rest, and raised my hands off the pie as Keegan announced that time was up.

After round three, each baker approached the judges to have his or her last pie critiqued. I faced the judges and audience. I was told my crust was undercooked and my filling questionable, but they loved my whipped topping. One judge questioned why I played it safe. She said they knew my reputation. I couldn't argue. I told them they were right but I played it safe because of the scope of this competition. I will never play it safe again.

Back in the green room, I told the other challengers that I had blown it. It was their game to win, not mine. I was devastated. I had such hopes, but at least I was asked to be in a Food Network Challenge.

We were called out for the announcement of the winners. Before the announcement I asked the group to hold hands. We had all gone through a great deal together and I thought it the right gesture. First, Keegan Gerhard announced the third place winner, who would receive a bronze Food Network medal. "John Michael Lerma!" I yelled, smiled a lot, and received my medal from Keegan. He placed it over my head. I don't remember the rest of the award ceremony after my win. I lost the $10,000 but I was now the owner of a Food Network medal. This was like winning an Oscar for cooking.

The following day we completed post-show interviews. Finally, I was sitting on an airplane going home and fell asleep. I woke as the flight attendant told the person sitting in front of me that I was wearing a Food Network medal. I grinned and retold my story of how I had won it. It was a very nice way to wake up from sleep.

In early spring 2008, the Food Network called me again to ask if I was interested in appearing in another Food Network Challenge to be filmed during the National Pie Championship at the American Pie Festival in Celebration, Florida. I, of course, said yes and immediately began planning for another adventure in the pie-baking world. This time Chad and I rented a fantastic three-bedroom house with a screen-enclosed spa and pool. We also began a new annual tradition of holding a Sunday morning potluck gathering for all the amateur and professional pie bakers. Everyone was welcome, and what a wonderful time we had. Imagine the best pie bakers in the nation, and they are bringing their favorite recipes to my potluck. We had a feast. I said it was like the happiest family in the world gathering together at Christmas. I was honored that the Food Network dropped by and filmed our first potluck gathering. We will always have film footage of this gathering and this special time. The challenge will air in September 2008, right before this cookbook is to be released. I hope my readers will enjoy it as much as I enjoyed filming it.

"I about dropped. The best pie bakers in the United States and I just placed a Bronze Medal. I couldn't believe it."

—JOHN MICHAEL LERMA (AFTER BEING AWARDED
THIRD PLACE) FOOD NETWORK CHALLENGE—
THE GREAT AMERICAN PIE COOK-OFF, NOVEMBER 2007

Wines for Pie

W INE, LIKE PIE, traces its origins back more than 4,000 years. Thought to have originated in Mesopotamia and following a similar path as pie, wine was also prevalent with the Egyptians, Greeks, and Romans. It is not far fetched to imagine the emperors and royalty of those nations eating pie, with their beverage of choice being wine. With water contaminated, and no soda or milk, it was wine that was enjoyed with their celebratory feasts. So if you are questioning why we have a chapter dedicated to serving wine with pie, the answer is that it has been done for centuries, so why would we not?

Fruit and Berry Pies

The first rule of thumb in pairing wine with dessert is that the wine needs to be at least as sweet as or sweeter than the pie so as not to detract from the experience and make the wine taste too acidic or dull. With this principle in mind, fruit and berry pies will require a very sweet wine that should be poured in smaller portions (usually 3-ounce servings).

Moscato d'Asti: From northern Italy, this is a great wine after a big meal. It exudes aromas and flavors of peach and pear with delicate, festive bubbles in the glass. This will pair exquisitely with peach- and apple-based pies. For raspberry and strawberry pies, try a Brachetto, Moscato's pink sibling. It is sweet, low alcohol, and bubbly with aromas and flavors of strawberries, raspberries, and fresh roses.

Riesling: Riesling is a wonderful all-around food wine. Look for a Spätlese or Auslese style, as these sweeter wines will pair well with dessert. Riesling shows gorgeous aromas and flavors of apples, ripe peaches, and poached pear and will work well with pies of the same. These wines are relatively low in alcohol and a great accompaniment to dessert.

Late-Harvest Chenin Blanc: For this dessert wine, look to South Africa for some great values, or for classic styles, look to the Loire region of Vouvray. Its beautiful fragrance of honeyed peaches and apricots will pair exquisitely with pies of the same, in particular the Peach Almond Pie.

Ice wines: Ice wine is one of the most fascinating wines made. The grapes are left on the vines to freeze well into the winter months, harvested, and then pressed to make a sweet, concentrated, intensely aromatic wine that exudes flavors of peach, apple, and pear. Look for ice wines from Canada, Austria, and Germany and pair them with any fruit pie.

Chocolate Pies

When it comes to pairing chocolate with wine, it's actually easier than you might think. The following are just a few of the wines that are classic companions to chocolate.

Brachetto: From the Piemonte region of northwestern Italy, Brachetto is classic with chocolate. Its low alcohol content and sweet flavors of raspberry and strawberry will work spectacularly well with the Chocolate Mousse Pie.

Vintage Port: Another rule in pairing wine with desserts is that we should look to wines that share similar weight and intensity, which we also do in matching dry wine and food. A dark, intense, rich chocolate dessert needs a rich, young vintage port with concentration, dark fruit, and some tannins. For budget options, look to other ruby-styled ports. This will be absolutely decadent with the Chocolate McDreamy Pie.

Late-Harvest Zinfandel: This wine was made with chocolate in mind. With a relatively high alcohol content, it should be served in 3-ounce portions. It is intensely flavorful with ripe, rich red and black berry flavors. Absolute perfection with the Chocolate Cherry Pie.

Banyuls: This wine hails from southern France. Banyuls is a fortified (higher alcohol content), Grenache-based dessert wine. It is known as a "little French love letter to chocolate," and you cannot go wrong pairing this wine with all things chocolate.

ƒ Citrus Pies

With citrus pies, the important thing to remember is that, if serving wine, you will need something with brisk, bright acidity to stand up to the zestiness of the citrus fruits. There are a couple of clear choices for these pies, though perhaps this is the toughest pie category for pairing wine.

Sauternes: From the Sauternes region of western France, Sauternes is produced from Sémillon, Sauvignon Blanc, and Muscadelle grapes. There is a beautiful balance of sweetness with the zest of acidity in these wines. For a lesser-priced alternative to Sauternes, look for wines from the neighboring regions of Cadillac, Monbazillac, Cérons, or Loupiac.

Beaumes de Venise: From southern France, this dessert wine is made with Muscat grapes, and it carries pure, distinctive aromas of flowers, tropical fruit, and honeyed sweetness. Its lively acidity will stand up to citrus pies.

⸕ Savory Pies

With pies in this category, we should look to a few other basic rules of food and wine pairing. First, we want to find wines that are lower in tannins. Tannins have a drying effect, and pairing them with salt, which also has a drying effect, will detract from the savory experience of these pies. Second, look for wines with lower alcohol content. High alcohol content paired with a heavily spiced pie or those with peppers, garlic, or onions, for example, will accentuate the heat.

Zinfandel: With California Zinfandel, look for one that is lower in alcohol content. Some of these Zins can now approach 17 percent alcohol. Look for a wine around the 13–14 percent level that has not spent much time in an oak barrel. These fruit-forward wines will work amazingly well with the Leftover Turkey Pie and Puddin' Pork Pie. As an alternative, for some of the Italian-inspired pies, try a Primitivo. Genetically, Primitivo is the same grape as Zinfandel and will maintain the Italian theme of the dish.

Pinot Noir: A great match for My Favorite Salmon Pie, Pinot Noir is a relatively thin-skinned grape that does not have heavy tannins. Look for a fruit-forward style here, and it will also pair nicely with ham, turkey, chicken, and sausage.

Valpolicella: For the That's Amore! Italian Pie, Real Pizza Pie, and Sage Sausage Pie, a Valpolicella red wine from northern Italy will lend a fruit-forward style, bright acidity, and low tannin to pair with the spices and the cheese.

Pinot Gris (Pinot Grigio) or other Italian white wine: With the lighter meat-based pies such as chicken or turkey, these bright, fruity wines have the mouthwatering acidity to cut through cream and butter and are also readily available in all price ranges. Look to Pinot Gris from Oregon, California, and Alsace in addition to those from Italy.

Chablis or other unoaked Chardonnay: Crisp, dry, unoaked styles of Chardonnay will also have the tangy acidity to stand up to butter, eggs, and cream without the overpowering flavors that come from oak barrel aging in so many Chardonnays.

🍴 Vegetable Pies

Here we turn again to another common food and wine principle. Some wine and vegetable matches are inherent in the flavors of the vegetables themselves. For example, if the pie contains mushrooms, look to an earthy-style Pinot Noir that is noted for its own signature forest-floor, mushroom bouquet. Or, the high acidity of tomatoes works well with the crisp acids of Sauvignon Blanc or Chianti. Other great red wines for veggies are the lighter, fruitier wines such as Beaujolais. Try Italian Barbera or Valpolicella for tomato-based pie fillings such as the Ratatouille Pie.

For something different, look to Greek wines. Their fuller-bodied red wines will pair well with the pies containing mushrooms or black olives. The white wines from Greece tend to have high acidity and will pair nicely with the Spinach Pie.

🍴 Holiday and Nut Pies

These pies are all about seasonal, warm, toasty spices, nuts, and other great fall and winter flavors. The pecan- and pumpkin-inspired pies will be heavenly with wines having the same nutty, caramel flavors stemming from barrel aging. Fortified wines, with around a 20 percent alcohol content, also will complement the warm spices in these pies.

Tokaji: This Hungarian wine has a wealth of history. With flavors of dried apricots and oranges and a sweet honeyed finish, Tokaji will go nicely with these pies. On a budget, look for Muscats and Tokays from Australia.

Tawny Port: Tawny Ports, which have been barrel aged, abound with the aromas and flavors of caramel, brown sugar, warm toasty vanilla, and spices. These fortified, higher-alcohol wines will pair well with the pecan pies and pumpkin pies. Another fortified wine, Sherry, will be sweeter than the Tawny Port, but with a richer texture. Look for a sweet Oloroso or Pedro Ximénez–style sherry. Warm, nutty, caramel, and toffee aromas and flavors will complement these holiday and nut pies.

Vin Santo: This little dessert wine is a gem from Tuscany, Italy. Vin Santo ("holy wine") has a sweet, nutty taste that will accentuate these pies and make your dessert absolutely divine.

✝ Kristen Kowalski

As proprietor and sommelier of The Wine Market, with two retail locations in Minnesota, Kristen Kowalski is able to use all of her skills as a businesswoman as well as share her love of wine and food with her customers. She prides herself on educating her customers about all aspects of wine. After more than fifteen years in the food and beverage industry at companies such as Kraft Foods, Coca-Cola, and General Mills, Kristen felt it was time to incorporate her passion for wine, culture, and history into a new business. Kristen received her sommelier certification from the International Sommelier Guild in 2006 and is one of only six women in the state to hold that title. Kristen graduated from the University of Minnesota Carlson School of Management with a bachelor's and master's degree in marketing. She was recently named one of 2008's "25 Women to Watch" by the *Minneapolis/St. Paul Business Journal.* www.thewinemarket.us.

Measurements and Equivalents

English Units

8 fluid ounces	equal	1 cup
2 cups	equal	1 pint
2 pints	equal	1 quart
4 quarts	equal	1 gallon

Approximate Conversions to Metric Measures from English Units

When You Know	*Multiply By*	*To Find*
fluid ounces	29.6	milliliters
cups	0.24	liters
pints	0.473	liters
quarts	0.946	liters
gallons	3.791	liters

Approximate Conversations to English Units from Metric Units

When You Know	Multiply By	To Find
milliliters	0.03	fluid ounces
liters	0.036	cubic feet
liters	2.1	pints
liters	1.06	quarts
liters	0.26	gallons

Approximate Conversions to Metric Measures from English Units

When You Know	Multiply By	To Find
ounces	28.3	grams
pounds	0.45	kilograms

Approximate Conversations to English Units from Metric Units

When You Know	Multiply By	To Find
grams	0.035	ounces
kilograms	2.2	pounds

Fahrenheit/Centigrade Conversion Table

TEMPERATURE

Formula:	Formula:
Degree C = $\dfrac{Degree\ F - 32}{1.8}$	Degree F = 1.8 x Degree C + 32

Acknowledgments

WRITING CAN BE SUCH A SOLITARY THING. I usually feel as if I'm under house arrest. It's the greatest job in the world and the worst job in the world. That's why I need to thank people for their contributions to my cooking, writing, and friendship.

Mike, Mona, Mollie, and Chloe Ahlf (our next-door neighbors to the east): The Ahlfs have tested many pies and other dishes that I've prepared, and they've been kind and constructive in their criticism. I remember Thanksgiving of 2007; they actually created a judging form and critiqued the pies I gave them. They wrote down everything they tasted or did not taste. This feedback meant the world to me and helped me at future pie events. Their tasting skills—and friendship—are very much appreciated.

Laura McCallum and her son Wyatt Miller: Wyatt appeared on the cover of my last cookbook and I would have loved to have him on again eating pie, but maybe the next cookbook. However, Laura and Wyatt have served as pie testers, too, and fortunately they live right across the street, so tasting results have a quick return time. Pleasing Wyatt's palate is no easy task, and I work hard to bake the best pies to pass his inspection. His mom, Laura, is simply happy to have home-baked desserts. I appreciate her brownies when I can't stomach another pie.

Linda and Rich Hoskins of the American Pie Council: I remember the first time I spoke with Linda on the telephone before my first APC Crisco National Pie Championship. We must have spent at least an hour talking. She told me everything I needed to know about entering the contest but also how much fun I would have. I was a nervous wreck and Linda was reassuring and nice. When I met her, we were instant friends. Rich has become a good friend and is amazing at organizing the pie judging each year. I have enjoyed working as a judge on his team. Thank you both for so much support and encouragement.

Nancy Mathieson of the American Pie Council: Nancy is a goddess. This woman is so many things to the America Pie Council and its members. She has also become a good friend, and her encouragement and support are thought of daily by me. No matter how busy this woman is, she will still find the time during the APC Crisco National Pie Championship to call me and make sure that I have not added any alcohol to my recipes. It's an inside joke, but I smile every time I think of it. Nancy is a wonder and I'm so glad that I can call her my friend.

Master Chef Dan "Klecko" McGleno: This man is a wonder. I once wrote a magazine article about him. He scared me the first time I saw him walking down a street at the Minnesota State Fair. Covered in tattoos, 6 foot 3 inches tall, size 13 black combat boots, and the nicest disposition of anyone I have ever known. From day one this man has protected me, watched out for me, and was always a friend. They don't make many like this one, and I'm glad he lives just a block and a half away from me.

Phyllis Bartholomew, Sarah Spaugh, and Dionna Hurt, "The Pie Goddesses": These three women don't know how much they influenced me. I was bedridden and very ill. I saw them on the Food Network at the APC Crisco National Pie Championship and dreamed what it would be like to bake next to them. Well, dreams come true and I have baked next to them many times. I always love hearing how Phyllis says good-bye: "Keep it flaky."

City of Braham, Minnesota, "The Homemade Pie Capital of Minnesota": Susan Severson, Valorie Arrowsmith, and Gary Skarsten have all invited me to be a part of this delightful annual celebration. Thank you for letting me spread the good word about pie in your wonderful community of east-central Minnesota.

High Noon Productions: Art Edwards, Deb Clime, Jennifer Adducci, Tricia Starcevich, Annie Rosenkranz, John, Andy, and George (camera and sounds guys), and everyone else I've worked with. You have been wonderful, and I can't tell you how exciting it is to simply be driving to the mall or grocery store and receive a call in the middle of the day asking if I would be interested in being on a Food Network special. You guys and gals of High Noon Productions rock!

Emile Henry: Thank you for providing the beautiful and colorful pie dishes for the cover and insert for this cookbook. Not only do you have the best pie-baking product available to the world, but it's stylish and wonderful to display in my home. Thank you, Tara!

Jennifer Fredericks Terrell: A good friend and professional photographer with whom I enjoyed working on this cookbook. I saw her work after she visited us in Italy. She and her husband took hundreds of photos—I believe fifteen hundred—and each one is a gem. I am so honored to have her eye focusing on my work—my pies and the beautiful pie dishes they are in. Also thanks to Brandon Terrell for friendship and being a very good PA.

Bret Bannon: I've known Bret for years as a professional chef, owner of Bret's Table (http://bretstable.com), friend, and food stylist. I couldn't be more thrilled to have Bret on our team as food stylist during the photo shoot for my cookbook. He's a perfectionist all the way. I have never seen anyone place lime zest as strategically on a pie with tweezers before. I knew I had the best person for the job. Bret and I also have the honor of being asked to offer food ideas twice at General Mills for their Ideation contest. Both times Bret and I tied with each other. I couldn't have been happier.

The Chef's Gallery and Stephanie Jameson: So many thanks go to the Chef's Gallery in Stillwater, Minnesota, for giving us a fantastic backdrop for our photo shoot for this cookbook. The Chef's Gallery gives my pies a permanent home in these pages. It looks lovely, and it is a lovely place to be. I have taught many cooking classes over several years and have cooked with hundreds of people from eastern Minnesota and western Wisconsin. Each of those classes holds wonderful memories for me. The anchor and spirit of the Chef's Gallery is Stephanie Jameson, who I wish would bottle her energy and enthusiasm and sell it. When I am happy and around Steph, I could rule the world. When I'm down and around Steph, I become glad again. Grazie mille amore mio!

Mary Byers: My editor and friend. Mary guided me through my first cookbook. It was a scary thing writing a cookbook for the first time, and she couldn't have been sweeter or kinder. I've missed our casual lunches and coffee breaks over the years, so I decided I had better write another cookbook to get back in touch. I am thrilled and honored to be whipped into shape (grammatically and professionally) by such a fine woman. Mary, thank you for reading my text, editing it, and redoing all of it so gracefully.

Maria Manske: I've decided that everyone needs a public relations person even if you are not in the business of writing. Maria is more than my PR person; she has become such a good friend and adviser. From the day I met Maria, before my first cookbook, I have trusted her opinions and insight. She has never let me down, and not only that, she makes me look really good. Maria, I thank you. (http://linwoodbookgroup.com)

The cast of characters on Isla Mujeres, Mexico: Steven Broin, owner of Casa Sirena Hotel Boutique (http://www.sirena.com.mx) is one of the dearest persons on this planet. He is the perfect host, friend, loves my pies, and threw me the best surprise birthday party of my life. Steven, I thank you from the bottom of my heart for putting up with me and my writing at the Casa. I know I can be difficult. Also, to the Princess of Power, Deb Harrington: thank you so such for friendship, incredible Spanish translation, and being such a delight in the air and on the ground. I think of us at Playa Norte often. And to Bev, Daniel, Dennis, Patsy, Jim, Ilse, Tom, and Brent—the rest of the cast—I miss you and can't wait to bake you more Coconut Cream Dream Pies on an island that is not known for its baking qualities.